THE KEYSTONE PROVINCE

The Keystone Province: Politics and Governance in Manitoba
© The Authors 2025

29 28 27 26 25   1 2 3 4 5

All rights reserved. No part of this publication may be reproduced or transmitted in any form or by any means, or stored in a database and retrieval system in Canada, without the prior written permission of the publisher, or, in the case of photocopying or any other reprographic copying, a licence from Access Copyright, www.accesscopyright.ca, 1-800-893-5777.

University of Manitoba Press
Winnipeg, Manitoba, Canada
Treaty 1 Territory
uofmpress.ca

For EU product safety concerns please contact Mare Nostrum Group B.V., Mauritskade 21D, 1091 GC Amsterdam, The Netherlands, gpsr@mare-nostrum.co.uk.

Cataloguing data available from Library and Archives Canada

ISBN 978-177284-122-0 (paper)
ISBN 978-177284-124-4 (pdf)
ISBN 978-177284-125-1 (epub)
ISBN 978-177284-123-7 (bound)

Cover design by Kirk Warren
Interior design by Karen Armstrong

The University of Manitoba Press acknowledges the financial support for its publication program provided by the Government of Canada through the Canada Book Fund, the Canada Council for the Arts, the Manitoba Department of Sport, Culture, and Heritage, the Manitoba Arts Council, and the Manitoba Book Publishing Tax Credit.

This book has been published with the help of a grant from the Federation for the Humanities and Social Sciences, through the Awards to Scholarly Publications Program, using funds provided by the Social Sciences and Humanities Research Council of Canada.

Funded by the Government of Canada | Canadä

THE KEYSTONE PROVINCE

Politics and Governance in Manitoba

Edited by
KELLY SAUNDERS AND CHRISTOPHER ADAMS

University of Manitoba Press

CONTENTS

Introduction Kelly Saunders and Christopher Adams _____ 1

PART 1   MANITOBA'S POLITICAL LANDSCAPE

CHAPTER 1 "All the Rights We Are Entitled To":
Louis Riel and the Creation of Manitoba
Robert Coutts _____ 17

CHAPTER 2 Political Culture in Manitoba
Jared Wesley and Lauren Hill _____ 38

CHAPTER 3 Structure and Change:
An Overview of the Manitoba Economy
Fletcher Baragar _____ 63

PART 2   INSTITUTIONS AND PROCESSES

CHAPTER 4 Westminster on the Prairies:
The Manitoba Legislature, Past and Present
Christopher Adams _____ 85

CHAPTER 5 Still Politicized? The Partial Evolution of Manitoba's
Crown Corporations
Malcolm G. Bird _____ 103

CHAPTER 6 Manitoba's Public Service under the Pallister/Stefanson
Government and Beyond
Andrea Rounce and Karine Levasseur _____ 121

CHAPTER 7	The News Media and Public Opinion in Manitoba *Curtis Brown and Mary Agnes Welch* ____146

PART 3	**POLITICS AND COMMUNITIES**
CHAPTER 8	Women, Gender, and Legislative Politics in Manitoba *Joan Grace* ____163
CHAPTER 9	Where in History? Indigenous Peoples and Rights in Twenty-First-Century Manitoba *Jeremy Patzer* ____182
CHAPTER 10	Municipal Government and Politics in Manitoba *Aaron Moore* ____204

PART 4	**PARTIES AND ELECTIONS**
CHAPTER 11	The Manitoba Progressive Conservatives *Royce Koop* ____227
CHAPTER 12	The Manitoba New Democratic Party *Christopher Adams* ____245
CHAPTER 13	The Manitoba Liberal Party *Kelly Saunders* ____259

Conclusion	*Kelly Saunders and Christopher Adams* ____277
Appendix A	Evolution of Voting and Elections in Manitoba____283
Appendix B	Manitoba Election Results, 1870 to 2023 ____288
Contributors	____295

INTRODUCTION

KELLY SAUNDERS AND CHRISTOPHER ADAMS

In their 2010 volume of collected essays on Manitoba politics, Paul Thomas and Curtis Brown write: "Lacking Quebec's cultural and linguistic distinctiveness, Ontario's traditional demographic and economic hegemony, or Alberta's combustible mix of prairie populism and oil wealth, Manitoba appears to blend into the background of the national family portrait, lacking the political importance, economic strength, or cultural effervescence of its larger and more colourful provincial cousins."[1]

This description suggests a Manitoba that is bland, unimaginative, and nondescript when compared with its provincial counterparts in other parts of Canada. The contributions contained in *The Keystone Province: Politics and Governance in Manitoba* challenge this narrative and paint a different picture of Manitoba, highlighting the many different and fascinating facets that comprise our province. Some examples of this distinctiveness include the history of Manitoba and how it entered into Confederation, the province's economy and the ways in which economic forces intertwine with geography, governing traditions and civil society, and its political parties, each with its own story of how it developed and evolved and continues to seek electoral support from voters. The opening chapter of *The Keystone Province*, written by contributing historian Robert Coutts, sets the stage for this debate by asking the question "Is the political history of Manitoba dull?" His answer is a resounding *no*. Coutts reminds us that the province's origins are rooted in resistance; in fact, Manitoba stands as the only province in Canada to enter Confederation through armed conflict, and the only one to do so led by an Indigenous people, the Métis under the leadership of Louis Riel. Subsequent chapters attest to the fact that Coutts's assessment of our province's political history—that it is neither as dull nor unremarkable as the abovementioned quote implies—also extends to contemporary politics and governance in Manitoba. Together, the chapters contained in *The Keystone Province* show that, while Manitoba may indeed be "in the middle" geographically, economically, and socially from a national perspective, this somewhat reductionist portrayal belies a province that is also home to a rich diversity of peoples and ideas, an entrepreneurial spirit, and an increasing willingness to punch above its weight on the country's intergovernmental stage.

Like other provinces in the country, Manitoba is home to a Westminster parliamentary system, a single member plurality electoral system, and a constitutional framework that provided the foundation for Canada as a federal liberal democracy. While these factors attest to a certain degree of convergence with other provinces in terms of basic structures and processes, Manitoba is also its own unique political, economic, and social community. We draw on the work of such scholars as David Elkins, Richard Simeon, and Jared Wesley[2] to position Manitoba as a "world among other worlds" with regards to politics and governance in Canada. Elkins and Simeon first coined the phrase "small worlds" in 1980 to advance the argument that there is no "one Canada" that describes the various social, political, and governing systems that exist across the country. Instead, we can think of Canada as comprised of ten political systems, reflecting the diversity of regions and provinces in the country, which Elkins and Simeon say is "a defining characteristic of the Canadian community itself."[3] Elkins and Simeon viewed each province as constituting a small world unto its own, within the larger world of Canada, shaped by its particular socio-economic cleavages, party systems, political cultures, and voting patterns.

As the responsibilities, budgets, and prominence of provinces continued to expand and grow in the decades that followed the 1980s, some scholars began to question whether the "small world" metaphor adequately captured the more robust, and powerful, presence of provinces in Canadian federalism. In his aptly named volume on provincial politics in Canada, *Big Worlds: Politics and Elections in the Canadian Provinces and Territories,* Jared Wesley maintains that, no longer the "small" (insular or diminutive) communities they once were, provinces and territories have emerged as "Big Worlds" in and of themselves. Whether we use the term "small world" or "big world," one thing is clear: the existence of unique political worlds in Canada. In this, Manitoba is no exception.

Yet, as many of the contributors to this volume suggest, what may be most remarkable about Manitoba are not the cultural, ideological, political, and economic differences and tensions that have constituted an underlying thread of the character of our province, and which differentiate us from our provincial cousins. Rather, it is how the province's political actors and structures have managed these conflicts, sometimes through accommodation and consensus and other times in response to external pressures from extra-institutional forces and the "other worlds" within Confederation and beyond. In the pages that follow, we will see examples of this provincial tendency to embrace accommodation and consensus in the face of challenge and conflict, as demonstrated by the role of international economic forces, national politics, technological developments, elections, party politics, and struggles over Indigenous, labour, and gender rights.

The lingering stereotype of Manitoba politics as lacklustre and indistinguishable from its provincial neighbours to the west and east has not been helped by the paucity of academic scholarship on the province and its political, social, and economic institutions. For many years, Murray Donnelly's 1963 work titled *The Government of Manitoba* was the only comprehensive book available to students on how politics and government operated in the province.[4] More recently, *Manitoba Politics and Government: Issues, Institutions, Traditions,* edited by Paul G. Thomas and Curtis Brown (a quote from which opened this introduction), was an exceptional addition to what has been available. Published in 2010, it provided a comprehensive examination of Manitoba society, elections, political parties, government bodies, and leading public policy issues of the time. Other excellent surveys of various aspects of Manitoba political life, notably in the area of electoral politics, have appeared. These include edited volumes by Andrea Rounce and Jared Wesley;[5] by Karine Levasseur, Andrea Rounce, Barry Ferguson, and Royce Koop;[6] and by Royce Koop, Barry Ferguson, Karine Levasseur, Andrea Rounce, and Kiera Ladner.[7] Other volumes include collected essays on public policy and the COVID-19 pandemic in Manitoba, edited by Andrea Rounce and Karine Levasseur;[8] and essays on Manitoba political culture by Jared Wesley.[9] In 2008 Christopher Adams, one of the two editors of this volume, came forward with *Manitoba Politics: Parties, Leaders, and Voters*,[10] which provided an insightful and thorough history of Manitoba's provincial parties and elections. As well, various political biographies have appeared, including those by Howard Pawley and Gary Filmon, who served as premiers of Manitoba from 1981 to 1988 and 1988 to 1999, respectively, along with former New Democratic Party (NDP) cabinet minister and MLA (Member of the Legislative Assembly) Gord Mackintosh.[11] While each of these volumes makes an important contribution to the literature on Manitoba politics, there is no up-to-date book that examines Manitoba's diversity of political institutions, processes, sectors, and actors initially captured by Thomas and Brown in their seminal volume, and, in particular, explores the unique, small/big world of Manitoba politics.

The Keystone Province: Politics and Governance in Manitoba seeks to fill this void. We bring together a diverse array of distinguished scholars from political science, history, sociology, gender studies, economics, public policy, and municipal politics, in addition to experts in the fields of media and public opinion polling, to share their perspectives and expertise in their respective areas. This book offers an informed and comprehensive insight into the main features of political, economic, and social life in Manitoba, from both an historical and a contemporary perspective. As such, we seek to build on the earlier work of Thomas and Brown, and explore what has changed—and what has remained the same—in Manitoba politics and governance over the past decade and a half. Certainly, much has changed for Manitoba, as indeed for the rest of the world, in the wake of the global COVID-19 pandemic. As Andrea Rounce and Karine Levasseur first articulated in their edited volume on Manitoba's policy response to the first wave of the pandemic, the wide-ranging impacts of COVID-19 touched every facet of Manitoba society and government.[12] The after-effects of this historic event will continue to linger for decades, if not generations, to come, in ways and means we have yet to realize. As we move through these first years of a post-pandemic world, it seems an opportune time to consider the past, present, and future of Manitoba's political, social, and economic institutions and their ability to accommodate and manage the pressing challenges of our time.

Throughout this volume we explore the concept of "Manitoba in the middle," a central premise of Thomas and Brown's work from fifteen years ago. While the physical geography of the province remains the same, in what ways does Manitoba still constitute the middle in economic, political, and social terms? And if this descriptor still holds, what are the consequences and implications of this middling status for how Manitoba, as its own small world, is seen by others and how Manitobans see themselves? Is our political culture still considered as moderate and centrist as it was in 2010, or has political pragmatism given way to increased polarization and the absence of cross-partisan collegiality? Does our economy, long described as stable, slow, and steady rather than boom and bust, still fit this portrayal? Moreover, are social relations in the province still able to be managed through accommodation and consensus as has historically been the case, or have our differences become too deeply entrenched? These are some of the questions we hope to untangle through the various chapters and sections of this volume. In so doing, we hope to illustrate that, like our political past, contemporary politics and governance in Manitoba are anything but boring and unremarkable. Indeed, we aim to show the myriad of ways in which Manitoba, historically and today, remains a vibrant, intriguing, and unique place within the national landscape—a world within worlds.

This collection is divided into four sections, with two appendices. The first section, "Manitoba's Political Landscape," explores questions related to the province's political history, culture, and economy. In Chapter 1, as noted previously, historian Robert Coutts deconstructs the assumption of Manitoba political history as "dull." He argues that this view ignores much of the province's past, a past born of a long history of Indigenous occupation and influence that continue today. Exploring this past, Coutts traces the historical development of Manitoba from the first Indigenous peoples to the arrival of European fur traders in the late seventeenth century. He describes some of the province's main political and governance structures in the decades preceding its entry into Confederation (notably Louis Riel's provisional government of 1869–70) and identifies some of the common governance traditions of pre- and post-contact Indigenous peoples in Manitoba. Central in this regard is the Cree and Métis concept of *wahkohtowin*, or "having or possessing good relations." As Coutts explains, wahkohtowin embodies shared cultural and community identities and values, the development of a broad social consensus, and the acceptance of authority through representation. He argues that wahkohtowin, as practised by Riel, played a major role not only in the Red River Resistance but also in helping bring people together. It solidified a common culture and group identity in the new province. As such, Coutts concludes that wahkohtowin, and the ways in which Riel interwove this principle with the traditions of Western statecraft, stands at the heart of democracy in Manitoba.

In Chapter 2, Jared Wesley and Lauren Hill interrogate another commonly held belief about Manitoba, that the province is "undeveloped" and lacks its own distinguishable political culture. The authors reject this theory, instead arguing that the province has a distinctive political ethos grounded in the concepts of modesty and moderation that make up its popular "middleman" image. They point to evidence of this ethos in the province's community symbols, such as the Manitoba emblem and provincial flag, as well as slogans and brands used to promote the province and its capital city, Winnipeg. Such phrases as "Friendly Manitoba," found on provincial licence plates, and "Made from What's Real," Winnipeg's official brand, speak to the values of accommodation, diversity, authenticity, and centrism that underline Manitoba's political culture. It is these values, they contend, that have gotten the province through times of crisis and conflict; whether it be 1919's Winnipeg General Strike or the most recent COVID-19 pandemic, "each of these events brought with it a spirit of sacrifice (modesty) and togetherness (moderation) in the face of steep challenges." The final section of the chapter examines the impact of political culture on individual and political elite attitudes in Manitoba. Wesley and Hill conclude that Manitobans tend to reflect a "centrist realism" in their views on government and the economy, while the most successful political leaders have been those who subscribe to an elite discourse based on progressive centrism, pragmatism, and flexible partisanship.

In Chapter 3, Fletcher Baragar provides a comprehensive picture of Manitoba's provincial economy. Reflecting the theme of "Manitoba in the middle," he describes the economy as one based on diversity, modesty, and stability. Included in this economic mix are such primary industries as agriculture, mining, and hydroelectricity; a manufacturing sector that has declined in recent years in the face of globalization and neo-liberalism; and a vibrant service sector (notably in the areas of real estate, health care, public administration, finance, and insurance), which constitutes an ever-increasing area of economic activity in the province. He adds that the varied and balanced nature of the Manitoba economy is augmented by a modestly growing population, thanks largely to international immigration. Together, these factors have resulted in Manitoba's having one of the lowest unemployment rates in the country. Despite this relative stability, however, the author maintains that "transformation and change in the Manitoba economy are ongoing." Manitoba's lower fiscal capacity relative to other provinces leaves it reliant on equalization payments and federal transfers from Ottawa, while its status as a small player on the national and international economic stage has forced it to adjust to externally generated developments and shocks. Baragar concludes that, while Manitoba has been relatively successful in making those adjustments, the burden of the adjustments and the consequent spoils have been distributed unevenly in the province.

The second section of the book, "Institutions and Processes," contains four chapters that examine the legislative and executive branches in Manitoba, Crown corporations, the provincial civil service, and the news media and public opinion polling sector. Christopher Adams opens this section with an examination of the workings of Manitoba's Legislative Assembly and cabinet in Chapter 4. He describes the development and evolution of the Westminster parliamentary system in the province, its main functions (namely, representing citizens, decision making, and passing legislation), and the role of cabinet. Originally consisting of a bicameral legislature with an appointed lieutenant-governor and electoral districts based not on representation by population but instead on the religious, linguistic, and cultural identities dominant at the time, Manitoba's electoral system now reflects those of the other provinces, Adams states, including a legislative system based on the British Westminster model. At the same time, Manitoba has had its share of political issues and turmoil. Adams recounts such events as the fall of Howard Pawley's NDP government in 1988 at the hands of a disgruntled NDP backbencher, the 2014 exodus of five cabinet ministers from the Greg Selinger administration, and, more recently, the 2021 resignation of the minister of Indigenous and Northern Relations that triggered the stepping down of former Progressive Conservative premier Brian Pallister a month later. As Adams reminds us, these events demonstrate that premiers in Manitoba, while remaining the dominant players in their caucuses, are not immune to caucus grievances and revolts.

In Chapter 5, Malcolm Bird discusses Manitoba's Crown corporations, focusing on the three largest in the province (Manitoba Hydro, Manitoba Public Insurance, and Manitoba Liquor and Lotteries). He describes these institutions as important policy actors in the province, deeply embedded in the provincial political economy and forming part of Manitoba's distinctive prairie culture and society. While Manitoba's Crown corporations have revised many of their internal operations and governance structures, he notes that they continue to be subjected to considerable political influence by provincial governments of all stripes. This has not only left them with less autonomy than state-owned enterprises in other parts of the country but has also lent a unique character to how Manitoba governments interact with their Crown corporations. The reasons for why Manitoba remains an outlier in this regard are not entirely clear, Bird recognizes, suggesting that it could be the result of the province's small size, have-not status, and parochial middling political culture; alternatively, it could simply be that Manitoba's Crowns are behind their contemporaries in the evolution of their governance practices. Regardless of the reasons, and despite this relative lack of autonomy, Bird concludes, "these Crowns serve the province and its citizens well by providing high-value goods and services and revenues to the state, and aid governments in meeting other vital policy goals."

Publicly funded services account for 25 percent of the Manitoba economy and employ approximately 12,000 people in the province. In Chapter 6, Andrea Rounce and Karine Levasseur consider the key elements, governance structures, and actors involved in Manitoba's public service; highlight some of the changes that have occurred; and identify the main challenges confronting the public sector as it looks to the future. They argue that the public service has undergone a period of "tremendous change" since the 2016 election of the Progressive Conservative (PC) government. New legislation passed in 2021 considerably expanded the scope of the public service to include the broader public sector, which some people saw as a conscious effort to extend the government's political reach. This was followed by targeted cuts and attempts by the governing Conservatives to impose wage freezes and maximum wage caps on the public service (causing the Manitoba Federation of Labour to sue the provincial government). Rounce and

Levasseur conclude that while public servants in Manitoba continue to provide "fearless and frank advice and loyal implementation" of public policy to the benefit of Manitobans, they have been faced with dropping morale, declines amongst their ranks, increasing demands, and significant changes in the political, economic, and labour relations environment in the province. If these challenges are not addressed, the authors predict, this situation will lead to further erosion of the public sector in terms of stress and morale, longer delays in program and service delivery, and an overall "weakening democracy" in Manitoba.

Chapter 7, written by two highly respected veterans in journalism and public opinion polling, Curtis Brown and Mary Agnes Welch, provides an overview of the contemporary news media and public opinion research sectors in Manitoba. The authors note the symbiotic relationship that exists between the two industries (notably, in the case of the *Winnipeg Free Press*, the province's largest daily newspaper, and Manitoba-based public opinion research firm Probe Research). While legacy print and broadcast media outlets in Manitoba, like elsewhere, have faced increased competition from Facebook and other online websites and forums, the authors argue that these traditional sources of news reporting nonetheless remain "influential conduits shaping how Manitobans learn and think about the province's major issues." Alongside the media, public opinion polling serves as a key gauge for how citizens feel about their government and the big policy issues of the day, and Manitoba has always played what Brown and Welch describe as an "outsized role" in the public opinion research industry. Indeed, Probe Research's quarterly omnibus poll on provincial party support in Manitoba remains a highly anticipated event amongst political observers in the province. It is used as a framing mechanism by reporters, columnists, and pundits, providing context to help explain government decision making and setting the stage for upcoming provincial election campaigns. Brown and Welch conclude that political coverage in Manitoba—still strong but shrinking—will continue to evolve with the times, as governments find new ways to communicate and listen to the public through both the media and polling.

The authors in the third section of the book, "Politics and Communities," assess the role of women and gender minorities in Manitoba politics and government, Indigenous-settler reconciliation, and municipal governance. History was made in the fall of 2021 when the PC Party chose Heather Stefanson to become the province's first woman premier. In Chapter 8, Joan Grace examines the participation of women and gender minorities in Manitoba provincial politics. She opens the discussion with an assessment of why gender representation matters in public office: by allowing for more voices and perspectives to be heard, enhancing the tone and tenor of political debate, and sparking larger institutional reforms. Grace notes that while Manitoba typically ranks in the middle in terms of gender representation compared with other provinces, the 2023 election saw a record number of women and gender-diverse individuals win seats in the Manitoba legislature. Manitoba has now exceeded the critical mass of 30 percent women/gender-diverse people in the Legislative Assembly, which is widely seen as key to instigating a more gender-friendly legislative chamber. While this is an important achievement, Grace cautions that gender diversity is not just about the numbers, drawing attention to the significance of critical actors in such key bodies as cabinet, the Speaker's office, and the premiership. She concludes that, with the increasing number of women and gender minorities elected to the Manitoba legislature, "more women are assuming important legislative leadership roles and are, in their own ways, regendering the assembly."

In Chapter 9, Jeremy Patzer explores the relationship between Indigenous peoples and modern Manitoba. As he reminds us, Manitoba has the largest proportional population of Indigenous peoples in the country, and is the sole province that was ushered into Confederation by an Indigenous leader. However, he argues that Manitoba has had difficulties keeping attuned to the shift towards reconciliation and Indigenous rights that began in Canada in the late twentieth century, to say nothing of leading the way toward the relationship sought by Indigenous nations in the twenty-first century. In advancing this argument, Patzer traces some of the state-imposed assimilationist policies and practices of the past, followed by the "Indigenous rights turn" that began in the country roughly fifty years ago and continues to this day. He contends that contemporary politics in Manitoba still demonstrates a persistent hostility to the assertion of rights by Indigenous peoples, and points to such examples as former premier Brian Pallister's inflammatory comments about Indigenous hunting rights and access to vaccines for Indigenous peoples during the COVID-19 pandemic. Patzer concludes that Indigenous peoples in Manitoba continue to deal with the consequences of colonialism, dispossession, and the harm suffered to their governance systems. While Manitoba should be leading the way in responsiveness to Indigenous nations, the province instead is lagging behind, a situation Patzer describes as emblematic of the "age-old settler colonial perception of Indigenous peoples as problematic obstacles to be removed in order to extract wealth from territory."

From policing and fire services to waste collection and road construction, municipalities have taken on an ever-larger share of responsibilities across the country. Nonetheless, they remain the creation of provincial governments and subject to the whims of premiers. In Chapter 10, Aaron Moore traces the history of municipalities in Manitoba and examines how municipal responsibilities and fiscal constraints, the structure of municipal elections and oversight, and provincial-municipal relations influence and shape municipal politics and governance. In so doing he draws attention to some of the challenges facing municipal governments, including fiscal constraints, the lack of electoral accountability and transparency, the struggle of councillors to maintain oversight of municipal staff, and the continual interference by the provincial government. He describes municipal politics in Manitoba as typified by parochialism, the conflicting desire to expand services while limiting tax increases, and an "amateurishness" that separates municipalities from senior levels of government. Together, these factors "serve to undermine any attempts to implement progressive, municipal-wide policies, and municipal governments' capacity to maintain transparency, oversight, and accountability." Moore cautions against simply placing blame for these failings at the feet of elected officials and municipal staff, however. For him, the fundamental issue is the lack of interest in municipal politics amongst the broader public. If change is to occur for the better at the municipal level, he argues, then voters must become more engaged and active in municipal affairs, otherwise breakdowns in governance, oversight, and accountability will continue.

The fourth and final section is "Parties and Elections." In Chapter 11, Royce Koop takes on the PC Party of Manitoba, providing an historical overview of the party's electoral and ideological record, leadership, and organizational performance. He notes that the leader has always occupied an important place in the PC Party; therefore, understanding the party requires understanding the personalities who have variously led it to both victory and defeat. He draws attention to the ongoing splits in the party between its rural and urban factions and progressive and conservative wings. These geographic and ideological tensions have remained in the party over time and under its many leaders, Koop argues, leading him to conclude: "The history of the PC Party of Manitoba is one of varying factions—urban versus rural, right wing versus Red Tory—rising and falling inversely to one another." Koop then turns his attention to the Brian Pallister and Heather Stefanson governments, noting that while Pallister's leadership of the party would lead the PCs back into power in 2016 and again in 2019 (the largest majority ever in Manitoba's history), that would come at a cost. As he reveals, despite a more moderate direction and the rebuilding of relationships that had been damaged by the previous leader, the hope that Stefanson could successfully rebrand the PC Party following Pallister's leadership failed to materialize in the 2023 provincial election.

Christopher Adams sheds light on the New Democratic Party of Manitoba in Chapter 12. He maps the party's roots to urban labour politics in the early twentieth century, followed by the Co-operative Commonwealth Federation (CCF), which in turn transformed into the NDP in the early 1960s, both federally and provincially. Adams describes how the NDP became one of the two main provincial parties in Manitoba following the 1969 breakthrough election that brought Edward Schreyer to power. Since then, the party has battled the PCs in each election, with political power alternating between them. In the late 1990s and into the 2000s, Gary Doer shifted the NDP towards the ideological centre, successfully winning women and middle-class swing voters, in addition to maintaining the party's traditional bastions of support in the province's North and working-class Winnipeg. Yet, despite this move to the centre, Adams notes, the NDP maintains formal links to organized labour. In addition to providing an historical account of the party and its ideological bases, the chapter outlines the NDP's organizational structure and how the party elects its leaders, including, most recently, Wabanakwut "Wab" Kinew. Adams concludes the chapter with an assessment of the NDP's performance in the 2023 election, notably its success in defeating a long-governing but unpopular PC party by appealing to mainstream voters in Winnipeg. As Adams argues, however, "time will tell whether Kinew and his party will be able to translate the party's success into successive victories."

In Chapter 13, Kelly Saunders explores what she calls "the conundrum" of Manitoba liberalism in her examination of the Manitoba

Liberal Party (MLP). Despite its dominance in Manitoba politics for the first seven-plus decades of its existence, Manitoba's centrist, moderate political culture, and the lack of viable alternatives for Manitoba voters outside of the NDP and PC parties, the MLP is rarely able to capture more than 15 percent of the popular vote in the province. To unpack this puzzle, Saunders describes the historical and geopolitical context that continues to shape Manitoba politics, followed by an assessment of the leaders, performance, and organization of the MLP, notably over the past three decades. She suggests that, despite the many factors that favour a more robust Liberal Party in Manitoba, the ability of the NDP and the PCs to broker geographic, class, and ethnic cleavages and claim the ideologically moderate centre has left little room for the MLP. This lack of ideological space has been compounded by the Liberals' perennial struggles on the organizational, financial, and leadership fronts, and by the internal conflict, factionalism, and dysfunctionalism that appear to be "an ingrained feature" within the party. Reduced to a single seat following the 2023 provincial election, and facing yet another leadership convention, the party's fortunes appear dim. This may change, Saunders notes, depending on how well the NDP government led by Wab Kinew is able to meet its 2023 election promises and whether the PC Party continues to shift to the right. Together, these two factors may open new ideological space for the Liberals down the road.

As the reader can see from this brief overview of the thirteen chapters gathered for this volume, whether the province is seen as a "big world" or a "small world," one thing is certain: Manitoba is a fascinating, unique, and anything-but-dull political community. A lot of ground is covered in this book, from the history of Manitoba to its political, economic, and social institutions and some of the communities that make up the province. We hope that readers walk away with a new-found respect, appreciation, and understanding for Manitoba, the Keystone Province.

We are deeply grateful to each of our authors who have contributed their time, energy, and insights to this volume. Truly, this project would not have been possible without their valued efforts. We would also like to thank the two anonymous peer reviewers who provided comments and suggestions on an earlier version of this manuscript, and whose feedback resulted in a stronger and more conceptually rigorous book. Last but not least, we thank Jill McConkey and all the staff at the University of Manitoba Press for their patience and diligence in helping guide this book through to its successful conclusion. We hope that this volume will help fill some of the gaps in our knowledge and understanding of politics and governance in this remarkable and distinctive province many of us call home.

Notes

1. Paul G. Thomas and Curtis Brown, "Introduction: Manitoba in the Middle," in *Manitoba Politics and Government: Issues, Institutions, Traditions*, ed. Paul G. Thomas and Curtis Brown (Winnipeg: University of Manitoba Press, 2010), 3.
2. See David J. Elkins and Richard Simeon, eds., *Small Worlds: Provinces and Parties in Canadian Political Life* (Toronto: Methuen, 1980); Jared J. Wesley, ed., *Big Worlds: Politics and Elections in the Canadian Provinces and Territories* (Toronto: University of Toronto Press, 2016).
3. Elkins and Simeon, *Small Worlds*, xvi.
4. Murray Donnelly, *The Government of Manitoba* (Toronto: University of Toronto Press, 1963).
5. Andrea D. Rounce and Jared J. Wesley, eds., *Disengaged? Fixed Date, Democracy, and Understanding the 2011 Manitoba Election* (Regina: University of Regina Press, 2014).
6. Karine Levasseur, Andrea Rounce, Barry Ferguson, and Royce Koop, eds., *Understanding the Manitoba Election 2016: Campaigns, Participation, Issues, Place* (Winnipeg: University of Manitoba Press, 2016).
7. Royce Koop, Barry Ferguson, Karine Levasseur, Andrea Rounce, and Kiera L. Ladner, eds., *Understanding the Manitoba Election 2019: Campaigns, Participation, and Issues* (Winnipeg: University of Manitoba Press, 2019).
8. Andrea Rounce and Karine Levasseur, eds., *COVID-19 in Manitoba: Public Policy Responses to the First Wave* (Winnipeg: University of Manitoba Press, 2020).
9. See Wesley's chapter on Manitoba in his edited volume *Big Worlds: Politics and Elections in the Canadian Provinces and Territories* (Toronto: University of Toronto Press, 2016); as well as Wesley's *Code Politics: Campaigns and Cultures on the Canadian Prairies* (Vancouver: UBC Press, 2011).
10. Christopher Adams, *Politics in Manitoba: Parties, Leaders, and Voters* (Winnipeg: University of Manitoba Press, 2008).
11. Howard Pawley, *Keep True: A Life in Politics* (Winnipeg: University of Manitoba Press, 2011); Gary Filmon, *Yes We Did: Leading in Turbulent Times* (Winnipeg: Heartland Associates, 2021); Gord Mackintosh, *Stories Best Left Untold* (Winnipeg: Great Plains Publications, 2017).
12. Rounce and Levasseur, *COVID-19 in Manitoba*.

PART 1
Manitoba's Political Landscape

CHAPTER 1

"All the Rights We Are Entitled To": Louis Riel and the Creation of Manitoba

ROBERT COUTTS

Is the political history of Manitoba dull? Traditionally, Manitoba has been viewed, at least by some people, as a province without a political identity or a distinctive political culture. According to political scientist Jared Wesley, it is often regarded as a fuzzy middle ground where East meets West; an "ambiguous mediocrity" and a buffer between the traditions of the older East and the populism of the "new west."[1] When writing about Manitoba's political tradition, historian Gerald Friesen asked former premier Duff Roblin what that provincial tradition might be. Replied Roblin, "I don't believe there is such a thing. You'll have to invent one."[2]

Yet, such views ignore much of the province's past, a past born of a long history of Indigenous occupation and influence—6,000 years ago and today. It glosses over early fur trade culture, over later class and ethnic controversy and conflict, the gaudy capitalism of early Winnipeg, impoverished immigrants, and over a labour movement either smouldering just below the surface or exploding in protest. Manitoba has its own political character, and if terms like "mediocrity" have been used to describe that character, they overlook the events and personalities who have fashioned a unique and stimulating past. Writing in the 1950s, historian William L. Morton called his native province "an unusual and fascinating place possessed both of a history of great interest and of a deep sense of history."[3] Not to be forgotten is that Manitoba originated in resistance, the only province to enter Confederation to the sound of guns.

An Indigenous Foundation

The earliest years of governance in Manitoba, or what would become Manitoba, involved Indigenous forms of authority. Long before the Council of Assiniboia nominally governed the old colony of Red River and Louis Riel organized his provisional government, the Indigenous peoples of Manitoba had developed unique histories, laws, and cultures as part of their relationship with traditional territories.

Over millennia, Manitoba's First Peoples employed different forms of governance that helped to regulate cohabitation, conflict, resource use, trade, and seasonal movement. In the plains, parkland, and boreal forest areas, some groups lived in small communities while others were organized into larger bands. In traditional Néhinaw and Maškékowak (Cree) society, for instance, the fall, winter, and spring months saw the organization of smaller family units, which facilitated hunting, and in summer several hunting groups would come together to form larger communities that were based on collective principles. As these groups moved northward into the boreal forest, the Ojibwa, part of the Anishinaabeg, came to occupy Manitoba's plains and parkland and were divided into politically autonomous bands that shared a common culture. Like the Cree, the Ojibwa organized into discrete family-based hunting groups in the winter months, re-forming as a larger assembly in late spring or early summer. Ojibwa society and governance relied on patrilineal totem-based clans. In the Far North, among Sayisi Dene peoples, leadership was a communal endeavour. Although an Elder was chosen as leader, or chief, many community decisions were made by consensus.[4]

The common factor with First Nations in Manitoba, both pre- and post-contact, was the importance of a communal voice in governance. Consensus approaches to decision making characterized virtually all areas of life, from family and clan relations to larger group decision making about issues both large and small. From this governance tradition, a tradition of unanimity, there emerged the concept of *wahkohtowin*, a Cree word meaning "having or possessing good relations." Later adopted by Métis peoples, it is a concept that arises from the core values relating to the nature of relationships that Indigenous peoples are required to live by—relationships that are both individually and collectively characterized by positive and affirmative connections with others.[5] Wahkohtowin also establishes protocols and frameworks for interaction and behaviour; it is the foundation for pursuing any economic, political, social, or cultural activity, and is essential for the creation of alliances and codes of conduct.[6] Linking community, family, culture, and land, wahkohtowin has much in common with representative democracy as it helps to define the way people can govern themselves within a broad social consensus. While Manitoba's current democratic culture owes much to the evolution of the Westminster system and parliamentary custom, we might also see parallels with traditional Indigenous forms of authority.

When viewing Manitoba's political origins and history from a diversity of cultural perspectives, we can appreciate that representative or parliamentary democracy is one type of collective function that has slowly gained status in the West. Governments were formed that involved the election of government officials, and as more people became included within this authority, there emerged the recognition of the freedom of assembly and association, freedom of speech and religion, and equality. Property rights have also been a foundation of representative democracy.

But in studying the Resistance of 1869–70, the passing of the Manitoba Act, and Manitoba's entry into Confederation, we can also see how Indigenous forms of government and the emergence of leadership in the province were related to wahkohtowin and traditional forms of consensus building. Historian Derrick Nault has recently argued that wahkohtowin helps to explain three interrelated aspects of the Red River Resistance: where it commenced, who participated in the first act of resistance, and, most critically, why Louis Riel emerged as leader of the Métis in the fall of 1869.[7] Nault's analysis of Indigeneity and the resistance of 1869–70 builds upon the work of M. Max Hamon, whose 2019 book *The Audacity of His Enterprise: Louis Riel and the Métis Nation That Canada Never Was, 1840–1875* provides a parallel perspective, one that sees Riel's encounter with the Canadian state as more dialogic than confrontational and involving multiple perspectives as well as leadership and negotiation skills. Riel, Hamon argues, had many cultural inspirations, including "Catholic and Métis spirituality, French traditions, English culture, British legal understanding, and American political rhetoric," all of which provided him with the intellectual and cultural training to help achieve Métis land rights while realizing a Métis Nation in the Northwest.[8] In helping to shape Confederation, Riel merged the media of communication of both Indigenous and non-Indigenous peoples. Arguably, it is here where Riel successfully wove Indigenous concepts of community with the traditions of Western statecraft.

Early Approaches: The Council of Assiniboia

The first non-Indigenous peoples to arrive in the region that is now Manitoba were European fur traders. French traders entered from the east through the Great Lakes in the early eighteenth century, and the English Hudson's Bay Company (HBC) began building trading posts along Hudson Bay in the late seventeenth century. The fledgling economy that was the early fur trade did not alter Indigenous forms of governing, although the position of "trading captains," as they were called, assumed a greater role in Maškékowak, Dene, and Ojibwa societies.

In 1812, with the arrival of the Selkirk Settlers to the confluence of the Red and Assiniboine rivers, a new form of governance was soon created. In what became known as the Red River Settlement, Scottish, Irish, French, and Métis settlers were nominally governed by a form of administration known as the Council of Assiniboia. Although the council enacted laws and maintained policing for the district, it was not a form of responsible government or a particularly democratic one, as members were appointed by the HBC. The Red River Settlement was governed according to the imperial traditions of the day. The Council of Assiniboia was created to provide a governing body for the District of Assiniboia, a territory that ran along the Red and Assiniboine rivers and included the forks of the two rivers. In the early years of the council, it was not directly governed by the Hudson's Bay Company, although the company maintained de facto control of the colony through the close relationship between Lord Selkirk and local HBC officers as well as George Simpson, the company's overseas governor. Several council members came from the ranks of the HBC officer class, who served along with local clergy and with members of the so-called leading settlers.

In 1836 the HBC purchased the District of Assiniboia from the estate of Lord Selkirk. Thereafter, councillors were appointed by the

HBC and the size of the council was increased from seven members to fifteen. Assiniboia was divided into four judicial districts, each with its own court with an appointed magistrate or justice of the peace. More serious cases in the district were referred to the General Quarterly Court, made up initially by the colony governor and council, and later presided over by an HBC-appointed lawyer called the recorder. Adam Thom, a lawyer from Montreal, was the first to occupy this position. The Métis peoples of the settlement (who made up the bulk of the population) strongly disliked Thom, who was very much anti-French in both his opinions and his rulings. Louis Riel's father, Jean-Louis Riel, who had emerged as a Métis leader and reformist in Red River by the middle part of the century, vehemently opposed Thom and organized a petition for his removal in 1849. Riel Sr.'s activism on behalf of Métis rights in the settlement helped persuade the HBC to end Thom's position as recorder in 1851.[9] With pressure from Jean-Louis and others in the settlement, the HBC was compelled to appoint francophone and Métis members to the Council of Assiniboia; Abbé Louis Laflèche was appointed a councillor in 1850, and the Métis François Bruneau in 1853. Although the Council of Assiniboia remained technically independent from the HBC for much of its existence, its members were appointed by the company and its limited jurisdictive responsibilities were strongly connected with the interests of the fur trade. With the creation of Louis Riel's provisional government in 1869, the council was disbanded.

Canada Looks Westward and Louis Riel's Emerging Leadership

By the 1850s central Canada had begun to look beyond its borders.[10] A mounting desire to annex portions of the West was due to several factors, including the growing scarcity of good farmland in the East and the opportunity to develop a railway that could exploit the rich resources of the hinterland that would become Manitoba and the Northwest. While some historians have depicted the settlement of Red River as weak and unstable by the middle of the century,[11] in fact the colony—largely French- and English-speaking Métis with some Europeans—was reasonably secure, if traditionally subject to the vagaries of climate and geography and the social tensions of its European inhabitants. However, as the once-isolated settlement became increasingly integrated into the wider world (the first steamboat in Red

River, the *Anson Northup*, arrived from Minnesota in 1859),[12] Canadian annexationists also began arriving in the West determined to link Red River and the Northwest with central Canadian interests. Once the HBC's nominal ownership of Rupert's Land had been extinguished, a new empire would arise. Not surprisingly, the occupation claims of the West's First Nations would be ignored, at least until the era of treaty making later in the century. Land once known as the commons became in essence common property resources and eventually regulated by private ownership. The Canadian Party, as it came to be known, under the leadership of John Christian Schultz, led the annexationist movement in Red River, with its arguments for joining the Canadas put forward through the *Nor'Wester*, which had been founded in 1859 as western Canada's first newspaper.[13]

As annexationist sentiments developed among the British and incoming Canadian settlers in the mid- to late 1860s, Métis residents grew uneasy with the promised influx of new colonizers, and questions over economic status and land ownership rights dominated the politics of the settlement.[14] Though annexation by Canada was the preferred alternative for many people in Red River, primarily among its European inhabitants, others preferred Crown colony status or amalgamation with the United States. While French-speaking Métis in the settlement were most suspicious of a new English ascendency, English-speaking Métis in Red River and beyond were also apprehensive about their land rights, although at one level they were less worried about a coming new order because of the commonality of language and religion. Louis Riel, born in Red River in 1844, stepped into the leadership vacuum that existed in Métis Red River. His education in Montreal provided the charismatic young man with the leadership and oratorical skills to oppose the Canadian Party when he returned to Red River in 1868.[15] If some English-speaking Métis remained suspicious of the settlement's new Indigenous leader, his movement would eventually unite the peoples of the region and their demands for adequate representation in Canada's hinterland.

The Riel-Lagimodière family had a long history in Red River and its kinship and social networks were broad. These kinds of networks, along with the concept of wahkohtowin, played a part in the establishment of community values and objectives as well as its political organization. Max Hamon describes how Louis Riel's upbringing in the Riel-Lagimodière family at Red River, along with his education and religious beliefs, influenced the Métis leader's character and personal magnetism and helped make him an effective politician with strong leadership qualities.[16] Derrick Nault adds that Riel's "kith and kin likewise viewed the world through the prism of *wahkohtowin*, ... [and] the obligation to support family and community members, whether [it was] Riel or others close to them."[17] Thus, Riel's leadership and political success at Red River during much of the resistance depended not simply upon his skills as a politician and orator but also on the community character that had developed from his father's leadership in the settlement, and even from the days of his grandparents, Jean-Baptiste Lagimodière and Marie-Anne Gaboury.

Resistance: Riel's Provisional Government

The March 1869 transfer of Red River and Rupert's Land to the new Canadian government brought considerable alarm to the settlement, especially among its Métis inhabitants, who were never consulted regarding the handover. John Schultz's Canadian Party, which was allied with the national Canada First movement, a British Protestant association organized in 1868, had lobbied for some time to have Assiniboia join the new confederation and continued to conspire against Métis interests in the settlement. Métis fears of dispossession and loss of rights were real, as Canada intended to govern the new territory not as a province equal to the others but as a colony with a lieutenant-governor and an appointed council, none of whom had ever set foot in the region. In October of 1869, shortly after forming the Comité national des Métis with John Bruce as president and himself as secretary, Louis Riel led a group to block the Canadian surveyors who had arrived in Red River. At the same time the comité also threw up a blockade on the trail to Pembina (a settlement located in the Dakota Territory), intending to stop the entry of William McDougall, an Ontario Member of Parliament appointed by Prime Minister John A. Macdonald as the lieutenant-governor designate of Assiniboia.[18] With this blockade, later to become famous as *La Barriere*, Riel wrote McDougall in Pembina that by order of the comité, McDougall was to be barred entry "sur le territoire du Nord Ouest sans une permission spéciale de ce comité."[19]

A month later, Riel occupied Upper Fort Garry with the support of Michif-, French-, and English-speaking Métis in the settlement.

Hoping to bring the English-speaking Métis of the community on board with his plans to stand up to Ottawa and its non-consultative and unilateral seizure of the settlement and the territory, Riel sent out a notice in early November inviting these English parishes to send twelve representatives to join the twelve French-speaking members of the comité. Titled "Public Notice to the Inhabitants of Rupertsland" and dated 6 November, Riel offered to "extend the hand of friendship to you our friendly Fellow Inhabitants" now that, as he wrote, "the Invaders of our rights being now expelled."[20] Riel's goal was to "form one body with the above Council [comité] consisting of twelve members to consider the present political state of the Country, and to adopt such measures as may be deemed best for the future welfare of the same."[21] On 16 November twelve delegates from the English-speaking parishes in Red River met with their French-speaking counterparts at Upper Fort Garry. Although only a small handful of the newcomers were Métis, their leader was James Ross, the Métis son of long-time settler and historian Alexander Ross and a lawyer by training. At one time a joint editor and proprietor of the *Nor'Wester* newspaper supported by the Canadian Party, Ross now generally favoured the goals of the resistance and the negotiation of better terms with Canada.

Negotiations between English- and French-speaking members of the committee dragged on for several days, as the anglophones considered the occupation of Fort Garry illegal and Riel's desire for a provisional government to be premature. Although both elements agreed on the need to present terms of negotiation to the Canadian government, and even agreed generally on what those terms should be, the English-speaking members wanted to engage with the Canadians only after McDougall had been installed as lieutenant-governor. Riel, for his part, was insistent that the necessary rights of the region's inhabitants be guaranteed first through an act of Parliament and that this be done prior to annexation. In one speech before the comité, Riel emphasized the necessity to "protect [our country] against the dangers which threaten it. We desire that the people of Red River will be a free people, let us join one another. We are all brothers and cousins. Don't let us be separated."[22] But while some people in the English-speaking Métis community in Red River continued to oppose Riel, and despite differences of language and religion, most people supported the Métis leader and his aspirations for the settlement.

On 1 December 1869, the day originally selected for the official transfer of Rupert's Land to Canada (but with McDougall still in Pembina), Riel convened a meeting at Fort Garry and, after hours of "disorderly discussion,"[23] the group emerged with the first draft of a "List of Rights." Over the next number of days, several versions of this list circulated throughout the settlement and thus began the various incarnations that would result in the final List of Rights that was delivered to Ottawa. In the initial list the consent of the local legislature to federal parliamentary acts was stipulated, and while some general guarantees regarding land were contained within the demands, they were less than explicit regarding Indigenous title.[24] Also, in early December 1869 members of the Canadian Party led by John Schultz armed themselves against the Métis but were soon taken as prisoners and jailed at Fort Garry. The next day Riel issued a "Declaration of the People of Rupert's Land and the North West" and announced the creation of a provisional government to replace the Council of Assiniboia.[25]

One of the seminal events of the resistance occurred at Fort Garry in the mid-January cold of 1870. At an outdoor gathering of over 1,000 locals, Donald Smith, representing Canadian interests (and, it was hoped by Ottawa, the man to stir up opposition to the new government), instead provided what historian Jack Bumsted has called a "*de facto* recognition to an extra-legal authority in the settlement," a move that Prime Minister Macdonald would later call "wretched physical cowardice."[26] For Riel, however, the assembly, made up of both French and English speakers, had recognized that the people of Assiniboia "claim no half rights ... but all the rights we are entitled to."[27] For his part, Smith agreed to take back to Canada the provisional government's terms regarding the acceptance of Canadian rule. The Fort Garry assembly then approved the creation of a Convention of Forty made up of elected representatives from the parishes of the settlement, which was the first elected body in Rupertsland. Charged with creating a final and comprehensive bill of rights, the convention passed a series of articles that focused on all the residents of Assiniboia and not solely the Métis Nation, arguing for a public administration that would be beyond simply a Métis government.[28] Many of the listed rights concerned basic matters of governance such as public expenditures for schools and public buildings, homestead laws, the creation of a railway to Lake Superior, representation in the federal parliament, and the negotiation of treaties with First Nations peoples. Most crucial, the final Bill of Rights called for the admission of Manitoba into Canada as a province rather than a territory. Such a provision, Riel argued, along with the demand for the respect and protection for all privileges, customs, and usages, would guarantee the new province crucial political, land, and language rights. No doubt it was expected that provincial control of resources would also fall under Manitoba's control upon its entry into Confederation, though that was not to be the case.

In February Riel appointed three emissaries—Father Joseph-Noël Ritchot, John Black, and Alfred Scott—"to proceed to the city of Ottawa and lay before the Dominion Government the accompanying list of propositions and conditions as the terms upon which the people of Assiniboia will consent to enter Confederation with the other Provinces of the Dominion."[29] Ritchot was a close advisor to Riel, especially in the early days of the resistance, and would take the lead in negotiations with Ottawa that ultimately led to the passage of the Manitoba Act.

That same month Riel released the prisoners still held at Fort Garry. Some, including John Schultz and Thomas Scott, had escaped the previous December, and had rallied in Portage la Prairie with other members of the Canadian Party. Under the direction of Major Charles Boulton, they planned a march on the fort to release the remaining prisoners, only to disband after hearing that the prisoners had been freed. A short while later, however, Riel had several of these staunch and armed opponents of the provisional government recaptured and again imprisoned at Fort Garry. Meanwhile, in Ottawa the federal government began preparing a military force made up of British regulars and Canadian volunteers to travel to Red River if required.[30]

The incident that is generally believed to be the turning point in the resistance, the execution of Thomas Scott, was soon to occur. For some historians, Scott, though a steadfast supporter of the Canadian Party, an enemy of Riel, and indeed a troublemaker, was basically an innocuous member of Riel's opposition, a "stranger" according to the Métis leader.[31] Others have been less kind to Scott. Jean Teillet writes that "Scott was an obnoxious bully boy. His character did not improve in captivity. He taunted and kicked the guards. He spat bitter racist slurs at them day and night...he said he would never be satisfied until he had walked through the blood of Louis Riel."[32] Historian Norma

Hall has referred to Scott as a sort of "*wihktigoo*," a murderous and infectious force in Ojibwa spirituality.[33] Regardless, it was decided after a brief trial to execute Scott, which was done outside the walls of Fort Garry on 4 March 1870. It was his execution that animated eastern opposition and certainly the ire of the Canada Firsters who made much of the killing in the Ontario press. And it surely provided the excuse for Ottawa to follow through on sending an expeditionary force to punish Riel and the Red River Métis for their challenge to a Canadian sense of manifest destiny.

Although the literature on Scott's death might offer various perspectives, one thing that is widely agreed upon is that the execution changed the whole course of the resistance. But did it? From the beginning, Ontario was adamant that Assiniboia (and the much larger Northwest) be part of the new country, although not necessarily on an equal footing. In part, this was to keep the region out of American hands, but most important was to keep it as a resource hinterland for eastern interests. There was little knowledge of the settlement and its people and little interest in negotiating with the Indigenous locals. Mounting a force against what was perceived to be a less than civilized Indigenous adversary was characteristic of an imperialist era, and a colonialist approach that was the lingua franca, or common language, among the British stock of nineteenth-century Ontario.

Despite Scott's death and the resulting furor in Anglo-Ontario, the negotiations between Riel's government and Ottawa went on.[34] Arriving at the capital in April 1870, Ritchot, Black, and Alfred Scott were not given official standing (as Ottawa still considered the provisional government to be without status), although they did carry on private negotiations, mainly at the house of MP Sir George-Étienne Cartier. New additions to the earlier Bill of Rights called for the admission of the territory to Canada as the "Province of Assiniboia" with a constitution like that of Quebec's, an official demand for amnesty for the members of the provisional government, and a clause demanding the institution of publicly funded separate schools.[35] The granting of amnesty, though promised verbally, was never made official and would come to haunt many people in Red River in the days after the arrival of the Wolseley Expedition (discussed below). During the negotiations, which dragged on for several days, John A. Macdonald wanted the region to enter Confederation as a territory with an appointed government, and only later to be made a province with an elected assembly. Eventually, Macdonald (reluctantly) and Cartier agreed to the concept of a province with two chambers, an elected Legislative Assembly and what proved to be a short-lived appointed council. A fledgling judicial branch was also to be part of the new government. The new province, to be called Manitoba, would be small, less than 30,000 square kilometres. The provision of 1.4 million acres (approximately 566,560 hectares) would be guaranteed to the children of Métis heads of families, as were bilingual language rights. Unallocated land in Manitoba was controlled by the federal government and later sold off to new immigrants to help support the construction of the Canadian Pacific Railway.

After debate in Parliament, the Manitoba Act was given royal assent on 12 May 1870 and came into effect on 15 July of that year. Manitoba thus entered Confederation as the young country's fifth province—the "postage stamp" province would have four members in the House of Commons as well as two senators. At Confederation there were 181 seats in the House. Unlike with the other provinces at the time, Canada maintained control of natural resources in the new province, in keeping with Ottawa's desire to develop a resource base and hinterland economy for the central provinces. Moreover, education and language rights that were guaranteed under sections 22 and 23 of the Manitoba Act were later swept aside by the Thomas Greenway government of the 1890s.

Notwithstanding the passage of the Manitoba Act, and the oral guarantee of amnesty, a military force under Colonel Garnet Wolseley was sent to Red River from Ontario, arriving in August 1870. Despite Ottawa's oral agreement of amnesty for Riel and his supporters, the expedition members arrived looking for revenge; Riel was forced to flee, and, in the early fall of 1870, Adams Archibald was formally installed as lieutenant-governor of Manitoba. Some members of Riel's provisional government were imprisoned, and a "Reign of Terror," or violence against the French-speaking Métis of the settlement, ensued.[36]

As Archibald had yet to enter Red River when the Wolseley Expedition arrived, the colonel advised that Donald Smith, the ranking Hudson's Bay Company officer who had met with Riel earlier, was to assume the role of acting lieutenant-governor. Shortly after Archibald's arrival in early September to take over the role of lieutenant-governor (much to the great relief of Donald Smith), a group under John Schultz broke into the offices of *The New Nation*, a Métis newspaper, and beat its editor, Thomas Spence. A week later Elzéar Goulet, one of the members of the Thomas Scott firing squad, was chased into the Red River, where he drowned. Soldiers searched and ransacked homes in the settlement. Locals such as François Guillemette and James Tanner were killed. Hugh Francis (Bob) O'Lone, a member of both the Convention of Forty and the Legislative Assembly of Assiniboia, and the owner of the Red Saloon, died after a barroom brawl. Others, such as Riel's cousin and Métis council member André Nault, were savagely beaten. After the aborted Fenian raids on Manitoba in the autumn of 1871,[37] many of the Wolseley troops left Manitoba, although some remained to take advantage of a promised 160-acre (64.7 hectares) land grant while others went into business or undertook successful careers as lawyers. As Canadian settlers—largely English-speaking—began arriving in the new province, the expedition members who remained behind enjoyed the fruits of the new colonial occupation.

In 1870 approximately 10,000 of the 12,000 inhabitants of the new province were Métis.[38] At the time the province's geographic size was a mere fraction of what it is today. The Manitoba Act provided land titles in the form of scrip be confirmed for Métis landowners. As well, 1.4 million acres in the new province were to be reserved for the children of Métis heads of households. Sections 30, 31, and 32 of the Act conceded ownership of the occupied territory in the settlement to the original inhabitants and their families.

Scrip is a document that entitles the bearer to certain rights. In 1870 the federal government devised a system of scrip, issuing documents redeemable for land or money and given to Métis people living in Manitoba in exchange for their land rights.[39] However, as land could not be acquired until a full survey had been completed—a process that took up to three years—many of the province's Métis people sold their scrip for far less than its true value. For many families who had lived for decades on the river lots of the old settlement, proving ownership of that land became difficult, especially when documentation of clear title did not exist. As well, those families that followed a mixed resource-extraction economy of buffalo hunting and limited agriculture found it difficult to assert claims to their traditional lands and migrated west.[40] As the scrip process itself was legally complex and its issuance disorganized and based for the most part upon the legal and financial systems of central Canada, the system was open to fraud. Land speculators began buying up scrip at much reduced prices, claimed the land, and then resold the titles for much higher prices to incoming settlers. Being redeemable for land, or its cash value, scrip, for the federal government, was a convenient process to acquire Métis rights in Manitoba, thereby clearing the province for white settlement.[41]

As for Riel, with the resistance over and Ontario troops still looking to lynch him, the Métis leader made his way south to the Dakota Territory. Although Métis candidates did well in the first Manitoba election in December of 1870, Riel was unable to return because of illness. He did manage, however, to raise enough Métis support to oppose Fenian plans orchestrated by his old lieutenant, William O'Donoghue, to attack Manitoba. Fearing Riel's return to Manitoba, John A. Macdonald offered the Métis leader a bribe to stay in the U.S. With the defeat of Cartier in Quebec in the federal election of 1872, Riel, who had been asked to run in the riding of Provencher, stood aside for the former Quebec MP to run in Manitoba.[42] When Cartier died in May 1873, Riel was persuaded to run in Provencher in a by-election he won easily. Afraid of prosecution, however, Riel never took his seat in the House of Commons. Riel lived for a time in New York State before travelling to Montreal, where he was committed by his uncle to an asylum at Longue-Pointe in 1876. In 1878 Riel was released and ended up in Montana, teaching school at St. Joseph's Mission in the Sun River District and becoming an American citizen. In 1884, however, a Métis entourage from Saskatchewan under the leadership of Gabriel Dumont travelled to St. Joseph's, where they convinced Riel to return with them to Batoche to oppose the new colonialist pressures that emanated from Ottawa.[43] The resulting North-West Resistance of 1885 under Riel's leadership would become a turning point in western Canadian, and indeed all Canadian, history.

Manitoba after Riel: Francophone Rights and the Manitoba Schools Question

With Manitoba soon to be under the control of the province's Anglo elite, the character and population of the province were about to be transformed. Although francophone leaders still maintained a hand in the politics of the province, within a few decades this would be altered as Ontarian and British immigration changed the makeup of the young province. An appointed upper house, or the Legislative Council of Manitoba, was created by the Manitoba Act. Based on the Quebec model of a bicameral legislature, ethnic and religious representation was a critical part of the council's function. Four of its members were Protestant and three were Catholic. As well, four members were Métis and represented ties to the "old settlers" and the heritage of the region. Its dissolution in 1876 helped to hasten the end of certain language rights in Manitoba, rights that Riel had insisted be central to the Manitoba Act.

The Legislative Assembly of Manitoba, consisting of twenty-four elected members, was created after the first general election in the new province in December 1870. Seventeen seats went to Lieutenant-Governor Adams Archibald's Government Party and the remainder were controlled by John Christian Schultz's Canadian Party, the government's opposition in the province. Although unelected, Archibald ostensibly fulfilled the role of "premier," or first minister, in essentially a non-partisan legislature and was followed in that role by Lieutenant-Governor Alexander Morris in 1872. Both positions were non-elected appointments by the federal government and demonstrated Ottawa's determination to control the administration of the new province, a situation different from that of the existing provinces and reflective of John A. Macdonald's belief that Manitoba should have entered Confederation as a territory rather than a province. The first legislative sittings were held in the former residence of Andrew G.B. Bannatyne on Main Street. In 1883 the second legislative building opened northeast of where the current building now stands. The Legislative Assembly of Manitoba grew quickly from its initial twenty-four seats to forty-nine by 1914; however, constituencies were inconsistent in their composition. A lack of common social or economic interests within constituencies made representation difficult. The great boom in immigration to the province in the last decades of the nineteenth century led to an increase in assembly seats and the expansion of Manitoba's borders in 1881 and 1912.[44]

With the massive influx of settlement after 1870—especially English-speaking Ontarians—francophones became a minority in the province. In 1890, under the premiership of Liberal Thomas Greenway, the provincial government denied the linguistic rights of francophones as the Legislative Assembly passed an Official Language Act that made

English the sole official language of the province. French was abolished as an official language in the assembly, in the courts, the civil service, and in government records.[45]

That same year, Greenway's Liberals under the leadership of Clifford Sifton, a member of Greenway's cabinet and the later federal minister of Immigration, eliminated the francophone Catholic denominational school system. Upon appeal, the Supreme Court ruled that the 1890 legislation contradicted the Manitoba Act of 1870. However, in 1892 the Judicial Committee of Britain's Privy Council, the highest court in the Commonwealth until 1949, overturned the Supreme Court decision and restored Greenway and Sifton's non-sectarian, publicly funded school system.[46]

The "Manitoba Schools Question," as it came to be known, which had created divisions within the province but had largely been settled in two provincial elections that supported the end of bilingualism and separate schools, became, interestingly, a national issue between English and French Canada. In fact, with Quebec wary of losing minority, or Catholic education, rights, the schools question became a major issue in the federal campaign of 1896, won by Wilfrid Laurier's Liberals. That same year the Laurier-Greenway compromise was reached, although Manitoba was represented mostly by Clifford Sifton. Little in the agreement satisfied Manitoba francophones as the province retained its public schools and public-school funding. Religious instruction could be offered for only one-half hour after regular school hours, and only when a sizable group of one faith in a particular school (Catholic or Protestant) existed. When ten or more students in a school spoke a particular language, instruction could be offered in that language. While the compromise worked early on in terms of French-language religious instruction, the French minority in the province failed to regain control over education. Later immigration of different ethnic groups to Manitoba, ironically encouraged by Sifton as minister of the Interior, created a demand for instruction in various languages.

Instruction in the French language in Manitoba continued until 1916, when the Legislative Assembly passed the Thornton Act, which repealed the Laurier-Greenway compromise and disallowed any language other than English in schools. Later legislation allowed for some use of the French language in schools but was not re-established as an official language in provincial education until 1970. In 1993 the

Supreme Court ruled that Manitoba's francophone minority had the right to control their own educational facilities, and through section 23 of the Canadian Charter of Rights and Freedoms in 1994, the Franco-Manitoban School Division (La Division scolaire franco-manitobaine) was created.

Within two decades after Manitoba's entry into Confederation, Greenway, as one historian has argued, presided over the final transition of Manitoba from a community-based political entity, where power was shared between the province's ethnic, linguistic, and religious communities, to a political culture, where partisan majoritarianism and liberal capitalism determined political power.[47] Along with the loss of land rights for many of the region's original settlers, in essence the unique quality of Manitoba as a province, and the foundation of its entry into Confederation as negotiated by Louis Riel, had all but ended.

Epilogue

I began this chapter by tracing some of the common governance traditions of pre- and post-contact Indigenous societies of present-day Manitoba, along with a brief discussion of the Cree and Métis concept of *wahkohtowin,* or "having or possessing good relations." In the case of the Red River Resistance, wahkohtowin helped to define how the role of kinship influenced not just the origins of the resistance but the cultural values that galvanized much of the community to oppose the annexationists and, more importantly, to organize support for Riel's leadership.

The Red River Resistance was, Derrick Nault argues, an event or series of events that for the Métis of Assiniboia involved "having positive relationships with others ... nurturing these relationships and supporting those in their network." As Louis Riel himself developed positive associations with those around him, Nault describes how "his kith and kin, besides needing his help, likewise felt duty-bound to assist Riel in his political aspirations."[48] M. Max Hamon contends that Riel drew upon Métis political legitimacy, where authority came from family relations and the land. "In Red River, like other Indigenous public spheres," Hamon writes, "authority was not drawn from clever words used by newspapermen expressing their opinions; rather it was about kinship and ties to the land."[49] At the same time, Hamon also argues, Riel had a foot in both worlds and derived his authority with the Métis from this fact. Hamon continues that Riel, resisting colonial power with intellectual force, "was also complicit in the transfer of authority from Indigenous ideas around kinship to a nebulous, but much more universal social identity that could serve as an umbrella for a much larger political community."[50] This would suggest that Indigenous forms of community governance are different from the Westminster style of majoritarian democracy. While in theory the Westminster system is representative, the anti-democratic nature of the colonial state in the nineteenth and twentieth centuries, with its many proscriptions on voting, representation, and rights, is less community-grounded than some traditional forms of governance.

The success of the Red River Resistance of 1869–70 in establishing the rights of the Manitoba Métis demonstrated this cohesion, even if many of those rights would be lost within a few short decades. As for the Canadians in Red River, and the Ontarian settlers who were to follow, their ascendency to positions of political and commercial power was consolidated by the 1890s. Manitoba, and especially Winnipeg, changed much in the years between 1869 and the turn of the twentieth century. Yet the spirit, and the abiding resolve of the year-long resistance, would remain woven into the fabric of the new province.

Notes

1 Jared Wesley, "Political Culture in Manitoba," in *Manitoba Politics and Government: Issues, Institutions, Traditions*, ed. Paul Thomas and Curtis Brown (Winnipeg: University of Manitoba Press, 2010), 43–44.
2 Gerald Friesen, "The Manitoba Political Tradition," in *Manitoba Politics and Government: Issues, Institutions, Traditions*, ed. Paul Thomas and Curtis Brown (Winnipeg: University of Manitoba Press, 2010), 21.
3 William L. Morton, *Manitoba: A History* (Toronto: University of Toronto Press, 1957), xiv.
4 Leo Pettipas, *"Other Peoples' Heritage": A Cross-Cultural Approach to Museum Interpretation* (Winnipeg: Association of Manitoba Museums, 1994), 47–49.
5 Harold Cardinal and Walter Hildebrandt, *Treaty Elders of Saskatchewan: Our Dream Is That Our Peoples Will One Day Be Clearly Recognized as Nations* (Calgary: University of Calgary Press, 2000), 14–15.
6 For a longer discussion of the meaning and origins of *wahkohtowin* as a social, cultural, and governance concept, see Brenda Macdougall, *One of the Family: Metis Culture in Nineteenth-Century Northwestern Saskatchewan* (Vancouver: UBC Press,

2010), especially Chapter 2, "The Bond that Connected One Human Being to Another," 51–85.

7   Derrick Nault, "Louis Riel, *Wahkohtowin*, and the First Act of Resistance at Red River," *Prairie History*, no. 8 (Summer 2022): 5–16.

8   M. Max Hamon, *The Audacity of His Enterprise: Louis Riel and the Métis Nation That Canada Never Was, 1840–1875* (Montreal: McGill-Queen's University Press, 2019), 7.

9   "Thom, Adam," in *Dictionary of Canadian Biography*, http://www.biographi.ca/en/bio/thom_adam_11E.html.

10 At the time of Confederation, Canada consisted only of Nova Scotia, New Brunswick, and lands surrounding the Gulf of St. Lawrence, the St. Lawrence River, and lands on the northern side of the Great Lakes. See Government of Canada, "Historical Boundaries of Canada," https://www.canada.ca/en/canadian-heritage/services/historical-boundaries-canada.html.

11 See, for instance, Frits Pannekoek, *A Snug Little Flock: The Social Origins of the Riel Resistance, 1869–70* (Winnipeg: Watson and Dwyer, 1991), who argues that Red River was a much-splintered colony with divisions between French-speaking and English-speaking Métis peoples that were exacerbated by Anglican-Catholic fault lines within the settlement. While some mistrust might have existed at various times between French- and English-speaking Métis, and the clergy of the opposing faiths in the settlement (most especially the Anglican clergy) did their best to inflame passions, Indigenous peoples in Red River lived in basic agreement. Those divisions that did exist in Red River were generally more class-based. See Robert Coutts, *The Road to the Rapids: Nineteenth-Century Church and Society at St. Andrew's Parish, Red River* (Calgary: University of Calgary Press, 2000), 131–51.

12 "Anson Northup (1859–1860)," https://www.gov.mb.ca/chc/archives/_docs/hbca/ships_histories/anson-northup.pdf.

13 Gerald Friesen, *The Canadian Prairies: A History* (Toronto: University of Toronto Press, 1984), 115, 119. See also Willliam Coldwell, "Founding the Nor'Wester," introd. Scott Stephen, *Manitoba History* 70 (Fall 2012): 53–58.

14 Jack M. Bumsted, *The Red River Rebellion* (Winnipeg: Watson and Dwyer Publishing, 1996), 31–38.

15 Riel's education at the Sulpician Collège de Montréal and his training for the priesthood are detailed in Hamon, *Audacity of His Enterprise*, 102–30; and in Maggie Siggins, *Riel: A Life of Revolution* (Toronto: HarperCollins Publishers, 1994), 46–66.

16 Hamon, *Audacity of His Enterprise*, 27–28.

17 Nault, "Louis Riel," 11.

18 Bumsted, *Red River Rebellion*, 55.

19 Louis Riel, "Letter to William McDougall," 21 October 1869, in *The Collected Writings of Louis Riel* (Edmonton: University of Alberta Press, 1985), 1:21.

20 Louis Riel, "Public Notice to the Inhabitants of Rupertsland," 6 November 1869, in *Collected Writings*, 1:22.

21 Ibid.

22 As quoted in Hamon, *Audacity of His Enterprise*, 171.

23 Bumsted, *Red River Rebellion*, 93.

24 Ibid., 93–94.

25 Louis Riel, "Declaration of the People of Rupert's Land and the North West," 69/12/08, in *The Collected Writings of Louis Riel* (Edmonton: University of Alberta Press, 1985), 1:42–44.

26 Bumsted, *Red River Rebellion*, 128.

27 As quoted in Hamon, *Audacity of His Enterprise*, 193.

28 Jean Teillet, *The North-West Is Our Mother: The Story of Louis Riel's People, the Métis Nation* (Toronto: HarperCollins Publishers, 2019), 197.

29 Louis Riel, "Letter to N.J. Ritchot, Winnipeg," 22 March 1870, in *The Collected Writings of Louis Riel* (Edmonton: University of Alberta Press, 1985), 1:64–65.

30 Jack M. Bumsted, "Red River Resistance," in *The Oxford Companion to Canadian History*, ed. Gerald Hallowell (Don Mills: Oxford University Press, 2004), 533.

31 See, for instance, Jack M. Bumsted, "Why Shoot Thomas Scott? A Study in Historical Evidence," in *Thomas Scott's Body and Other Essays on Early Manitoba History* (Winnipeg: University of Manitoba Press, 2000), 197–209.

32 Teillet, *North-West*, 214. Teillet does not provide a source for this statement except to write "By all accounts ..."

33 Norma Hall, "'Perfect Freedom': Red River as a Settler Society, 1810–1870," MA thesis (University of Manitoba, 2003), 158, as quoted in Hamon, *Audacity of His Enterprise*, 198.

34 Louis Riel, "Letter to N.J. Ritchot, Winnipeg," 22 March 1870, in *The Collected Writings of Louis Riel* (Edmonton: University of Alberta Press, 1985), 1:64–65.

35 Bumsted, *Red River Rebellion*, 169.

36 For a detailed, if somewhat embellished, account of the "Reign of Terror" following the arrival of the Wolseley Expedition, see Siggins, *Riel*, 185–94.

37 "Fenian" is the name of the old Irish National Militia that hoped to liberate Ireland from the English and establish a republic. One of the ways the Fenians proposed to do this was by capturing Canada and using this as a lever to free Ireland. Unsuccessful Fenian raids from the United States occurred in central Canada between 1866 and 1870. Hoping to gain the favour of Manitoba's Métis peoples, the Fenians, with a handful of men, decided to invade the new province in 1871. They captured the trading post at Pembina, a place of dispute as to whether it was in Canada or the United States, but were quickly captured themselves by the United States army. Troops in Manitoba did gather to defend the province from the small group of Fenian invaders but never saw action.

38 Gerald Friesen, "Manitoba," in *The Oxford Companion to Canadian History* (Don Mills: Oxford University Press, 2004), 383.

39 "Métis Scrip in Canada," in *The Canadian Encyclopedia*, https://www.thecanadianencyclopedia.ca/en/article/metis-scrip-in-canada.

40 See Coutts, *Road to the Rapids*, 194.

41 A debate has long simmered as to whether this exodus was caused by the loss of Manitoba properties, or the appeal represented by the buffalo robe trade in the Northwest. Though referred to as the "push-pull debate," it is clear that the Canadian government never intended to establish an equal relationship with the Manitoba Métis, a fact demonstrated by the language used in section 31 of the Manitoba Act. Approximately only 15 percent of the 1.4 million acres was ever distributed to Manitoba Métis families.

42 "Cartier, Sir George-Étienne," in *Dictionary of Canadian Biography*, http://www.biographi.ca/en/bio/cartier_george_etienne_10E.html.
43 Rod C. Macleod, "North-West Rebellion," in *The Oxford Companion to Canadian History* (Oxford: Oxford University Press, 2004), 451–53.
44 Friesen, "Manitoba," 383.
45 James Mochoruk, "Thomas Greenway, 1888–1900," in Barry Ferguson and Robert Wardhaugh, eds., *Manitoba Premiers of the 19th and 20th Centuries* (Regina: Canadian Plains Research Center Press, 2010), 92.
46 Ibid., 94.
47 Ibid., 101–2.
48 Nault, "Louis Riel," 11.
49 Hamon, *Audacity of His Enterprise*, 171.
50 Ibid., 202.

CHAPTER 2

Political Culture in Manitoba

JARED WESLEY AND LAUREN HILL

Introduction

Compared with the popular impression of other Canadian provinces, Manitoba's political culture remains undeveloped in the minds of many observers. In the words of Rand Dyck,[1] "Manitoba is a province without a distinctive political culture. If Manitobans have a self-image, it is probably one of a moderate, medium, diversified, and fairly prosperous but unspectacular province."[2]

Dyck is not alone. Many people define Manitoba by its ambiguity rather than by any unique political personality. Manitoba is the "keystone province," after all; it is the geographic centre of North America, the "Heart of the Continent," and the buffer between the "old" country of the east and Canada's "new west." Its population and economy are among the country's most diverse, and both are of average size. Relative to other major Canadian centres, even its capital city, Winnipeg, is viewed, Chris Read writes, as a "balance between exotic and obscure."[3] In short, Manitoba is Canada's "middling" province, positioned between east and west, old and new, exciting and bland.

Yet, such views distort the precise nature of Manitoba politics. As Douglas Marshall has written, the province "is more than a fuzzy middle ground where the East ends and the West begins."[4] It has its own, distinctive political ethos, which is grounded in the very concepts of modesty and moderation that make up its popular "middleman" image.

Modesty and Moderation

Some people regard it as a form of prudent pragmatism—an unpretentious, unassuming, conciliatory approach to politics that holds as its principal goals the accommodation of diversity, the preservation of order and tradition, and the protection of Manitoba's median position in Confederation. Others view the province's culture as a brand of prudish pessimism—a sign of Manitobans' quiescence on divisive issues or reticence on the national stage. Some see humility and realism in Manitoba's political culture, where others see meekness and resignation.

Whatever the case, there is little doubt Manitoba has always been "a land of steady ways" in which "the simple, sturdy virtues of hard work, thrift and neighbourliness have been cherished and transmitted."[5]

Reflecting these tendencies, Marshall writes, Manitobans, "though driven to strike out in new ways in politics, [have] remained fast wedded to the old ways in manners and morals."[6] In this sense, Manitoba politics has featured a stronger strain of traditionalism than Canada's other two prairie provinces, Saskatchewan and Alberta. This tendency is embodied in the province's political culture of modesty and moderation—a shared sense of identity that has both reflected and shaped the community's political evolution. But where do we find evidence of Manitoba's political culture—those unspoken norms that guide politics in the province?

Symbols

In order to sketch the contours of Manitoba's political culture, we must distinguish the indicators of the community's overarching values from their potential causes and consequences. Individual attitudes, beliefs, and behaviours of residents and elites cannot be used as indicators; they may stem from culture or reflect it but only imperfectly. (Culture is a collective phenomenon that exerts its influence on these individual actors. A community, or culture, is more than a sum of its parts.)

For evidence, we must turn to a community's symbols.[7] As James Johnson suggests, "culture consists of inter-subjectively shared symbols, deployed in ritual or other cultural practices, which actors invest with meaning in the process of imposing conceptual order on the social and political world."[8] In its broadest sense, culture may manifest itself in cultural and social artifacts like folk songs, popular novels, children's stories, television shows, music videos, movies, school textbooks, contracts, greeting cards, statutory holidays, popular leisure activities, or public prayers.[9] From this perspective, "the social," "fowl supper," and "potluck dinner" are indicative of collective spirit embodied in Manitoba's broader social culture.[10] Symbols like these both reflect and reinforce culture, in that, once the values become well established, they take on "a life of their own," independent of the forces and factors that contributed to their rise.[11]

Consider Manitoba's official emblems. Adopted in 1905, the Manitoba coat of arms signals the province's history of cultural conservatism, accommodation, and diversity (see Figure 2.1). As tribute to its settler colonial roots, British and Canadian icons are displayed, including the royal crown, the Cross of St. George (of England), and maple leaves. Indigenous symbols are also incorporated, albeit much more subtly. The Red River cart wheel pays homage to Métis roots, for example, and bead and bone decorations adorn the pair of unicorns in the crest, a reference to Manitoba's First Peoples. Lily flowers (fleurs-de-lis) symbolize the province's French-Canadian heritage. The province's economic diversity is represented at the bottom of the arms, marked by the presence of wheat, timber, and water. Most prominent, however, are the province's primary figurehead—the bison—and the provincial motto, *Gloriosus et Liber* (Latin for "Glorious and Free"). Borrowed from one of the country's early anthems, "O Canada," the maxim reflects Manitoba's ties to Canadian culture more generally.[12]

Manitoba also has a provincial tartan, the pattern of which reflects similar principles. According to the government's description of the official plaid: "Each colour has its own significance: Dark Red Squares—natural resources of the province; Azure Blue Lines—Lord Selkirk, founder of the Red River Settlement (Winnipeg); Dark Green Lines—the men and women of many races who have enriched the life of the province; and Golden Lines—grain and other agricultural products."[13] Of note, Manitoba is the only province in Canada to make specific reference to the intermingling of cultures in its tartan—a sign of the extent to which ethnic diversity forms a unique part of Manitoba's political culture.

Historically, the bison epitomizes Manitoba's roots as a plains society. It hearkens back to the time when the buffalo outnumbered humans in the region, or to the province's origins in the fur trade.

Figure 2.1. Manitoba Coat of Arms. Image courtesy of the Government of Manitoba, https://www.gov.mb.ca/legislature/visiting/docs/symbolsofmanitoba.pdf.

More abstractly, the bison symbolizes Manitoba's stolid, yet vulnerable, presence in Confederation. The animal's own history speaks of scars, while its future remains optimistic, if uncertain. Yet, for anyone who has seen a herd up close, the bison carries a respectful and respectable air. As W.L. Morton has indicated, this same sense of self can be felt among Manitobans in general. While Manitobans and their leaders may lack the bravado of their western neighbours, their quiet confidence speaks volumes of the nature of their pride. Alberta has its cowboy and Saskatchewan its wheat farmer, just as Quebec has its fleur-de-lis and

Ontario its maple leaf. As a community of communities, Manitobans cherish all these symbols, yet stake their collective identity on none of them. If Manitoba has its own symbol, it is the bison.

While the bison figures prominently, it is not the only symbol of note on the Manitoba flag. As history reveals, the Union Jack is equally important. The province's present flag was adopted on 12 May 1966, amid a nationwide debate over symbols and heraldry. A year earlier, then prime minister Lester Pearson's Liberal government had adopted Canada's Maple Leaf flag, sparking resentment among those committed to retaining British symbols, particularly the Union Jack.[14] Galvanized by federal Progressive Conservative leader John Diefenbaker, opposition to "Pearson's pennant" was fiercest in (rural) Ontario and Manitoba.[15] Tory governments in both provinces endorsed this sentiment by adopting a Red Ensign template for their respective new provincial flags, eschewing Canada's drift towards being a bilingual and bicultural country. As historian David Grebstad put it, the Manitoba flag symbolized "ninety-six years of the establishment and preservation of British cultural hegemony in Manitoba."[16] Modelled on the Canadian Red Ensign—the country's unofficial flag prior to 1965—each province's flag features the Union Flag in the upper left corner (or canton), defaced by the provincial shield to the right (or in the fly) (see Figure 2.2).

To some, the new Manitoba flag signified a form of loyalist protest against the severing of symbolic ties to the British Empire.[17] Whereas most other provinces abandoned the ensign in designing their new flags in the 1960s, Manitobans had it emblazoned on theirs.[18] To others, the new flag represented a more positive statement of the province's identity, rooted as it was in the trappings of its British colonial past. Either way, by endorsing the province's roots and traditions, the Manitoba Red Ensign remains a symbol of the province's modest, "steady ways." The flag has never been without its critics. The province's sesquicentennial offered a moment for reflection on Manitoba's heraldry. Some found a lack of diversity and inclusivity in the flag,[19] sparking a defence from the Progressive Conservative government of the day.[20]

The province's penchant for moderation also finds its voice in its political slogans. Engraved on its licence plates since 1976, the moniker "Friendly Manitoba" serves as the province's unofficial motto,[21] drawing

Figure 2.2. Flag of Manitoba. Image courtesy of the Government of Manitoba, https://www.gov.mb.ca/legislature/visiting/docs/symbolsofmanitoba.pdf.

on Manitoba's reputation as a community of diversity, and as W.L. Morton states, "understanding and agreeableness."[22]

Moderation is also reflected in Winnipeg's 2022 adoption of a new official brand and slogan: "Made from what's real." Rooted in Manitoba's embrace of modesty, the slogan seeks to highlight Winnipeg's genuineness, centredness, and groundedness, in modest, down-to-earth ways. During their public consultations, Travel Manitoba and Economic Development Winnipeg found Winnipeggers used words like the following to describe their city: authentic, real, warm, innovative, independent, connected, strong, diverse, industrious, creative, and centred.[23] According to the branding website, "Winnipeg is authentic to the core. Genuine experiences abound here. We don't sugar-coat; we problem-solve." And, "The Winnipeg story is changing," "What stays the same is our authenticity."[24] The new Winnipeg emblem also incorporates these elements: "Some see a sun on the horizon, a fitting symbol of our radiating optimism and warmth. [Or] A snowflake, reflecting a steely determination crystalized over generations. [Or] A cog for our industrious roots."[25] This down-to-earth, non-pretentious self-conception extends beyond the city limits to the rest of the province, as well. Like many other civic rebrands, the exercise was not without its critics. It is telling, however, that most of the criticisms were directed at the choice of logo and colours (red, instead of the historic blue for Winnipeg), and not the brand's authentic personality.[26]

The same "spirit" had been expressed during Manitoba's corporate branding exercise in 2006. That year the government launched the "Manitoba Image Project"—a highly publicized attempt to forge "a fresh, new image for Manitoba; a way of communicating our province's unique identity to raise our profile and tell the world that Manitoba is an exceptional place to live, work, visit and invest in."[27]

As the Manitoba Promotion Council argued: "Manitoba's image is often based on our own self-deprecating attitudes. We need to change the way we see ourselves, so we can do a better job of selling ourselves to the world.... It's time we redefined who we are. It's time we told the world how proud we are to call Manitoba home."[28] In this vein, their choice of slogan—"Spirited Energy"—aimed to capture "the truth about our province, and the way we want everyday Manitobans, businesspeople, and visitors to think about Manitoba." In particular, the brand was meant to embody "Manitoba's rich history of diverse cultures, varied climate, and northern location [which] has instilled a unique energy that radiates in from the hearts and minds of our people. From the birthplace of many successful artists, musicians and entrepreneurs who compete on the world stage, to the natural resources that fuel our economy, Manitoba is a wellspring of energy. Manitoba's spirited energy propels our province and its people, and drives our success. A rich past, a vibrant future—it's ours."[29] While it evokes a greater sense of dynamism and vibrancy than the other, more established symbols, nonetheless, the new "Spirited Energy" brand was intended to draw on many of the same core principles.

Manitobans' reaction to the new brand was mixed, at best, ranging from support to indifference to outright hostility. Among those in the latter category, some people felt that the new slogan departed too drastically from the province's more modest, moderate unofficial motto: "Friendly Manitoba." Despite opposition from those whose position appeared grounded in the province's penchant for "steady ways," the Spirited Energy campaign suggested that the province's identity lies in its accommodation of diversity and its future retains strong links to its past. This is the very essence of Manitoba's ethos of "moderation and modesty." That the province has, to date, not replaced "Spirited Energy" with another slogan reinforces this reluctance to change.

Origins

The question remains: Where did these values originate? Political cultures are neither entirely primordial nor entirely constructed. They do not simply "exist" but require definition and cultivation by members of the community. By the same token, they are not entirely "invented." Would-be mythmakers do not have a blank canvas upon which to paint their visions of a society; when proselytizing, they must take into account their community's social, ethnic, geographic, economic, historical, and other characteristics. In short, political culture contains both structural elements that appear inherited and agential elements that must be experienced.

Fragments

On the inherited side, one approach examines how early immigration patterns contribute to the development of a community's political culture. Fragment theory posits that, when colonizing, dominant settler groups import certain values from their parent cultures.[30] The character of these values depends on both the point and time of the group's departure, such that the settlers will transplant only a "fragment" of their original political culture, which is determined by both the dominant values present among the group's members and the point in the ideological evolution of the parent culture. Thereafter, the settler society becomes severed from its parent, effectively "freezing" in its stage of ideological development and spawning a unique political culture.

As John Ralston Saul argued, many of the values of conciliation, accommodation, and egalitarianism that pervade political culture in Canada more generally were "absorbed" by European settlers when they came in contact with Canada's First Peoples.[31] The same is true in Manitoba, where many white pioneers were exposed to the principles (and necessity) of negotiation with the region's first inhabitants. In this sense, Manitoba's political culture may be seen to predate the formal establishment of European political institutions.[32]

In terms of colonization, Manitoba's founding fragment was decidedly British. Beginning with the opening of the West in the late nineteenth century, Manitoba drew the vast majority of its immigrants from the province of Ontario, whose foundations and leading political figures were, according to Rand Dyck, only "slightly more progressive and politically experimental" than central Canadian liberalism.[33]

This "progressivism" brought with it a penchant for social and political reform, including the extension of suffrage, individual rights, and temperance. Yet, these British-Ontario pioneers brought with them a "Tory-touched liberalism" not found in other parts of the prairies.[34] This Toryism—also known as "classic," "traditional," or "Burkean" conservatism—has a long, if disputed, history in Canadian politics.[35] Compared with the "new right" (or "neoliberal") conservatism of today, Toryism involves a higher level of deference to authority, a stronger preference for social order, a keener reverence for the past, a deeper affinity for the United Kingdom, and a greater willingness to use the state to serve the public good. In addition to the many British symbols found in Manitoba's emblems, the presence of this Tory strain also helps to explain Manitoba's aversion to populism and radicalism. If the province inherited its "progressive" streak from the Ontario Grits and western Canadian farming community (by far the most dominant fragment), Manitoba inherited its "steady ways" from these early Ontario Tories.[36] Thus, in the late nineteenth century, its combination of western liberal-progressivism and eastern Tory-conservatism made Manitoba a sort of ideological melting pot of Confederation.

Fragment theory has been challenged on ethical and moral grounds for its colonial tendencies; the notion that European settlers arrived in "the New World" and imprinted their own ideological approaches *terra nullius* is obviously contestable.[37] Viewed through the lens of the state, however, it is clear how Manitoba's first settlers set up institutions and symbols to perpetuate their dominance over Indigenous peoples and, eventually, newcomers.[38] In this sense, political culture is a homogenizing force, both a product and a cultivator of settler colonialism.[39]

Transformative Events

From a second perspective, we might interpret political culture as a product of the community's shared experiences. One school of thought suggests that societies like Manitoba experience certain formative, and transformative, events throughout their history. As pioneers of this approach, Gabriel Almond and Bingham Powell, suggested, "Certain events and experiences may leave their mark on a whole society," compelling individuals to "acquire new conceptions of the role of politics in their lives."[40]

Some of these episodes are exogenous to the community, imposed by outside forces. Wars, epidemics, global economic trends, natural disasters, and other occurrences may fall under this category. Others are endogenously created, fostered by forces or actors within the community itself. These may include scandals, budget crises, social turmoil, or other, more localized events. Regardless of their origination and regardless of their political, economic, or social character, these transformative events leave a lasting imprint on the community's political culture.

Manitoba has experienced more than its share of such critical junctures. Since its violent entry into Confederation in 1870, the province has played host to some of the country's most divisive political debates, many with lasting ramifications for the country as a whole. From the Riel Resistance and the Manitoba Schools Question to the periodic but heated debates over biculturalism and the province's place in Confederation, Manitoba has been a "polity on the edge" at various points in its history.[41]

Nowhere is the importance of transformative events clearer than in the case of the 1919 General Strike. The violent suppression of the uprising constituted a major turning point in the province's history. The event helped to polarize and eventually mute the radical elements of the province's business and labour movements, and set the stage for the success of more moderate parties like the Liberal-Progressives, Progressive Conservatives, and New Democratic Party.[42]

Numerous other episodes could be cited as pivotal in Manitoba's history, of course. The two World Wars, the Great Depression, the Red River floods of 1950 and 1997, or the scandals surrounding the construction of the legislative building (1915) and the administration of northern election campaigns (1995) spring to mind. The COVID-19 pandemic also has the potential to reshape Manitobans' views of themselves, their politics, and their society. Each of these events brought with it a spirit of sacrifice (modesty) and togetherness (moderation) in the face of steep challenges, be they to the security of Manitobans' way of life, the future of the provincial economy, or the quality of Manitoba democracy. Dark days, like the opening of the Panama Canal in 1914—which ended Manitoba's reign as the sole gateway to the Canadian West—also served to reinforce Manitobans' humility and modesty.

From this perspective, an understanding of modern Manitoba politics begins with an appreciation for the periods of intense confrontation and disappointment that punctuate its past.

Economy

Manitoba's political culture may also be linked to the nature of its economy. Manitoba's first economic activity—the fur trade—helped forge (and in many ways challenge) the province's penchant for intercultural compromise. Since that time its lack of ideological tilt may reflect the absence of a dominant economic activity or "staple."

In a second, related, sense, Manitoba maintains Canada's most diversified economy, "balanced among various primary industries and among primary, secondary, and tertiary sectors. Although this economy is not outstanding in any particular respect, the province manages to remain relatively stable and prosperous."[43] Besides creating a heterogeneous community of interests, classes, and occupations, the structure of its economy has insulated Manitoba from the boom-and-bust cycles experienced by other provinces. As a result, by avoiding the depths of the Depression or heights of economic growth experienced in Alberta and Saskatchewan, for example, Manitoba has not been subject to the same type of radical "utopian sorties" led by parties such as Social Credit and the Co-operative Commonwealth Federation.[44] In this sense, Manitoba's stable, diversified economy has contributed to its ethos of moderation.

Third, the average size and growth rate of the Manitoba economy place it consistently near the national mean. Since the modern equalization program was introduced in 1957, Manitoba has maintained a "have-less" position relative to other, more prosperous members of Confederation. As discussed in greater detail below, this fiscal status helps to explain Manitoba's moderate, cautious approach to either expanding or contracting social programs or its modest, conciliatory tack toward the balance of power between the provincial and federal orders of government.

Combined, these distinct settlement patterns, transformative events, and economic factors have all contributed to the development of Manitoba's modest, moderate ways. Those are the primary sources of the province's political culture, but what of its effects?

Constraints on time and space here do not permit a complete examination of the full impact of Manitoba's political culture. As others in this volume attest, political culture leaves its mark on all political institutions, including government programs and organizations, as well as on political parties and party systems. Of note in this chapter, political culture also affects all members of a community, from those at the grassroots to those in the halls of power.

Impacts on Individual Attitudes

On the first count, political culture is reflected, according to Gabriel Almond and Sidney Verba, in "the specifically political orientations—attitudes toward the political system and its various parts, and attitudes toward the role of the self in the system."[45] Thus, political culture manifests itself in community members' "psychological orientation toward social objects ... as internalized in the cognitions, feelings and evaluations of [the] population."[46] An examination of public polling data reveals this is certainly the case in Manitoba. While reliable province-wide surveys are difficult to come by, existing data support the notion that Manitobans' attitudes have long reflected a modest and moderate political culture.[47]

There is a noticeable strain of realism in Manitobans' orientation toward the economy, for instance. Findings from a spring 2008 Canada West Foundation survey revealed that, compared with their western Canadian neighbours, Manitobans were far more modest in their assessments of the health of their economies than were residents of Alberta and Saskatchewan.[48] Some may argue that these views flow directly from the "realities" of Manitoba's diversified, consistent, steady, yet "unspectacular" economy. However, Manitobans' perceptions of these "realities" are crucial; and this is where political culture plays a critical intervening role. Manitobans could just as easily be more pessimistic (defeatist) or optimistic (delusional) about their economic prospects. Instead, and in large part, they have chosen to accept their economic standing. The modesty embedded in Manitoba political culture is the fount of these perceptions.

Manitobans are also quite centrist on most matters of public policy, according to research from the Comparative Provincial Elections Project, which studied Canadians' attitudes between 2011 and 2014. Their responses to major matters of public policy tend to be nearer to the centre of the political spectrum and closer to the Canadian average than their counterparts' in Alberta and Saskatchewan (Table 2.1). And when asked to place themselves on the left-right spectrum, the average Manitoban is closest to the centre line (5) (Figure 2.3).

Table 2.1. Attitudes toward Public Policy Issues by Province, 2011–2014.

	AB	SK	MB	Cdn Avg
Favours raising taxes to increase public services (0) vs. favours cutting public services to cut taxes (10)	5.0	5.2	5.5	5.2
Favours more traditional policies on matters such as abortion, homosexuality, and euthanasia (0) vs. favours less traditional policies on matters such as abortion, homosexuality, and euthanasia (10)	6.3	5.5	6.0	6.1
Favours high levels of regulation and control of the market (0) vs. favours deregulation of markets at every opportunity (10)	5.3	5.5	5.4	5.2
Supports protection of the environment, even at the cost of economic growth (0) vs. supports economic growth, even at the cost of damage to the environment (10)	4.6	4.9	4.8	4.6
Advocates that government should provide universal free health care (0) vs. advocates that medical expenses should be paid by individuals and private insurance plans (10)	3.3	3.3	3.1	3.0

Note: Cell figures represent the average self-placement of respondents on a 0-to-10-point scale. Source: Adapted from Jared Wesley, "Introduction," in *Big Worlds: Politics and Elections in the Canadian Provinces and Territories* (Toronto: University of Toronto Press, 2012).

This sense of centrist realism is connected to Manitoba's fiscal and political position within Confederation. Compared with other regional residents, Manitobans are less attached to "Western Canada" as a distinct political identity, for example, and are more content with their province's treatment in the federation. Indeed, Manitobans are still significantly less attached to their regional identity than are their neighbours in Saskatchewan and Alberta (see Table 2.2). In terms of "western alienation," Manitoba's distinctiveness is even clearer. In 2019 most Manitobans felt that their province was treated with the respect it deserves in Confederation. Manitobans are less likely to assume a province-first identity compared with their counterparts in Alberta and

Saskatchewan; they are also less likely to want to see the West or their own province separate from Canada. In all of these areas, Manitobans sit "sandwiched between the highly satisfied Ontario and the highly dissatisfied Saskatchewan."[49] This lack of western alienation reflects the province's age-old penchant for moderation.

Table 2.2. Attitudes toward the West and Confederation, by Province, 2019–2021.

	AB	SK	MB
The West is a distinct region*	89	90	84
Province has less than fair share of influence in important national decisions****	62	65	62
The west usually gets ignored in national politics*	81	85	72
Federal government should make a greater effort to address western alienation*	69	73	60
I feel more attached to my province than I do to Canada**	46	47	31
The rest of Canada does not care about the West*	53	64	56
My province does not get its fair share from Confederation**	62	54	40
I feel less committed to Canada than I did a few years ago**	34	29	18
Province is not treated with respect it deserves in Canada****	57	59	50
Province receives less than its fair share of federal spending****	60	59	50
Western Canada should separate from Canada***	45	47	40
My province would be better off if it separated from Canada**	25	18	6

Note: Cell figures represent percentage of respondents agreeing or strongly agreeing with the statement.

Sources: *Adapted from Environics Institute, "2019 Survey of Canadians: Canada: Pulling Together or Drifting Apart?" (2019). **Adapted from Ipsos, "Western Alienation on the Rise? Not So Much" (2018). ***Adapted from Environics Institute, "2021 Survey of Canadians: Respect, Influence, and Fairness in the Canadian Federation" (2021). ****Adapted from Environics Institute, "2022 Survey of Canadians: The Evolution of Prairie Discontent" (2022).

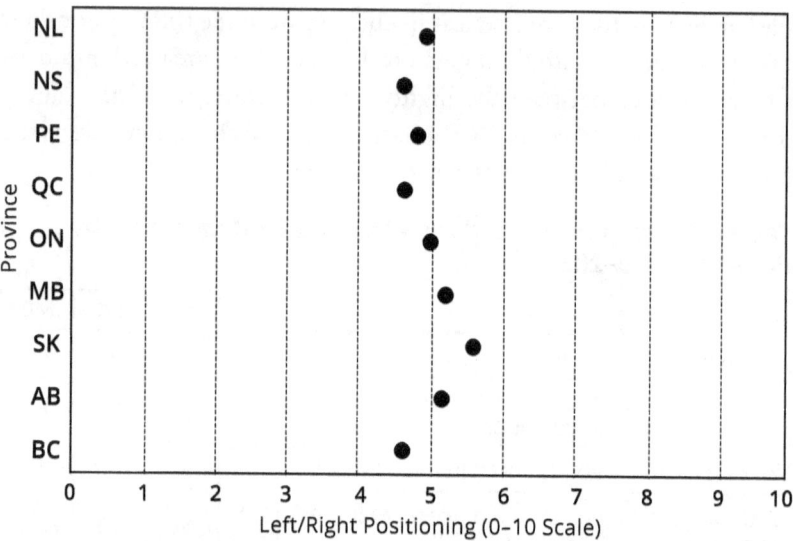

Figure 2.3. Ideological Self-Placement by Province, 2011–2014. Adapted from Jared Wesley, "Introduction," in *Big Worlds: Politics and Elections in the Canadian Provinces and Territories* (Toronto: University of Toronto Press, 2012).

Impacts on Elite Politics

Beyond the grassroots, a community's shared values also affect the way elites approach politics. Specific cultural factors make a community more conducive to certain sets of ideas and their carriers, for example. By the same token, situational factors may also make a community more receptive to a given message or messenger. As discussed above, crises like the Great Depression or World Wars may create the opportunity for a re-evaluation of a society's leadership.

Overall, however, the presence of a stable, guiding ethos—like modesty and moderation—makes a community such as Manitoba more susceptible to certain types of leadership. As David Bell describes, political culture "provides a range of acceptable values and standards upon which leaders can draw in attempting to justify their policies. Thus, political culture shapes the perception of the politically relevant problems, thereby affecting both the recognition of these problems as issues requiring some sort of governmental action and the diagnosis of what sort of action is appropriate."[50] This is certainly true in Manitoba, where a political culture grounded in modesty and moderation has spawned an elite discourse based on three related principles: progressive centrism, pragmatism, and flexible partisanship.

Progressive centrism constitutes the foremost element of "high politics" in Manitoba. Leading politicians in Manitoba have consistently stressed the importance of avoiding extreme ideological positions in favour of pragmatic, middle-of-the-road, incremental policies and programs.[51] This is not to say that Manitoba parties have been unprincipled or devoid of ideological commitment. Manitoba parties have taken distinct left-wing and right-wing positions throughout history.[52] Yet, the differences between them have been much more subtle than those found in Saskatchewan and Alberta.

Ultimately, the persistence of this theme of moderation goes some way in explaining why—with the notable exceptions of Ed Schreyer and Sterling Lyon—most of Manitoba's party leaders have been praised for their competence and congeniality, as opposed to their vision and charisma. They have been viewed as both reformist—adopting change when necessary and where popular—and conservationist—standing by established ends and means, and relying on compromise and patience. As Morton put it, Manitoba leaders have tended to be "hard-headed, practical men [sic] who took life as they found it, were skeptical of reform and . . . indifferent to idealism."[53]

The search for the progressive centre is related to the second component of Manitoba elite politics: pragmatism. Since Manitoba lost its status as the commercial and transportation gateway to the Canadian West with the opening of the Panama Canal, Manitoba politicians have adopted a modest, cautious view of Manitoba's economic and political future. This practicality underlies the incrementalism that pervades major party platforms in Manitoba, both in terms of their policy pledges and their rhetoric. With few notable exceptions, the focus of party elites has been on convincing voters they offer a "better administration" of government, rather than a fundamentally "better way" of doing politics. This is not to say Manitoba leaders are pessimistic or defeatist, as others have implied—far from it.[54] The realism found in Manitoba elite discourse merely reflects a belief that, with its stable and diversified economy and society, a "better Manitoba" is more attainable and desirable than an unrealistically "ideal" one.

A final related element of Manitoba "high politics" is flexible partisanship. In their campaign rhetoric, Manitoba elites have tended to promote a more fluid conceptualization of party interaction than have their counterparts in Saskatchewan or Alberta. At times, the Manitoba narrative has defined politics as a "non-partisan" affair, as the efforts to create broad, formal coalitions in the early twentieth century attest, or as "multi-partisan," as seen during periods of negotiation over Manitoba's constitutional position in later decades.

Some attribute this partisan flexibility to a form of "politicophobia"—a concern over contesting controversial issues in the partisan arena for fear of dividing the province or losing elections.[55] Others view the approach as placing provincial interests above partisan ones. Either way, this form of "stewardship"[56] has been practised by Manitoba's most successful premiers, beginning with John Norquay, who "believed that the government should represent not a party but a province, both to conciliate groups within it, and also to strengthen the province in negotiations with Ottawa."[57]

On the latter point, moderation in Manitoba has also extended to the realm of federal-provincial relations, where links between Winnipeg and Ottawa have been far friendlier than those in other western Canadian capitals.[58] Even prior to achieving provincehood, Manitoba had always held a central place in Canadian nation building, and its founding settlers, elites, and institutions were drawn predominantly from Ontario. As a result of this, and its historic position as a have-not province, Manitoba has been more closely tied to central Canada than either of its prairie neighbours.[59] Consequently, its elites have lacked the same "oppositional reflex" as found in Alberta,[60] and, compared with either of its western neighbours, Manitoba election campaigns feature the lowest level of provincial patriotism.[61]

All three elements of Manitoba elite discourse—centrism, pragmatism, and partisanship—speak to the same spirit of conciliation and accommodation embodied in the province's political culture. Notable breakdowns have occurred, of course. Tumultuous periods surrounding the Winnipeg General Strike, recessions in the 1970s and 1980s, and the Meech Lake Accord featured much more acrimony than so-called normal times. The COVID-19 pandemic exposed tensions within and between the province's main political parties, as well. But, due largely to Manitoba's political culture, these episodes have been exceptions to the rule. The province's guiding ethos, as cultivated by elites bent on stability, mitigates the intensity and duration of these "punctuations."

This final point speaks to the two-way relationship between political culture and political leadership—politicians are shaped by their culture but also help reinforce and recraft it through their rhetoric.

Conclusion

Manitoba's "mediocre" image is well earned, if undervalued or misinterpreted. Rather than being a default classification, the label reflects an ethos of modesty and moderation that is deeply ingrained in the province's political culture. These values are embodied in the province's core symbols, including its flag, logos, mottos, and slogans. They are rooted in Manitoba's early, Tory-touched liberal settlement patterns and highly diversified economy, and have been tested and reinforced through several transformative events, ranging from the Riel Resistance to the Winnipeg General Strike and more recent debates over Manitoba's position in Confederation. This culture of modesty and moderation is not only reflected in Manitobans' attitudes toward the economy and the province's place in Confederation. It is also manifested in the behaviour of the province's elites, who have emphasized the importance of progressive centrism, pragmatism, and flexible partisanship throughout much of the province's history.

Without doubt, the anti-radical tendencies of Manitoba's political culture mask tensions and inequalities of power. The go-along-to-get-along quality of the province's political norms downplays the challenges faced by traditionally marginalized communities to achieve influence over government. The flashpoints noted above reveal how such tensions remain barely below the surface. The gradual but painfully slow rise of workers, women, visible minorities, and Indigenous people to positions of power reflects the incrementalism embedded in Manitoba's political culture. It takes generations, not years, for new conceptualizations of what is "moderate" to develop, culminating most recently in the ascendancy of Manitoba's (and Canada's) first premier of First Nations descent, Wabanakwut "Wab" Kinew, and the province's first non-white majority and gender-balanced cabinet in 2023.

Somewhat ironically, these values of accommodation and humility are a sense of pride to many Manitobans. This suggests they are rather immodest in terms of their modesty. And not all people agree with the nature of Manitoba's political culture. To some, Manitobans' quiet confidence manifests itself in an unhealthy form of complacency. A self-image based on moderation and compassion can lead Manitobans to underestimate the challenges and discrimination that still face many members of their community. To others, Manitoba's moderate, modest predisposition is almost defeatist. By accepting the province's middling status, the culture holds Manitoba back from greater aspirations and progress as a society.

For better or worse, the story may seem familiar to students of Canadian politics more generally. And it should. From the time of European settlement, and in many ways, Manitoba remains the "microcosm" of Canada: "it is both rural and urban, with urbanization being the trend; it contains an ethnic mosaic anchored by an internally diverse Anglo-Saxon charter group; its economic life and institutions reflect a hinterland status; and its politics are perhaps best noted for their typically Canadian moderation."[62] Manitoba is, in short, the "matrix" of Canada. As Douglas Marshall says, "For Manitoba is Canada in miniature. Imagine all our complex problems and potential—numbing distances, the untapped North, biculturalism and bilingualism, teeming cities and deserted farms, the need for investment capital and the concern about where it comes from—condensed and reduced to one twentieth of scale, you would have something that looks a lot like Manitoba."[63]

In these ways, Manitoba is the country's quintessentially Canadian province. Yet, this does not mean it lacks a distinctive identity. The province's modest and moderate ethos is derived directly from that image, and, as a result, its political culture is defined by its own unique symbols, sources, and consequences.

Notes

1 Rand Dyck, *Provincial Politics in Canada* (Scarborough: Prentice-Hall, 1996), 381.
2 As Dyck describes, "Manitoba has in many ways become Canada's median or average province. The 'gateway to the West,' it is centrally located and traditionally served as the location where eastern manufactured goods were exchanged for western raw materials. In modern times, the decline of railways, the advent of air travel and telecommunications, and the emergence of substantial manufacturing capacity in the West have reduced Manitoba's role in interprovincial trade. It is still the median province in terms of size, and is more advanced economically than the Atlantic region but behind the three richest provinces. It has a relatively balanced economy, not being identified with any particular industry, and is somewhat 'average'

in terms of its ethnic distribution, with a medium-sized francophone community." Ibid., 373.
3   Chris Read, "From Scranton to Winnipeg: The Office Goes North," *CBC News Online*, 23 October 2008, https://www.cbc.ca/news/entertainment/from-scranton-to-winnipeg-the-office-goes-north-1.697048.
4   Douglas Marshall, "How Manitoba Turned 100 by Standing on its Head," *Maclean's* 83, no. 12 (1 December 1970): 31.
5   W.L. Morton, *Manitoba: A History* (Toronto: University of Toronto Press, 1957), viii.
6   Marshall, "How Manitoba Turned 100 by Standing on its Head," 382.
7   Clifford Geertz, "Ideology as a Culture System," in *Ideology and Discontent*, ed. D.E. Apter (New York: The Free Press, 1964), 193–229; Clifford Geertz, *The Interpretation of Cultures* (New York: Basic Books, 1973). Lowell Dittmer suggests political culture lies in the "system of political symbols," which itself "nests within a more inclusive system that we might term 'political communication.'" See Lowell Dittmer, "Political Culture and Political Symbolism: Towards a Theoretical Synthesis," *World Politics* 29 (1977): 566. For other examples, see Elisabeth Jean Wood, *Insurgent Collective Action and Civil War in El Salvador* (Cambridge: Cambridge University Press, 2003); and James C. Scott, *Weapons of the Weak* (New Haven: Yale University Press, 1985), 28–47.
8   James Johnson, "Conceptual Problems as Obstacles to Progress in Political Science," *Journal of Theoretical Politics* 15, no. 1 (2003): 99.
9   See Stephen Chilton, "Defining Political Culture," *The Western Political Quarterly* 41, no. 3 (September 1988): 436; Robert Putnam, *Bowling Alone: The Collapse and Revival of American Community* (New York: Simon and Schuster, 2000).
10 Gerald Friesen, *The West: Regional Ambitions, National Debates, Global Age* (Toronto: Penguin Group/McGill Institute, 1999), 185.
11 Sheri Berman, "Ideas, Norms, and Culture in Political Analysis: Review Article," *Comparative Politics* 33, no. 2 (2001): 234.
12 "O Canada" did not become Canada's official national anthem until 1980, and the official English translation of the song was not written until 1908. Any reference to the terms "glorious and free" must have been adopted from popular versions of the song that were in circulation to that point.
13 Government of Manitoba, Residents Portal, accessed 21 January 2025, https://residents.gov.mb.ca/reference.html?d=details&program_id=5909#.
14 For the record, many alternative flag designs included British symbols alongside French (e.g., the fleur-de-lis) or Canadian (e.g., the maple leaf) symbols.
15 Alaistair B. Fraser, "A Canadian Flag for Canada," *Journal of Canadian Studies* 25, no. 4 (1991): 64–80.
16 David Grebstad, "The Flag of Our Fathers? The Manitoba Provincial Flag and British Cultural Hegemony in Manitoba, 1870–1966," *Raven: A Journal of Vexillology* 23 (2016): 56.
17 In particular, some interpret the new flag as a partisan protest by Manitoba Progressive Conservatives, following Diefenbaker's defeat at the hands of the Pearson Liberals in Parliament over the national flag.
18 In 1960, prior to the national flag debate, British Columbia adopted its flag, which incorporates the Union Jack.
19 Bryce Hoye, "Is Manitoba's 150th a Chance to Redo Province's Flag?" *CBC News*, 2 February 2020, https://www.cbc.ca/news/canada/manitoba/manitoba-150-provincial-flag-design-1.5446653.

20 Steve Lambert, "Manitoba Flag Called Outdated, a 'Relic,'" *Winnipeg Free Press*, 26 February 2009, https://www.winnipegfreepress.com/breakingnews/2009/02/26/manitoba-flag-called-outdated-a-relic.

21 Prior to 1976, the provincial licence plate featured the slogans "100,000 Lakes" and "Sunny Manitoba" or featured a bison icon.

22 Morton, *Manitoba: A History*, viii–ix.

23 "Winnipeg Brand: Winnipeg: Made from What's Real," accessed 23 August 2022, https://realwinnipeg.com.

24 Ibid.

25 Ibid.

26 Ryan Stelter, "Winnipeg's New Slogan Has Not Been Well-Received," *Winnipeg Sun*, 11 June 2022, https://winnipegsun.com/opinion/columnists/stelter-winnipegs-new-slogan-has-not-been-well-received.

27 Manitoba Promotion Council, *Manitoba's New Image*, 2008, http://www.mbpromotion.ca/spirited_energy_message.php; and Manitoba Promotion Council, *Why Change Manitoba's Image?* 2008, accessed 28 October 2008, http://www.mbpromotion.ca/spirited_energy_why_brand.php. The effort was coordinated by the Premier's Economic Advisory Council (PEAC). See also, "Manitoba's New Brand: 'Spirited Energy,'" CBC News, 15 June 2006, accessed 26 March 2025, https://www.cbc.ca/news/canada/manitoba/manitoba-s-new-brand-spirited-energy-1.626226; and Government of Manitoba, "Private Sector Takes Lead in Promoting Manitoba," 6 November 2008, accessed 26 March 2025, https://news.gov.mb.ca/news/index.html?item=4714#:~:text=A%20new%20organization%20known%20as%20the%20Manitoba,Swan%20and%20Premier%27s%20Economic%20Advisory%20Council%20(PEAC).

28 Manitoba Promotion Council.

29 Ibid.

30 See Louis Hartz, *The Founding of New Societies* (New York: Harcourt, Brace and Jovanovich, 1964). Space does not permit a detailed appraisal of fragment theory here. For a recent critique, see Jared J. Wesley and Sylvia Wong, "Beyond Fragments: The Canadian State and the Origins of Alberta Political Culture," *International Journal of Canadian Studies* 60, no. 3 (2022): 60–87.

31 John Ralston Saul, *A Fair Country: Telling Truths About Canada* (Toronto: Penguin Canada, 2009).

32 Nelson Wiseman, *Social Democracy in Manitoba: A History of the CCF-NDP* (Winnipeg: University of Manitoba Press, 1983), 3–5.

33 Dyck, *Provincial Politics*, 381.

34 Grounded in the semi-feudal, traditionalist tendencies of the country's Loyalist heritage, Toryism represents Canada's "old right." As a unique mixture of seemingly disparate philosophical elements, Toryism has attracted criticism as being non-ideological (H.D. Forbes, "Hartz-Horowitz at Twenty," *Canadian Journal of Political Science* 20, no. 2 [June 1987]: 287–315); politically expedient (Roger Gibbins and Neil Nevitte, "Canadian Political Ideology: A Comparative Analysis," *Canadian Journal of Political Science* 18, no. 3 [September 1985]; 577–98); unscientific (Janet Ajzenstat and Peter J. Smith, "The 'Tory Touch Thesis: Bad History, Poor Political Science," in *Crosscurrents: Contemporary Political Issues*, ed. Paul Barker and Mark Charlton, 5th ed. [Scarborough: Thomson Nelson]; and even mythical (Rod Preece, "The Myth of the Red Tory," *Canadian Journal of Political and Social Theory* 1, no. 2 [1977]: 3–28).

To some critics, for all its usage in political circles, mass media, popular culture, and academia, the term "Toryism" remains too vaguely defined (see Rod Preece, "The Anglo-Saxon Conservative Tradition," *Canadian Journal of Political Science* 13, no. 1 [1980]: 3–32; Kenneth Dewar, "Toryism and Public Ownership in Canada: A Comment," *Canadian Historical Review* 64, no. 3 [1983]: 404–19). Despite these criticisms, the principles of Toryism do conform to the characteristics of ideology employed in the present analysis. Granted, it may be a "recessive strain" in Canadian political ideology (see William Christian and Colin Campbell, *Political Parties and Ideologies in Canada*, 3rd ed. [Toronto: McGraw-Hill Ryerson, 1990], 9; Ian Stewart, "All The King's Horses: The Study of Canadian Political Culture," in *Canadian Politics: An Introduction to the Discipline*, ed. Alain-G. Gagnon and James P. Bickerton, 2nd ed. [Peterborough: Broadview Press, 1994], 78–80); but even its harshest critics have noted the continued resonance of Toryism as a key theme in Canadian politics. See Charles Taylor, *Radical Tories: The Conservative Tradition in Canada* (Toronto: House of Anansi Press, 1982), 115.

35 This Tory-touched fragment not only helps to explain the long-term survival of the Progressive Conservative Party in Manitoba. It also suggests why socialism found a toehold in Manitoba in the form of the Independent Labour Party, Co-operative Commonwealth Federation (CCF), and, most recently, the New Democratic Party (NDP). According to fragment theory, when combined with the reform-minded philosophy of liberalism, the organic sense of community embodied in Toryism produces an environment conducive to socialism. See Louis Hartz, *The Founding Of New Societies: Studies in the History of the United States, Latin America, South Africa, Canada, and Australia* (Boston: Mariner Books, 1969); G. Horowitz, "Conservatism, Liberalism and Socialism in Canada: An Interpretation," *Canadian Journal of Economics and Political Science* 32, no. 2 (May 1996): 143–71; James McAllister, *The Government of Edward Schreyer: Democratic Socialism in Manitoba* (Kingston: McGill-Queen's University Press, 1984), 90–93. British Labourites, whose brand of Fabian socialism found a sympathetic ear among the province's working-class population, seized this opportunity, establishing the partisan foundations for the modern NDP. See Wiseman, *Social Democracy in Manitoba*, 4–9. In short, Wiseman says, "Manitoba had enough Ontario in it to have sustained the only provincial Conservative party west of Ontario that has never collapsed. But it also had enough of modern Britain and Continental Europe to provide CCFer J.S. Woodsworth and Communist leader W.A. Kardash with parliamentary seats." Wiseman, *Social Democracy in Manitoba*, 149.

36 Gabriel Almond and G. Bingham Powell Jr., *Comparative Politics: A Developmental Approach* (Boston: Little, Brown and Co., 1966), 65. Seymour Martin Lipset is another pioneer of the formative events approach. See his *Revolution and Counterrevolution: Change and Persistence in Social Structures* (New York: Basic Books, 1968) and *Continental Divide: The Values and Institutions of the United States and Canada* (New York: Routledge, 1990).

37 James Holt, "Louis Hartz's Fragment Thesis," *The New Zealand Journal of History* 7, no. 1 (1973): 3–11.

38 Shauna Wilton, "State Culture: The Advancement of 'Canadian Values' Among Immigrants," *International Journal of Canadian Studies* 42 (2010): 91–104.

39 Walter Soderlund, Ralph C. Nelson, and Ronald H. Wagenberg, "A Critique of the Hartz Theory of Political Development as Applied to Canada," *Comparative Politics* 12, no. 1 (1979): 63–85.

40 Gabriel A. Almond and G. Bingham Powell, Jr. *Comparative Politics: A Developmental Approach* (Boston: Little, Brown and Company, 1966), 65.

41 Wiseman, *Social Democracy in Manitoba*, 8–9; Nelson Wiseman and K. Wayne Taylor, "Class and Ethnic Voting in Winnipeg during the Cold War," *Canadian Review of Sociology and Anthropology* 16, no. 1 (1979): 62. See also Morton, *Manitoba: A History*, 362–72; and McAllister, *Government of Edward Schreyer*, 89–90.

42 The opening of the Panama Canal in 1914 "sap[ped] the traffic that fed [Winnipeg's growth]," elevating Vancouver as the primary gateway to the West. See Morton, *Manitoba: A History*, 308.

43 Nelson Wiseman, *In Search of Canadian Political Culture* (Vancouver: UBC Press, 2998), 217. See also William L. Morton, "The Bias of Prairie Politics," in *Riel to Reform: A History of Protest in Western Canada*, ed. G. Melnyk (Saskatoon: Fifth House Publishers, 1992), 17; Christopher Dunn and David Laycock, "Saskatchewan: Innovation and Competition in the Agricultural Heartland," in *The Provincial State: Politics in Canada's Provinces and Territories*, ed. Keith Brownsey and Michael Howlett (Mississauga: Copp Clark Pitman, 1992), 225.

44 Gabriel Almond and Sidney Verba, *The Civic Culture: Political Attitudes and Democracy in Five Nations* (Princeton: Princeton University Press, 1963), 10.

45 Ibid., 13. It is crucial to note that Almond and Verba (and their many followers in the psycho-cultural school) consider political culture to *be* these attitudes. To them, culture is simply an aggregation, or average, of these individuals' beliefs and opinions. In this chapter, we consider individual attitudes to be *consequences—not* indicators—of political culture. This is done for several reasons. First, as Durkheim argued, culture is more than simply an aggregation of individual behaviours. Rather, it lies in the broader social structure—what he terms the "collective conscience" of a society, or the "repository of common sentiments, a wellspring from which individual conscience draws its moral sustenance." See Émile Durkheim, *Suicide: A Study in Sociology* (New York: Free Press, [1897] 1965, 16). By the same token, a community's culture—by definition, its *shared* values and norms—is more than a simple aggregation of individuals' beliefs. In technical terms, Almond and Verba fall victim to what is known as "false aggregation" or "the reverse ecological fallacy." Just as we cannot use macro-level data (e.g., census statistics) to make valid inferences about micro-level actors (e.g., individual residents of a census district), we cannot do the reverse. In short, as Johnson argues, analysts "gain little by treating the distribution of 'orientations' among a population as 'political culture' rather than, for example, simply as a 'mass belief system' or, more prosaically still, as 'public opinion.'" See Johnson, "Conceptual Problems," 99.

Second, political culture is less transitory than public opinion. Just as descriptions of the weather offer us only limited glimpses into the climate of a particular community, one-off surveys of individual residents offer us only a "snapshot" of a community's beliefs and orientations. Wiseman concurs, noting that the definition of "culture" as an aggregation of individual attitudes misconstrues the term's true meaning, which "is rooted in a specific group or nation and is cross-generational. It does not come and go like fashion. It is relatively stable and enduring. Studies purporting to deal with political culture, therefore, must strive to bring an historic, dynamic perspective to their analysis." See Nelson Wiseman, "The Use, Misuse and Abuse of the National Election Studies," *Journal of Canadian Studies* 21, no. 1 (1986): 31. Moreover, he notes, "'Political culture,' however defined, persists over substantial periods of time: hence the power and significance of the concept. Do variables such as 'efficacy' and 'trust' meet this test? The evidence suggests not." Wiseman, "Use, Misuse and Abuse," 32–33.

For these reasons, individual attitudes are considered consequences, rather than indicators, of (group) culture. This is not to say that Almond and Verba's approach is useless in the study of political culture. While it may be misused as an indicator of political culture, their methodology is very valuable in terms of measuring the *effects* of political culture on individual attitudes.

46 Ibid.
47 Aside from a pair of diligent polling firms—Probe Research Inc. and NRG (formerly Western Opinion Research)—and an outstanding think tank in the Canada West Foundation, few surveys are conducted with enough consistency and significant sample sizes to allow for a close examination of Manitoba political attitudes (a notable exception is Christopher Adams, *Politics in Manitoba: Parties, Leaders, and Voters* [Winnipeg: University of Manitoba Press, 2008], which draws upon Probe Research's polling data). Historically, the Canadian Election Study incurs just such a shortcoming. With sample sizes of just over 200 respondents in Manitoba, these surveys are difficult platforms from which to judge Manitoba political attitudes. For the pitfalls of this approach, see Wiseman, "Use, Misuse and Abuse."
48 Cited in Gartner, *State of the West*, 17. For a similar assessment, see Probe Research Inc., *Economic Outlook and Job Security in Manitoba* (Winnipeg: Probe Research, 2008).
49 Gartner, *State of the West*, 8.
50 David V.J. Bell. "Political Culture in Canada." In *Canadian Politics in the 21st Century*, edited by M. Whittington and G. Williams (Scarborough: Nelson, 2000), 277.
51 See Jared Wesley, "The Collective Centre: Social Democracy and Red Tory Politics in Manitoba," paper presented at the Canadian Science Association Annual Meeting, Toronto, 2006; and Jared Wesley, "In Search of Brokerage and Responsibility: Party Politics in Manitoba," *Canadian Journal of Political Science* 42, no. 1 (2009): 211–36.
52 Morton, *Manitoba: A History*, 335.
53 Ibid.
54 K.W. Taylor and Nelson Wiseman, "Class and Ethnic Voting in Winnipeg: The Case of 1941," *Canadian Review of Sociology and Anthropology* 14, no. 2 (1977): 176.
55 Morton, *Manitoba: A History*, 197.
56 Ibid., 459–60. The term "stewardship" is borrowed, in part, from Morton's description of the Liberal/Liberal-Progressive approach toward public ownership of hydroelectricity.
57 Ibid., 197.
58 Ibid., 420–21, 470–71.
59 Friesen, *The West*, 9.
60 Jared Wesley, *Code Politics: Campaigns and Cultures on the Canadian Prairies* (Vancouver: UBC Press, 2013). This moderation may be a reflection or a source of the many examples of cross-level jumping by Manitoba party elites. A number of Manitoba politicians have made careers at both the federal and provincial levels. While the following list is by no means exhaustive, prominent examples of level jumping among Manitoba politicians include Conservatives Joy Smith, Rick

Borotsik, Vic Toews, and Duff Roblin; Liberals Tobias C. Norris, Stuart Garson, Jon Gerrard, Gil Molgat, Lloyd Axworthy, Sharon Carstairs, and Reg Alcock; and New Democrats Bill Blaikie, Jim Maloway, Judy Wasylycia-Leis, and Ed Schreyer. Others have crossed not only levels but party lines, most notably John Bracken.

61 Jared Wesley, "Code Politics and the Prairie Paradox: Party Competition in Alberta, Saskatchewan and Manitoba," paper presented at the Prairie Provinces Political Science Association Annual Meeting, Regina, 2008.

62 Wiseman, *Social Democracy in Manitoba*, 148.

63 Marshall, "How Manitoba Turned 100," 31.

CHAPTER 3

Structure and Change:
An Overview of the Manitoba Economy

FLETCHER BARAGAR

Historically, Manitoba has been identified as one of Canada's western provinces, but the longitudinal centre of the country stretches north-south across provincial territory. The "western" designation reflects in part the pronounced geographic separation between Manitoba's eastern boundary and the country's political, demographic, and economic hub located in the southern Ontario-St. Lawrence River region. Geography, however, also acts to insulate Manitoba from the pull of the Pacific Ocean and the Pacific Rim, and the resulting outbound maritime outlook characteristic of British Columbia is largely absent in Manitoba. Furthermore, the massive flows of foreign capital and technology that have been funnelled into the oil and gas industry, and the concomitant export of these staple products to southern markets—forces that are driving factors in the economies and political culture of Alberta and Saskatchewan—are not prominent in Manitoba. As a result, the economic structure and political orientation of Manitoba are substantially different not only from the provinces that lie to the east but also from those of each of its western neighbours.

Geography and history lie at the heart of those differences, but the local conditions are profoundly shaped by the play of external economic forces. Indeed, Manitoba's economic history since the seventeenth-century contact between Europeans and peoples indigenous to territory coterminous with the present-day province is in large part a tale of ongoing adjustment and, at times, profound socio-economic transformation as external forces bear down on local and regional peoples and practices. For Manitoba, the present-day outcome of this historical process is a diversified industrial economy with a standard of living that aligns well with that of other first-world industrialized nations. Manitoba's economy is well integrated into both the national and international economies. The long-term trend of both economic and population growth is positive although relatively modest. The overwhelming majority of the province's 1.41 million inhabitants reside in the southern-agricultural region, and the dominance of Winnipeg (2022 population 783,096; 2022 metropolitan area population 871,778) is pronounced.[1] The northern half of the province, by contrast, is a vast area with low population density. The terrain in this region, home to many First Nations communities, is defined by the Canadian Shield and the surrounding parkland area on its southern-southwestern flank, and the Hudson Bay lowlands in the northeast. Raw resources incidental to the physical geography of the region have long been exploited by interests external to the region.

The private sector, primarily in the form of corporations or owner-operated businesses, commands the lion's share of market-oriented production of goods and services, but the public sector is also a major component of the Manitoba economy, comprising 32 percent of provincial GDP in 2022.[2] Residents of Manitoba have access, albeit uneven, to a wide range of public services. Public funding is prominent in health and education. Both areas are under the jurisdiction of the provincial government, and it is significant that spending by the province in these two fields absorbs roughly 50 percent of the provincial budget.[3] Disparities between regions as well as between households with respect to wealth, income, and the standard of living are omnipresent, however, as myriad political and economic forces interact to both ameliorate and exacerbate existing inequalities.

The following sections of this chapter offer a more detailed presentation of major structural elements of the Manitoba economy along with consideration of some recent trends and contemporary challenges. The first section provides an overview of the industrial structure of the province, identifying major industries and their relative importance in the provincial economy. The second section turns its attention to the provincial labour market, including employment and earnings. The macroeconomy and fiscal policy are the focus of the third section. The chapter closes with a brief conclusion.

Industries

Real GDP for Manitoba in 2022 was $73.7 billion, which amounts to a 3.1 percent share of that for Canada as a whole.[4] The flow of production captured in the GDP statistics refers to the output of both goods and services. The share of total GDP generated in the goods-producing sector has been declining for decades, a phenomenon common to most high-income industrialized countries. For Manitoba, goods-producing industries accounted for 25 percent of provincial GDP in 2023, down from 29 percent in 1997.[5]

Figure 3.1 provides a more detailed breakdown of the respective shares of provincial GDP generated by subsectors of the goods-producing industry, along with that of transportation and warehousing and the rest of the service sector.

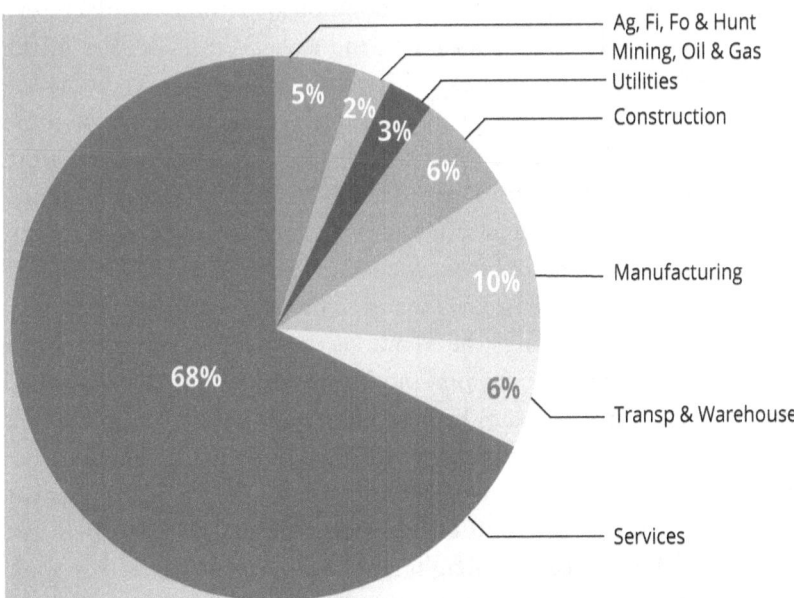

Figure 3.1. Share of GDP by Major Industrial Sectors in Manitoba, 2023. Source: Statistics Canada, Table 36100402, Gross domestic product (GDP) at basic prices, by industry, provinces and territories, annually, released 1 May 2024, https://www150.statcan.gc.ca/t1/tbl1/en/tv.action?pid=3610040201.

As shown in the chart, the primary industries of agriculture, fishing, forestry, trapping, mining, quarrying, and oil and gas production account for 7 percent of provincial GDP. These industries underscore the importance of the natural resource endowment of the province. Agriculture is the largest of the province's primary industries and, in many respects, it is Manitoba's most important industry. Agriculture's share of provincial GDP has, in recent years, fluctuated between 4.4 percent and 5.8 percent, but these figures understate its value. Bulk transport of agricultural products has been instrumental in shaping the ground transportation network across the province and remains a key determinant in the economic performance of the transportation and warehousing sector. Key agricultural products, such as canola, wheat, soybeans, potatoes and vegetables, and hogs, are among Manitoba's leading export commodities.[6] Agricultural production induces substantial backward linkages as a consequence of the industry's demand for inputs, including agricultural machinery, fertilizer, and feed for livestock. At the other end, forward linkages have developed as agricultural output offers ample and accessible flows of inputs for manufacturers, particularly in the food-processing industry. Manufacturers in the province have had success in exploiting these linkages. Food processing is the largest manufacturing subsector in the province, of which more than one-third is meat-product manufacturing.[7] Pork exports from Manitoba to other countries exceeded $1.2 billion in 2023 and exports of oil from canola and other oilseed crops soared to more than $1.4 billion.[8] Exports of farm machinery for 2023 were valued at $776 million.[9]

Agriculture also exemplifies many of the larger structural features and challenges incidental to the Manitoba economy. As indicated above, a substantial portion of the province's agricultural output is destined for the export market, and, in particular, international exports. That puts a premium on the importance for the industry of an efficient and reliable transportation system. The importance of the railway for the shipment of bulk commodities has been reflected historically in the national politics concerning freight rates and the problems of monopoly in the grain handling and transportation system. Disruptions to the system in the form of labour disputes, bad weather and natural disasters, and bottlenecks and backlogs at saltwater terminals have direct adverse implications for net earnings of Manitoba producers. Efforts of the province to promote an alternative outlet via the rail connection to Churchill have, due to a combination of factors,[10] had very limited success. A second significant challenge is that commodity exports destined for global markets are essentially sold at externally determined world prices, that is, prices beyond the effective control or influence of domestic producers. Changing supply-and-demand conditions in global markets result in price changes, including changes that can be quite sharp and sudden, which in turn directly affect the cash receipts of Manitoba producers. For agriculture, crop yields, including hay and other crops relied on for animal feed, are sensitive to weather conditions, thereby affecting output prices for crop producers and input prices for livestock production. A third challenge is that international trade can be a casualty of disruptions precipitated by health concerns or diplomatic disputes. Recent instances of disruptions of this sort affecting Manitoba agriculture include the U.S. country-of-origin labelling (COOL) that decimated beef and hogs exports to the U.S. from 2008 to 2010, and China's temporary ban on Canadian pork products in 2019.

These challenges underline the fact that, to a considerable degree, the revenue flows and, to a lesser extent, net receipts of producers in this major industry are highly dependent on factors well beyond the control of the producers. Some sectors within the industry, such as dairy and egg producers, operate in a supply management system that helps stabilize product prices and net incomes. It is significant, however, that neither eggs nor dairy is export oriented, and the supply management system is currently under pressure from other industrial sectors, consumers' groups, and international trading partners to relax and dismantle its distinctive institutional arrangements in favour of a more open, less regulated market. Outside of supply management, futures markets offer some opportunity for hedging by producers against the vagaries of the global market, but nonetheless a range of income support programs have been developed and relied upon to cushion substantial drops in market incomes.[11] The challenges of farming have also been met through increased capital investment and, to better exploit the economies of scale, increasing farm size. This phenomenon was especially evident in the latter half of the twentieth century, but the trends have continued into the twenty-first century as well.[12] The growth in the size of the farm in Manitoba has coincided with marked reduction in the number of farms: from 52,383 in 1951 to 21,071 in 2001 to 14,543 in 2021.[13]

The primacy of an export market and the attendant vulnerability of domestic producers to externally driven changes in market conditions are circumstances that also pertain to Manitoba's mining and oil production industry. Here, though, an additional constraint is imposed by the quality and quantity of the mineral deposit. New technological developments can augment the quantity of recoverable reserves that are, at any moment, economically viable, but the constraints imposed by the deposits are an effective reminder that these resources are non-renewable. As indicated in Figure 3.1, mineral and oil production in Manitoba constituted 2 percent of provincial GDP in 2023 (with a value of $1.5 billion in 2017 dollars) but is now an industry in decline. In mining, relative depletion of exiting reserves has precipitated the closure of a number of mines within the last ten years, including the Bucko Lake mine (nickel) in 2012, the Birchtree mine (nickel and copper) in 2017, the True North Gold mine (gold) in 2018, and Flin Flon's 777 mine (copper and zinc) in the summer of 2022.[14] Real GDP in metallic mining in Manitoba reached $931 million in 2000, but the industry has been on a downward trajectory since then, with real GDP sliding down to $390 million for 2023.[15] Oil production in the province benefited from strong prices and the development of new extraction techniques, resulting, after 2005, in a mini-boom and a surge in production. Production rose from 4.0 million barrels in 2004 to a peak of 19.2 million barrels in 2012.[16] The remainder of the decade saw production levels decline. By 2020, annual production had slipped to 13.8 million barrels, down 28 percent from 2012. Production levels have exhibited a measure of stability since 2020, with annual output hovering around the 14-million-barrel mark. In 2023, 14.5 million barrels were extracted. That year, real GDP in the oil producing industry was $725 million, a substantial sum but down 25 percent from the industry's peak in 2012.

Backward and forward linkages are not especially strong in the oil industry in Manitoba, as capital equipment is largely imported and the output exported for refining and subsequent processing elsewhere. For mining, however, metal smelting and refining in the mining centres of Flin Flon and Thompson generated considerable employment and value added in the North. Over the course of the last decade, however, declining metal production in northern Manitoba in conjunction with consolidation in the global metallic mining and processing industry resulted in the downsizing and phasing-out of these industrial activities in Manitoba. The copper smelter in Flin Flon closed in 2012,[17] and in 2018 it was the turn of Vale's smelting and refining operations in Thompson.[18] The combination of corporate rationalization with respect to their global operations, less than propitious global market conditions, and a diminishing resource endowment have thus reduced the level of economic activity in, and the strength of the fiscal resources available to, these northern communities. Mineral exploration activity continues in the North, and possibilities for new developmental projects, especially with enhanced local participation and ownership stakes, continue to be discussed and explored, but present conditions suggest that the expansion phase of the metallic mining and processing industry in Manitoba has given way to an era of contraction and decline.

The share of provincial GDP attributed to the other primary industries in Manitoba is miniscule: for forestry and logging, fishing, hunting, and trapping combined, their share in 2023 was less than 0.06 percent.[19] These low figures, however, understate the importance of these activities for households and communities across the province, and especially in the vast non-agricultural areas of the North and eastern regions. Real GDP for forestry and logging in Manitoba was only $20.3 million in 2023, but this industry provides the raw material for sawmills and paper manufacture, which in turn provide inputs for further processing and manufacturing activities. Early moves by capital to exploit the province's forestry resources led to the establishment in the 1920s of a paper complex at Pine Falls in eastern Manitoba, and, in the 1960s, of a sawmill and pulp and paper complex at The Pas in the west. In the twenty-first century, however, changing market conditions and moves by corporate capital to rationalize and consolidate operations resulted, in a scenario similar to that of the metal smelting and refining industry, in the closure of the paper complex at Pine Falls in 2009 and the 2009 cessation of the sawmill operations at The Pas. The Pas's paper mill was scheduled to close in 2016, but a change in ownership and an infusion of new capital rejuvenated the business with production destined for both domestic and international markets.[20] For many households, and especially for those in remote communities, hunting, fishing, trapping, and forestry activities are often conducted outside the realm of the market and "formal" economy. In these cases, the outputs are not included in the industry's GDP figures.

The physical geography of the province is favourable for the development of hydroelectric power generation. In the early decades of the twentieth century, investments in dams and generating capacity along the Winnipeg River provided electricity for Winnipeg and, with expansion of the electrical grid, to a growing portion of southern and eastern Manitoba. In the 1960s, attention was directed to the power potential of the Nelson River. Large-scale projects to develop generating and transmission capacity characterized the decades of the 1960s, 1970s, and 1980s. The accompanying inflow of capital and labour into the North provided economic spinoffs in the form of employment and demand for provision of goods and services but also environmental damage to parts of the area and disruption and upheaval in many local communities. The Churchill River Diversion and the flooding of South Indian Lake proved especially damaging to the communities directly affected. After a lull in the 1990s, a new wave of construction of generating capacity and transmission lines was launched. Manitoba Hydro capital expenditures in its electricity division rose from $462 million in 2006 to $1,038 million in 2010, to $1,949 million in 2015, and then to a peak of $2,924 million in 2018.[21] With the partial completion and a general winding down of major capital projects and a moratorium on new dam construction on the Nelson River, Manitoba Hydro's capital expenditures have been diminishing since their 2018 peak. For 2021, electricity division capital expenditures were $1,275 million. In 2023, these expenditures had dropped to $630 million.[22]

Hydroelectricity generation and the distribution of both electricity and natural gas in Manitoba are the responsibility of Manitoba Hydro, a provincial Crown corporation. The corporation is a major player in the provincial economy. Figure 3.1 indicates that the utilities sector produces 3 percent of the province's GDP, and virtually the entire sectoral contribution is that of Manitoba Hydro. The high levels of capital investment over the last fifteen years have been a powerful engine for economic growth in the province. Electricity is a major export for Manitoba. Hydro exported 13.3 million kilowatt hours of electricity in the 2022–23 fiscal year, earning $1.13 billion in revenues.[23] For domestic users, according to its annual report, Hydro's "domestic electricity rates continue to be among the lowest overall in North America."[24] Cheap electricity eases the cost-of-living for Manitoba households. Cheap and abundant electricity is an advantage for Manitoba businesses.

Access to power at a reasonable rate was a factor in establishing such energy-intensive manufacturing operations as metal ore processing in Thompson and pulp and paper at Pine Falls, but energy costs are only one of many factors in play in the decisions by businesses of where to locate, and it does not seem to be of anything approaching decisive importance for most of Manitoba industry. More significant, economically, are the economic rents that Manitoba Hydro provide for the provincial government. These rents, which are essentially transfers from the corporation to the government, include water rental charges and charges for the provincial guarantee of the corporation's debt. For the 2022–23 fiscal year, these particular rents were $84 million and $118 million, respectively.[25]

The manufacturing share of provincial GDP was 10.0 percent in 2023. In 1997, manufacturing's share stood at 13.4 percent. This drop of approximately three and one-half percentage points in roughly a quarter of a century reflects in part the growth of the service sector, but it also points to the challenges manufacturing industries have faced in the neo-liberal era. Increased international mobility of capital, widespread reductions in trade barriers, and lower transportation costs consequent to the increase of container shipments have induced a sharp rise in manufacturing capacity in lower wage countries and, from the standpoint of high-income industrialized countries, a concomitant rise in offshore production and geographically extended supply chains. For Canadian manufacturers, a low exchange rate (vis-à-vis the U.S. dollar) through the period from 1994 to 2002 provided considerable protection and helped level the competitive playing field, but after 2002, appreciation of the domestic currency intensified competitive pressure on Canadian producers, leading to upheaval and restructuring across this broad industrial sector. In Manitoba, some sectors were hit especially hard. For example, real GDP in textile manufacturing dropped from $55 million in 1997 to $21 million in 2012. Clothing and leather manufacturing plummeted from $181 million to $48 million over the same period, although this sector has since had a strong recovery. In general, though, restructuring and reinvestment have acted to sustain Manitoba manufacturers through the first two decades of the twenty-first century. Some industries, such as chemical manufacturing, enjoyed strong growth over this period.[26] Among the high-profile industries, machinery manufacturing recovered in the years following the 2008–09 financial crisis and real GDP for transportation equipment manufacturing reached its highest levels from 2017 to 2019, the tail-end of the pre-COVID era.[27] Overall, the net result is that the real (i.e., inflation-adjusted) value of manufacturing output in Manitoba in the early 2020s is at a level substantially above that generated at the turn of the century. The GDP levels for this sector in post-COVID years (2022 and 2023) have exceeded the production peaks of the previous quarter-century. The restructuring achieved real productivity gains, but it is significant that these gains were accompanied by reductions in employment. In 2000, manufacturing industries in Manitoba employed 66,800 workers, but employment in the industry has not exceeded 60,000 since 2008 (the year of the financial crisis). Employment levels for 2023 stood at 58,300.[28]

The diversity of the industries comprising the service sector defies easy categorization, but the sector as a whole continues to grow in terms of both GDP and employment. Real GDP for the Manitoba service sector (including transportation and warehousing) rose from $32.7 billion in 2000 to $51.3 billion in 2023,[29] an increase of 57 percent. Employment in this sector rose from just under 400,000 in 2001 to over 522,000 in 2023. The largest industries, in terms of GDP, within the service sector are real estate, rental and leasing (real GDP $9,671 million in 2023), health care and social assistance ($6,795 million), public administration ($6,062 million), finance and insurance ($4,159 million), and retail ($4,228 million).[30] All of these large industries have experienced substantial and persistent growth since the turn of the century, with finance and insurance, real estate, and retail essentially doubling in size since 1997.

The Labour Market

The prime determinant of the size of the provincial labour force is the number of people in the province. Statistics Canada estimates the Manitoba population at 1,474,439 for January 2024.[31] Annual population growth in the province has been consistently positive for over seventy years, but the growth rate for much of this period has been relatively modest. With low and stable rates of natural increase, short- to medium-term fluctuations in the size of the provincial population are the result of changes in net immigration.

There are two components to the net flows of migrants in and out of the province: interprovincial migration and international migration. Institutional barriers to interprovincial migration are virtually non-existent, allowing for relative freedom of movement for individuals and families between provinces. International migration, however, is highly restricted and is regulated by federal authorities.

For forty-nine of the last fifty years, net interprovincial migration for Manitoba has been negative. The size of the net outflow shows significant variation year to year. Over the interval from 2010 to 2020, the annual net interprovincial outflow has ranged from a low of 3,517 persons in 2010 to a high of 9,685 in 2020, and the decade-long trend has unambiguously been in an upward direction.[32] It is too great a simplification to say that the youth move to Toronto and Alberta while seniors relocate to British Columbia, but the prospects of higher earnings and superior career opportunities for younger adults and the appeal of less inclement weather for retirees are undoubtedly factors that do not play to Manitoba's advantage.

Given the net interprovincial outflow, population and labour force growth in Manitoba consequently depends heavily on international immigration. For Manitoba, the net international flows have consistently been positive, but for most of the 1980s and 1990s, the net international inflow rarely exceeded 3,000 persons.[33] That changed in the first decade of the twenty-first century with the establishment and growth of the Manitoba Provincial Nominee Program.[34] Under the program, the flow of immigrants rose rapidly, pushing annual net international immigrations totals into the 11,000 to 16,000 range for the period from 2008 to 2019. Immigration flows decreased to 9,482 in 2020,[35] largely because of the COVID-related restrictions on international travel. The lack of equivalent restrictions on interprovincial movement resulted in a situation where, for the first time since 2005, net international inflows were less than net interprovincial outflows. The consequent tightening of labour force growth became a contributing factor in the sudden acute worker shortage of 2022.

The phenomenon of persistent net population outflow from Manitoba to other provinces in conjunction with Manitoba's positive and relatively stable rates of economic growth contributes to labour market conditions conducive to relatively low unemployment. In general, Manitoba's unemployment rate lies below the Canadian average and the monthly unemployment statistics usually list Manitoba as one of two or three provinces with the lowest rates in the country.[36]

Within provincial boundaries, Winnipeg's population growth rate has exceeded that of the province as a whole, thereby intensifying the "dominant metropole" character of the provincial economy. The city and other urban centres have gained from the massive rural to urban migration movement that characterized the province's agricultural regions in the second half of the twentieth century. The following statistics indicate the relative magnitude of this transformative migration. In 1951, the rural Manitoba farm population was slightly above 219,000 and comprised 28 percent of the total provincial population. By 2006, the farm population was less than 63,000, comprising 5.5 percent of the total.[37] The trend has continued in the new century: reported farm population in 2016 stood at 44,175.[38] The first two decades of the twenty-first century have seen strong employment and population growth in areas in relatively close proximity to Winnipeg, and especially southeast of the city and in the north-central and south-central areas. From 2001 to 2020, the population aged fifteen years and over—the demographic segment from which the labour force is drawn—increased 20 percent in the north-central and south-central region, and an impressive 44 percent in the southeastern region.[39]

Growth in these southern regions has benefited from their geographical proximity to the Winnipeg metropolitan area, but other important factors include the regions' productive agricultural base, a good transportation network, strong community and business organization and leadership, and the role played by local and regional financial institutions, especially credit unions, in providing financial resources. The situation is very different in the North, where distance and the realities of geography elevate costs of transport, and where, historically, the mode of development had been oriented more towards externally driven large-scale projects involving resource extraction rather than alternatives associated with principles of community development. The recent difficulties experienced by prominent staple industries in northern Manitoba, along with the winding down of construction activity by Manitoba Hydro, have induced net out-migration from the North. In the northern and parkland regions, the size of the population cohort fifteen years of age and over decreased by 15 percent between 2001 and 2020.[40]

Average weekly earnings (excluding overtime) for Manitoba workers in 2023 was $1,072.28, an increase of 4.5 percent over the previous year.[41] The annual rates of increase for these weekly earnings have exceeded 3 percent every year since the COVID outbreak in early 2020, a phenomenon reflecting the relative scarcity of available workers during the initial COVID period, followed by widespread pressure to raise wages in the wake of the sharp rise in consumer prices in 2022 and 2023. For the decade preceding the COVID crisis, however, the average annual increase in weekly earnings was a more modest 2.2 percent. That modesty becomes even more pronounced when these nominal earnings are adjusted to changes in the cost of living, as measured by changes in the Consumer Price Index. When that adjustment is made, real average weekly earnings for Manitoba workers increased, on average, a meagre 0.32 percent per year between 2009 and 2019. For the 2020 to 2023 years, the higher nominal earnings garnered by Manitoba workers were wholly offset by higher prices, so the relative constancy of real average weekly earnings (again, excluding overtime) characteristic of the 2009 to 2019 decade has proven to be a feature of the early 2020s as well.[42]

In the Manitoba labour market, labour compensation levels tend to be below the Canadian average. Over the last thirty years, average weekly earnings (excluding overtime) for Manitoba workers have generally hovered between 88 percent and 93 percent of the Canadian average.[43] The persistence of this gap is a factor underlying the chronic net outflow of people from Manitoba to other provinces. The relatively robust growth of the Alberta economy prior to the post-2015 downturn in energy prices fuelled wage and salary increases in the Alberta labour market. One consequence was the widening of the disparity in weekly earnings between Manitoba and Alberta. In 1995, average weekly earnings for Manitoba workers were approximately 93 percent of the Alberta level. By 2014, the average for Manitoba workers amounted to only 77 percent of that in Alberta. The trend was reversed with the post-2015 slowdown of the Alberta economy, and the Manitoba to Alberta earnings ratio had climbed back to the 87 percent level by 2023. This interprovincial gap in average earnings, however, can be expected to widen once again with the return of higher energy prices and the consequent revival of the Alberta economy.[44] These developments underscore the fact that the dramatic ups and downs of the resource-driven, and especially energy-driven, economies of neighbouring provinces have direct implications for Manitoba. Boom times in Alberta, for example, place more pressure on the Manitoba labour market as westward labour migration becomes more attractive. Similarly, an Alberta government flush with strong flows of resource-related revenues finds itself in a fiscal position to offer comparatively more and better services and/or tax advantages, which are also factors that can affect interprovincial flows of capital and labour.[45]

The Macroeconomy and Fiscal Policy

In 2020, there was a 4.1 percent fall in real GDP for the Manitoba economy. In 2022, there was a 3.3 percent increase.[46] Sharp movements of this magnitude in provincial GDP are, for Manitoba, nowadays a relatively rare occurrence. Since the mid-1990s, Manitoba GDP growth is best characterized as modest and stable. Stability in this context does not imply the complete absence of fluctuations in the rate of growth of provincial output, and neither does it imply the elimination of the business cycle. It suggests instead that the amplitude of the business cycle is muted and that scenarios of macroeconomic boom and bust are not readily applicable to the Manitoba situation.

Comparisons of GDP growth rates between Manitoba and the national macroeconomy illustrate the phenomenon. The 1980s and early 1990s were a period of macroeconomic stress and economic restructuring. Both Manitoba and Canada experienced severe recessions in 1982 and 1991, but both economies had recovered by 1994. In the ensuing twenty-five years leading up to the COVID crisis of 2020, real GDP for Canada rose 74 percent. The corresponding increase in real GDP for Manitoba was a more modest 68 percent.[47] The final years of the century were marked by strong growth—a condition not unique to Canada but shared by the United States and numerous other industrialized countries. For the years 1997 to 2000, inclusive, real GDP growth rates in Canada averaged 4.9 percent per year. For Manitoba, annual average growth was 3.6 percent per year. The financial crisis that erupted in the fall of 2008 induced a recession in late 2008 and into 2009. For the national economy, real GDP dropped 3.1 percent in 2009. In Manitoba, by contrast, the 2009 decline was a very mild 0.2 percent.

This relative stability in the Manitoba macroeconomy is largely attributable to the relative diversity of the provincial economy. Among primary industries, agriculture dominates, but it is less than 5 percent of total provincial GDP. Crop production (64.5 percent of farm cash receipts in 2023) is, to a considerable extent, balanced by livestock production (32 percent of farm cash receipts in 2023), and the prominence of both canola and wheat (and, to a lesser extent, soybeans) lessens the risks that are associated with a more specialized, monoculture-like practice.[48] Manufacturing has retained its place as a significant sector in the provincial economy (producing 10 percent of provincial GDP), and the sector itself is remarkably diverse and is not dominated by the presence of a massive industry along the lines of Ontario's automobile and automotive parts manufacturing. Exports comprise close to 50 percent of provincial GDP, but leading exports are comprised of a mix of agricultural and manufacturing products, as well as electricity. In addition, although the United States is the most important single export market, aggregate Manitoba exports are roughly equally divided between international exports and exports to other provinces. In general, diversity reduces exposure to risk, and although the impact of external shocks potentially can be very substantial for particular subsectors of the economy, economic diversity acts to cushion and dilute the impact of those shocks on the economy as a whole.

The GDP per capita in Manitoba has consistently been below the Canadian average. As a result, the fiscal capacity of the provincial government is less than that of higher income provinces. Federal transfer payments, including equalization payments, act to offset this disadvantage. Notwithstanding what are at times perverse anomalies in the equalization formulas, Manitoba tends to be a net recipient of equalization payments, and federal transfers constitute a substantial portion of the province's budgetary revenues.[49]

The fiscal challenges of provinces such as Manitoba that possess a relatively smaller per capita fiscal base can be substantial. It is hard to avoid invidious comparisons with fiscally stronger provinces regarding levels of services and tax burdens. Fiscal resources, including borrowing capacity, must be available to the provincial government to meet various exigencies that arise from time to time, including recessions, natural disasters, and health crises such as pandemics. Budgetary deficits and extensive provincial borrowing in both domestic and international financial markets have been primary tools relied upon by Manitoba governments when faced with such exigencies. In Manitoba, when spared the arrival of new exigencies, periods of stronger than average economic growth have enabled the provincial government to run budgetary surpluses and thereby engage in debt reduction and/or in the accumulation of savings in the form of designated funds or programs. Propitious conditions have not in general prevailed over the last twenty years. The budgetary surpluses in the first decade of the new century disappeared with the irruption of the 2008–2009 financial crisis. The Manitoba response was aggressive fiscal spending, including capital investment from Manitoba Hydro. That helped mitigate the impact of the crisis on Manitobans, but budgetary surpluses were replaced by deficits. Post-crisis plans to return to a surplus position were dashed in part by extensive flooding in 2011, and as deficits continued, debt accumulated. Relatively slow economic growth through the years from 2015 to 2019 impaired the ability of the government to run surpluses, and governments had to assess the economic and political cost of forcing their way to surpluses by means of austerity measures or tax increases or some combinations of both. The province has been fortunate that this period of debt accumulation coincided with an era of historically low interest rates, but the post-pandemic rise in rates has underscored the temporary and contingent nature of the low-interest macroeconomy. The fiscal implications of having to refinance tranches of existing debt in a potential environment of rising interest rates and a deteriorating credit rating remained and remain a concern for Manitoba finance ministers. The COVID crisis of 2020 exacerbated the fiscal situation of the province, but management of the fiscal situation has been aided by the robust response of the federal government. To a considerable degree, the cost of the crisis has materialized in the form of public debt at the federal level.

Conclusion

Transformation and change in the Manitoba economy are ongoing. Manitoba remains very open, with innumerable ties to the national and international economies, but Manitoba is a small player on both the national and international stages and has been compelled to adjust to externally generated developments and shocks. The historical record suggests that, overall, Manitoba has been relatively successful in making those adjustments, although the burden of adjustment and the consequent spoils have been distributed unevenly. The role of the federal government, in both altering the larger institutional and economic environment, on the one hand, and assisting in the process of adjustment, on the other, cannot be underestimated.

Notes

1. Statistics Canada, Table 17100142, Population estimates, 1 July, by census subdivision, 2016 boundaries, annually (Persons), released 11 January 2023, https://www150.statcan.gc.ca/n1/en/catalogue/17100142; Table 17100135, Population estimates, 1 July, by census metropolitan area and census agglomeration, 2016 boundaries, annually, released 11 January 2023, https://www150.statcan.gc.ca/t1/tbl1/en/tv.action?pid=1710013501.
2. Statistics Canada, Table 36100222, Gross domestic product, expenditure-based, provincial and territorial, annual (x1,000,000), released 7 November 2024, https://www150.statcan.gc.ca/t1/tbl1/en/tv.action?pid=3610022201. "GDP" refers to the money value of final goods and services produced for the market in a specified period of time.
3. Province of Manitoba, Department of Finance, *One Future. One People. One Manitoba. Budget 2024, Estimates of Expenditure for the Fiscal Year Ending March 31, 2025*, https://www.manitoba.ca/budget2024/.
4. Statistics Canada, Table 3610022. For real GDP, the money value is expressed in terms of constant dollars, which means that the figures have been adjusted to neutralize the effect of price changes that occur from one time period to the next. The Statistics Canada figures for real GDP used in this chapter are, unless otherwise indicated, expressed in terms of 2017 dollars. An increase in real GDP is a widely used indicator of economic growth.
5. Statistics Canada, Table 36100402, Gross domestic product (GDP) at basic prices, by industry, provinces and territories, annually, released 1 May 2024, https://www150.statcan.gc.ca/t1/tbl1/en/tv.action?pid=3610040201. Following the classification categories adopted by Statistics Canada, the transportation and warehousing industry is categorized as a subgroup of the service sector. If this subgroup was instead considered as part of the goods-producing sector, then the share of provincial GDP generated in the goods-producing industry in 2023 would be 32 percent, down from 35 percent in 1997.
6. In 2023, the market value of international exports from Manitoba of wheat, canola, potatoes and vegetables, soybeans, and hogs amounted to $4.33 billion, comprising 20 percent of the total value of Manitoba exports to other countries. Figures are from Province of Manitoba, Manitoba Bureau of Statistics, Business, Industry and Trade, Manitoba international trade database, released 8 May 2024, https://www.gov.mb.ca/mbs/.
7. Statistics Canada, Table 36100402.
8. Manitoba Bureau of Statistics, Manitoba international trade database.
9. Ibid.
10. These factors include a limited shipping season, minimal inbound cargo, increased rail line maintenance costs due to permafrost thawing, and the demise of the Canadian Wheat Board.

11 Direct payments to Manitoba farmers from various income support programs rose to $634 million in 2022, up significantly from the $295 million and $418 million payments, respectively, for 2020 and 2021. Statistics Canada, Table 32100045, Farm cash receipts, annual, annually (Dollars), released 29 May 2024, https://www150.statcan.gc.ca/t1/tbl1/en/tv.action?pid=3210004501.

12 Average acreage per farm for Manitoba rose from 338 in 1951 to 1,192 in 2016. Statistics Canada, Table 32100152, Number and area of farms and farmland area by tenure, Census of Agriculture historical data, 1921 to 2016, every five years, released 11 December 2017, https://www150.statcan.gc.ca/t1/tbl1/en/tv.action?pid=3210015201.

13 Ibid.; Statistics Canada, Table 32100166, Farms classified by farm type, Census of Agriculture historical data, every five years (Number), released 11 May 2022, https://www150.statcan.gc.ca/n1/en/catalogue/32100166.

14 Martin Cash, "Manitoba Mining Industry Losing Its Lustre," *Winnipeg Free Press*, 24 May 2018, https://www.winnipegfreepress.com/business/2018/05/24/manitoba-mining-industry-losing-its-lustre; Martin Cash, "Hudbay Will Be Gone from Flin Flon by Summer," *Winnipeg Free Press*, 8 July 2022, https://www.winnipegfreepress.com/business/2022/03/08/hudbay-will-be-gone-from-flin-flon-by-summer, B5.

15 Statistics Canada, Table 36100402.

16 Province of Manitoba, Department of Economic Development, Investment, Trade and Natural Resources, "Oil & Gas Statistics," accessed 17 July 2024, https://www.manitoba.ca/iem/petroleum/stats. Production volumes are given in units of cubic metres (m^3). Cubic metres are converted into barrels at the ratio of $1m^3$ = 6.2898 barrels.

17 Bill Redekop, "Flin Flon Facing Trying Times," *Winnipeg Free Press*, 10 February 2018, https://www.winnipegfreepress.com/business/2018/02/10/flin-flon-facing-trying-times.

18 Cash, "Manitoba Mining Industry."

19 Statistics Canada, Table 36100402.

20 Sheila North, "During Global Pandemic, Paper Produced at Northern Manitoba Mill in High Demand," *CBC News*, 27 October 2021, https://www.cbc.ca/news/canada/manitoba/canadian-kraft-paper-the-pas-1.6226462.

21 Manitoba Hydro, Annual reports, 2017–18, 2018–19, 2019–20, https://www.annualreports.com/Company/manitoba-hydro. Annual statistics refer to the fiscal year ending March 31.

22 Manitoba Hydro, *Strategically Adapting to Our Changing Future, Annual Report 2020–21*, https://www.annualreports.com/HostedData/AnnualReportArchive/m/manitoba-hydro_2021.pdf; and Manitoba Hydro, *Manitoba Hydro-Electric Board 72nd Annual Report: Energy for Life, 2022–23*, https://www.hydro.mb.ca/docs/corporate/annual_report_2022_23.pdf, 46.

23 Manitoba Hydro, *2022–23 Annual Report*, 40.

24 Manitoba Hydro, *Annual Report, 2020–21*, 37.

25 Manitoba Hydro, *2022–23 Annual Report*, 42, 85. As noted in the report, the provincial government reduced the provincial debt guarantee fee by 50 percent, effective 1 April 2022. For the 2021–22 fiscal year, this fee was $229 million.

26 Real GDP in chemical manufacturing in Manitoba increased from $398 million in 1997 to $807 million in 2023. Statistics Canada, Table 36100402.

27 Annual real GDP in machinery manufacturing fluctuated over the $560 million to $680 million range between 1999 and 2010. Beginning in 2011, GDP in the industry

consistently exceeded the $740 million mark until the COVID outbreak precipitated a relative slowdown in 2020. The GDP in the transportation equipment sector exceeded $1.2 billion in 2018. Statistics Canada, Table 36100402.
28 Statistics Canada, Table 14100202, Employment by industry, annual, annually (Persons), released 28 March 2024, https://www150.statcan.gc.ca/t1/tbl1/en/tv.action?pid=1410020201.
29 Statistics Canada, Table 36100402.
30 Ibid.
31 Statistics Canada, Table 17100009, Population estimates, quarterly, quarterly (Persons), released 19 June 2024, https://www150.statcan.gc.ca/n1/en/catalogue/17100009.
32 Statistics Canada, Table 17100008, Estimates of the components of demographic growth, annual, annually (Persons), released 23 September 2023, https://www150.statcan.gc.ca/t1/tbl1/en/tv.action?pid=1710000801.
33 Ibid.
34 The Manitoba Provincial Nominee Program was established in agreement with the federal government and actively seeks out potential immigrants who possess specialized skills that are in demand in the provincial labour market. Province of Manitoba, *Manitoba Immigration Facts Report, 2016*, accessed 2 January 2025, https://immigratemanitoba.com/data/facts-report-2016/.
35 Statistics Canada, Table 17100008.
36 In June and July 2022, the Canadian unemployment rate was 4.9 percent, matching what Statistics Canada referred to as an "historic low." Manitoba's rate for these months was 3.8 percent and 3.5 percent, respectively, the lowest in the country and well below the national average. Statistics Canada, *Labour Force Survey, July 2022*, released 5 August 2022, https://www150.statcan.gc.ca/n1/daily-quotidien/220805/dq220805a-eng.htm. Two years later, a slowdown in the provincial and national economies raised unemployment rates, but Manitoba's relative position remained as before. For June 2024, the Canadian unemployment rate was 6.4 percent. The June Manitoba rate was 5.1 percent and again was the lowest in the country. Statistics Canada, *Labour Force Survey, June 2024*, released 5 June 2024, https://www.150.statcan.gc.ca/n1/daily-quotidien/240705/dq240705a-eng.htm.
37 Statistics Canada, 2001 Census of Agriculture, Agriculture-Population linkage data, Data tables, Table 14—Farm and non-farm Populations, 1921–2001, https://www150.statcan.gc.ca/n1/pub/95f0303x/t/html/4153161-eng.htm. Statistics Canada, 2006 Census of Agriculture, Highlights and analyses, Manitoba's farm population: changes over a lifetime, https://www150.statcan.gc.ca/n1/ca-ra2006/agpop/mn-eng.htm.
38 Statistics Canada, Table 32100004, Farm population classified by marital status, sex and age, every 5 years (Persons), released 27 November 2018, https://www150.statcan.gc.ca/t1/tbl1/en/tv.action?pid=3210000401.
39 Statistics Canada, Table 14100090, Labour force characteristics by province, territory and economic region, annual, inactive, annually, released 8 January 2021, https://www150.statcan.gc.ca/t1/tbl1/en/tv.action?pid=1410009001.
40 Ibid.
41 Statistics Canada, Table 14100204, Average weekly earnings by industry, annual, annually (Current dollars), released 28 March 2024, https://www150.statcan.gc.ca/t1/tbl1/en/tv.action?pid=1410020401.

42 Between 2019 and 2023, average weekly earnings (excluding overtime) of Manitoba workers increased 15.2 percent. Over that same period, the Consumer Price Index for Manitoba increased 15.9 percent. Statistics Canada, Table 14100204; Statistics Canada, Table 18100005, Consumer price index annual average, not seasonally adjusted, annually, released 16 January 2024, https://www150.statcan.gc.ca/t1/tbl1/en/tv.action?pid=1810000501. Author's calculations.

43 Statistics Canada, Table 14100204.

44 Ibid.

45 On 15 August 2022, Alberta premier Jason Kenney announced a $2.5 million advertising campaign, dubbed "Alberta is Calling," designed to induce skilled workers from other provinces to relocate to Alberta. The campaign, planned to extend through to October, explicitly extolled the province's relatively low taxes and higher wages. See Jim Wilson, "Alberta Launches Major Recruitment Campaign," *HRReporter*, 22 September 2022, https://www.hrreporter.com/focus-areas/recruitment-and-staffing/alberta-launches-major-recruitment-campaign/370066. A new, second campaign was announced by the Alberta government on 13 March 2023. See Alanna Smith, "Alberta Government to Expand Ad Campaign Attracting Workers from out of Province," *Globe and Mail*, 13 March 2023, https://www.theglobeandmail.com/canada/alberta/article-alberta-government-to-expand-ad-campaign-attracting-workers-from-out, A6.

46 Statistics Canada, Table 36100222.

47 Ibid.

48 Statistics Canada, Table 32100045.

49 *Budget 2024* states that federal transfers for the 2023–24 fiscal year are forecast to be $7,104 million, which works out to 33.1 percent of the anticipated total budgetary revenue of the province. Just under half (i.e., $3,510 million) of these federal transfers will come in the form of equalization payments. Province of Manitoba, Department of Finance, *One Future*.

PART 2
Institutions and Processes

CHAPTER 4

Westminster on the Prairies:
The Manitoba Legislature, Past and Present

CHRISTOPHER ADAMS

Introduction

This chapter seeks to fill a current gap in the existing literature on provincial parliamentary systems by focusing on the history and operations of the Manitoba provincial legislative assembly and cabinet.[1] The secondary literature is neither large in volume nor up to date. Christopher Dunn's *The Institutionalized Cabinet: Governing the Western Provinces* was published in 1995 and provides an historical focus on the premiers and cabinets in the western provinces, with focused pieces on each province.[2] In their edited 2010 volume, *Manitoba Politics and Government: Issues, Institutions, Traditions*, Paul G. Thomas and Curtis Brown have included two chapters on this topic: Jean Friesen's "The Manitoba Legislature: A Personal Reflection" and Paul Vogt's "The Manitoba Cabinet."[3] My own book, *Politics in Manitoba; Parties, Leaders, and Voters*, which appeared in 2008, focuses on leaders, party politics, and elections. However, it pays little attention to how the legislature and cabinet operate as governing institutions.[4]

This chapter focuses first on the Westminster system, sometimes referred to as the Westminster "model," and how it has operated as both a representative and governing entity in Manitoba. In his work *The Paradox of Parliament*, Jonathan Malloy writes about two main functions of a parliament: to serve as a body of elected representatives and to pass laws and make decisions, usually in accordance with the wants of the government of the day.⁵ The reader will see that this, too, is the case in Manitoba. The discussion begins with the province's birth in 1870 as part of Confederation, and proceeds to the evolution of its representative assembly, how it functions in passing laws, the role of cabinet, and how power has shifted from the cabinet towards the premier.⁶

Entering Confederation

The Westminster system is an import from Great Britain. It includes an executive branch and legislative branch. According to Robert MacGregor Dawson, the 1947 author of Canada's first comprehensive political science textbook: "The executive power in Canada has always borne a strong resemblance to executive power in Great Britain, from which it is, of course, in very large measure derived."⁷ The executive consists of two main elements. First, it has a "formal" executive that consists of the Crown, which is Canada's head of state and is represented by the governor general. The second element is the "political" executive, which deals with what Robert Jackson and Doreen Jackson refer to as the "realities of power." It includes the prime minister as the head of government, and the cabinet.⁸

The Westminster model's legislative branch includes a bicameral system for passing laws: an upper house (or upper chamber), which consists of the House of Lords in Great Britain and the Senate in Canada, and a lower house, which is the House of Commons in both Great Britain and Canada. Historically, the upper house has represented the aristocracy, and the lower house represented taxpaying communities (hence "communes").⁹ In Canada, this was set out in section 91 in the 1867 British North America Act (now renamed the Constitution Act, 1867). As do the other Canadian provinces, the Manitoba government is modelled on the Westminster system, with the Crown represented by a lieutenant-governor as the head of state. The political executive consists of the premier, who serves as the "first minister" among cabinet ministers, and those MLAs (Members of the Legislative Assembly) who are appointed to cabinet.

The 1870 Manitoba Act, which brought Manitoba into Confederation, was the outcome of negotiations between Ottawa and Louis Riel's provisional government of Assiniboia. It established that Manitoba would have an upper house, titled the Legislative Council, and a lower house, titled the Manitoba Legislative Assembly.¹⁰ The

Legislative Council, with seven appointed members in its first year, was deemed a way by which minority rights, including those of Métis peoples and francophones, would be protected in the anticipated wave of anglophone Protestant settlers arriving from Ontario.

In the province's early years, Manitoba did not have a premier. Adam G. Archibald, Manitoba's first lieutenant-governor, served as both the formal and political head of government. Balancing the interests of the francophone and anglophone populations, he appointed to the cabinet Alfred Boyd as provincial secretary and Marc-Amable Girard as provincial treasurer.[11] He then appointed seven individuals to the Legislative Council. These were drawn from both the Catholic and Protestant populations, as well as Métis peoples.[12] As I write elsewhere, the first two lieutenant-governors, Archibald followed by Alexander Morris, "served as the Crown's symbolic representative and as direct leaders of the provincial government. Their activities included general administration, putting forward legislation, amending provincial bills, and reserving legislation for review by Ottawa."[13] In 1876, with provincial revenues at $7,000 (which would be close to $240,000 in current dollars)[14] and operational expenditures exceeding $50,000, the Legislative Council was abolished by legislation passed in the lower house and approved by the upper chamber. The council's vote split between anglophone Protestants who favoured abolition and the francophone Catholics who were opposed.

Provincial Elections

Upon entering Confederation, Manitoba was one-eighteenth the size it is now.[15] The original electoral boundaries for choosing the MLAs were based on the old parishes of the Red River region and population numbers derived from a census that was held in 1870. Twenty-four electoral divisions, with equal representation for francophone and anglophone populations, were created in 1871.[16] In 1874, the old English and French parishes gave up two seats each to provide more representation to the outlying regions comprised largely of new English-speaking settlers. This changed again in 1875 with the province redistributed according to three main populations: French voters, including Métis; already established English-speaking settlers (including English-speaking Métis and Selkirk colonists); and new settlers who were chiefly arriving from Ontario.[17] Therefore,

Manitoba's religious, language, and cultural identities superseded the principle of representation by population.

Divisions in the legislature in the 1870s were considered factions representing different interests and demographic groups rather than formal political parties. During the 1878 provincial election, there was a push to introduce federal party labels, which was successfully but temporarily resisted. Parties, modelled on those at the federal level, became a permanent feature of the political landscape from the 1880s onwards.[18] Another feature absent in the early years was the secret ballot. It was only in 1872 that the first MP (Member of Parliament) in Great Britain was elected by secret ballot,[19] while in Canada voting procedures for federal elections, including the use of the secret ballot, were left to the provinces to determine until 1885.[20] Manitoba followed the British example by introducing mandatory secret balloting in 1875. However, this became optional for voters in time for the 1878 provincial election. Politicians wanted to ensure their supporters were indeed voting for them.[21] Expressing the views of the day, John H. Cameron, the MP for the Ontario riding of Peel, remarked on 21 April 1874 in the House of Commons: "Elections cannot be carried without money. Under an open system of voting, you can readily ascertain whether the voter has deceived you. Under vote by [secret] ballot, an elector may take your money and vote as he likes without detection."[22] The mandatory use of secret ballots in Manitoba was reintroduced permanently in 1888.[23]

Manitoba's geographic size changed radically during the province's first half-century, hence the scope of the governing institutions changed. Nicknamed the "postage stamp province" due to its tiny size, in 1881 Manitoba's boundary lines were extended in three directions (east, west, and north). The eastern boundary was subject to dispute, however, as both Ontario and Manitoba claimed Rat Portage (now Kenora) as in their own jurisdiction. Therefore, in the 1883 provincial elections of both Ontario and Manitoba, representatives were elected to both Queen's Park in Toronto and the Manitoba Legislative Assembly, including James Andrews Miller, Manitoba's attorney general. This was resolved by the British courts in 1884 to Ontario's benefit.[24] In 1912 Manitoba's boundaries were expanded again, thereby creating its current dimensions (see map, Figure 4.1).

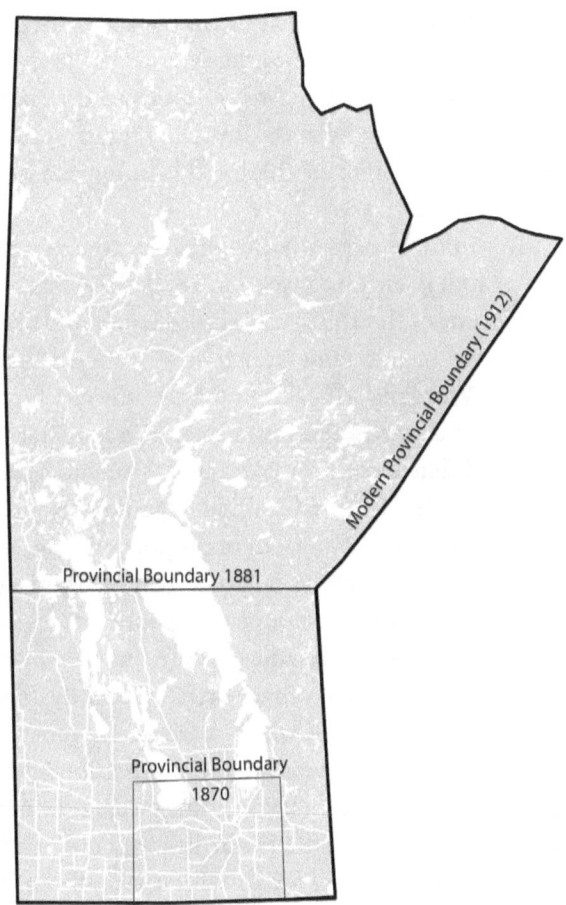

Figure 4.1. Map showing Manitoba's boundaries throughout late nineteenth and early twentieth centuries. Source: Gordon Goldsborough, *With One Voice: A History of Municipal Governance in Manitoba* (Portage la Prairie: Association of Manitoba Municipalities, 2008), 7. Used with permission.

The Manitoba Legislative Assembly

Since 1870, the Legislative Assembly has occupied three buildings. The first assembly was in a log building, originally the home of Andrew G.B. Bannatyne (a prominent merchant and member of Louis Riel's provisional government), located at the corner of McDermot Avenue and Main Street in Winnipeg. After its destruction by fire in 1873, the assembly moved about among a variety of buildings until 1884, when a second building was established on land just north of the current building. The current home is the Manitoba Legislative Building, which was opened in 1920.[25] As I write elsewhere, the "new" building was the centre of a major scandal involving fraud and kickbacks, which resulted in the downfall of the long-reigning Conservatives under Rodmond Roblin.[26]

As the province expanded in size, so too did the Legislative Assembly. From twenty-four seats in 1870, the assembly had grown to forty by the time of the 1892 provincial election, and then to forty-nine in 1914. It was in this same year that a new system was introduced for electing Winnipeg MLAs.[27] It divided the city into three regions, each with two elected representatives. Voters in each riding would choose a candidate from a list for the "A" seat and a candidate from a different list for the "B" seat. Candidates could not run in both lists. In 1920, this was replaced by a form of proportional representation with the entire city made into one electoral district. This lasted until 1949, the same year that the assembly was expanded to its current number of fifty-seven seats. The principle of representation by population was undermined by the fact that urban voters were vastly under-represented in the assembly, while rural voters were overly represented. In 1968 the Electoral Boundaries Commission redistributed seats in a more equitable manner. Almost half the ridings were now in Winnipeg and its suburbs. This was a major factor in producing the breakthrough election of Edward Schreyer in which his labour-oriented New Democratic Party (NDP) won its first provincial election.[28] Since that time, Winnipeg has been the chief battleground during each provincial election.

As in the federal House of Commons, the party with the most elected members forms the provincial government. The party with the second-most number forms the Official Opposition, leaving any other parties in the assembly deemed simply as the "Opposition." To hold party status in the provincial assembly, a party must elect at least four MLAs. In the 2023 Manitoba election, the NDP, led by Wabanakwut "Wab" Kinew, won thirty-four seats, thereby forming the government. The Progressive Conservative Party (PC), under Heather Stefanson, won the second-most seats (twenty-two), thereby forming the Official Opposition. The Liberals won only one seat, leaving it without party status.[29] Having official party status is significant, in that this provides more opportunities to sit on committees, for support to hire staff, and for speaking in the assembly.

While the Legislative Assembly must meet for at least one session each year, there are now usually three "sitting periods" per year: 1) the November Sittings, which commence with a Speech from the Throne and begin a new session; 2) Spring Sittings, which continue the November Sittings; and 3) the Fall Sittings, which bring the session to a close.[30] The November Sittings, in which the throne speech is presented and debated, commence the first Tuesday following the Remembrance Day (which falls on November 11) week and lasts until the first Thursday in December. The Spring Sittings commence on the first Wednesday of March, and usually go until sometime in June. It is during this period that the annual budget is presented. If there is leftover business at the end of this period, four additional days are allowed. The Fall Sittings usually commence in late September and last until the week just prior to Remembrance Day (November 11). The assembly might meet outside these periods when the government makes a special case to the Speaker or if the house leaders of the official parties agree to have the assembly sit on other days.

As is the case with the Canadian parliament, the Crown's representative opens each provincial session with a Speech from the Throne. This is written by government officials and sets out the priorities and plans for the coming session. Just prior to the commencement of the November Sittings, the lieutenant-governor will issue a proclamation proroguing (i.e., terminating) the session that commenced the previous fall.[31] The lieutenant-governor is also responsible for dissolving the legislature, on advice from the premier, to precipitate a general election. Since 2010, Manitoba has operated with a fixed day for holding provincial elections. These must be called at least every four years. Bending the rules, in terms of the spirit of the legislation, in 2019 Premier Pallister called an election one year earlier than was required. The October 2023 provincial election was held in accordance with the legislation.

The Legislative Assembly Act dictates that, after an election, on the first day the assembly meets, the MLAs are to elect a member to serve as its presiding officer, otherwise known as the "Speaker," who will oversee in an impartial manner the assembly and its business. This includes ensuring that proper protocols are followed, time limits are upheld, and members behave appropriately.[32] Although this person is an elected MLA, the Speaker does not vote except in the case of a tied vote. The selection of the Speaker is done by secret ballot and prior to the throne speech.[33] Following the 2023 provincial election, Tom Lindsey, the MLA for Flin Flon, was elected to serve as the Speaker.

Each party leader designates a "House Leader" who is expected to have a solid understanding of the rules of procedure and who determines the party's priorities when conducting business in the assembly. The government house leader consults with the other house leaders to discuss everyone's priorities and to increase the efficiency of the assembly's business. Each party's house leader works closely with their party's "whip," who is responsible for informing their MLAs about how they should proceed in dealing with the assembly's business, while ensuring their attendance and maintaining party discipline during votes.[34] As in the House of Commons, members follow the directions of their leaders and rarely speak out against decisions made in their caucus, or, for those on the government side of the house, against their premier.[35]

While it is rare that MLAs who are part of a governing caucus speak out against decisions made by their own leader or government, it does happen. In 1988, with Premier Howard Pawley's NDP holding power by a slim minority, disgruntled MLA Jim Walding voted against his own government's budget. It was enough to bring down the government, thereby triggering a provincial election, which brought Gary Filmon's PCs to power, where they remained for the following eleven years.[36] In 2014, the so-called Gang of Five walked out of Premier Greg Selinger's cabinet in protest for what they perceived to be their leader's heavy-handed behaviour.[37] Seven years later, in July of 2021, MLA Eileen Clark resigned her post as minister of Indigenous and Northern Relations in response to insensitive remarks made by Premier Pallister regarding Indigenous protests and the tearing down of statues: "The people who came here to this country—before it was a country and since—didn't come here to destroy anything. They came here to build. They came to build better."[38] A month later the premier announced he would not run in the next election. Following the 2023 election, NDP MLA Mark Wasyliw publicly demonstrated his disappointment in being left out of Kinew's first cabinet. However, a month later he stepped into line by publicly expressing support for his leader and caucus.[39] All of this indicates that even with all the disciplinary powers a governing leader may have, including the power to promote or demote caucus members, they are not limitless for fully containing caucus grievances.

Creating Laws

In accordance with how the Westminster system operates, a major task of the Manitoba Legislative Assembly is to create laws.[40] To do this, a "bill," which is a proposed law, is put forward and, if passed by a majority vote of MLAs, is then given Royal Assent by the lieutenant-governor to become law. At this point it has become an "Act" or "statute." The stages of legislation for passing laws in Manitoba are similar to those that occur in the House of Commons.[41] "Private members' bills" are those put forward by MLAs rather than by the government and do not involve public spending. This is because bills relating to spending must originate with the government. An example of a private member's bill would be the creation of a specific holiday. In Manitoba, each party in each session can select up to three private members' bills for a second reading debate and a vote.[42] Independent members (i.e., those who are not part of an official party) can select one bill per session for second reading. "Public bills" are those that apply to policies. They can be put forward by either MLAs or the government. Those that are considered "government bills" are put forward by cabinet ministers. Only cabinet ministers are allowed to put forward bills relating to spending, taxation, and other financial matters.

For a government bill to succeed, it must go through three "readings." Specified bills must be approved by the time the assembly rises at the end of its Spring Sittings. Designated bills must be approved by the end of the fall session. The Opposition can choose up to five bills to be "designated" in order that they can be debated and reviewed later in the Fall Sittings. Controversial government bills are sometimes chosen so that they can remain in the public's eye. An example of this was Bill-64, the Education Modernization Act, which was introduced in 2010 and which drew much public criticism and was later withdrawn (more is said about this in the next section). Financial bills are usually adopted without being specified or designated, and, subject to negotiation with the Opposition, other government bills that are neither specified nor designated may also be passed.

When a bill is given its first reading, it is introduced by the MLA who is putting forward the motion. It is not debatable. When given a second reading, the bill is subject to debate and either approved or rejected by a vote. If approved, the bill is then sent to a "standing" or "special" committee (both of which are comprised of government and Opposition MLAs) or is reviewed by a "committee of the whole" (i.e., comprising all MLAs). Usually, the government house leader, in consultation with the Opposition house leader(s), determines the type of committee that will do the work. At this stage the public and advocacy groups are given the opportunity to provide input into the proposed legislation. It also allows the committee to review the bill in greater detail.[43] The committee then submits any proposed amendments it feels are needed to the assembly, and after consideration is given to any amendment from either the committee or other MLAs, the bill is put forward for a third reading. If approved, the bill is passed and then awaits Royal Assent by the lieutenant-governor.

An important part of the day-to-day operations is "question period," by which the Opposition seeks to hold the government accountable. As is the case in the House of Commons,[44] questions posed by the Opposition in the provincial assembly are planned in caucus, and can arise from a media story, a citizen's complaint or concern, a government leak, or research (including the results of access-to-information requests) conducted by the MLAs and their staff.[45] The Opposition may focus its questioning on a particular issue on which the government may be particularly vulnerable. Recent examples include issues surrounding hospital overcrowdings due to the pandemic and the emergency departments closures. Of course, MLAs on the government side are allowed to ask questions, which invariably are of a "softball variety," providing an opportunity for a cabinet minister to speak positively about government policy or actions. Question period is limited to forty minutes; MLAs are allowed forty-five seconds to ask their question (leaders of recognized parties are allowed sixty seconds), followed by a maximum of one or two supplementary or additional questions. Answers are limited to forty-five seconds, with sixty seconds for leaders of recognized parties.[46] Exchanges between the Opposition and cabinet ministers or the premier will sometimes receive significant attention. In March 2022, NDP leader Wab Kinew asked the premier for a public inquiry into the case of an Indigenous woman who died in the care of health authorities in 2021. Rather than answering the question, the premier began praising her son's hockey team that recently won a championship.

As she transitioned her response to then address the question, she was cut off by the Speaker, who informed the premier her allotted time had expired.[47]

As is the case in the House of Commons, while a party is in opposition, certain MLAs are assigned to serve as a "critic" for specific policy areas. This allows an MLA to focus on a particular area of concern, such as health or Indigenous issues, and to be responsible for raising questions in this area during question period.[48] Those who serve this role for the Opposition take part in what is informally called a "shadow cabinet," which has two main purposes: to show the public that the Opposition party is capable of governing, and to prepare MLAs to eventually become cabinet ministers.[49] In 2023, with the change of government, most of those who served in the shadow cabinet transitioned into their respective portfolios on the government side.

Another important part of governing is preparing the annual budget. The funds required to run the province's finances are called "appropriations" and this is presented by the minister of Finance in the annual budget speech. The annual budget is presented during the Spring Sittings, and usually, but not always (as was the case in 2024), follows the federal budget. The timing is connected to the announced plan for the flow of federal funds to the provincial coffers. For the media and other observers, both the throne speech and the budget speech provide windows into the government's plans and priorities for the session and the coming year. In the 2022 budget speech, delivered by Finance Minister Cameron Friesen, the government emphasized tax cuts and additional expenditures aimed at resolving surgical backlogs in the health sector.[50] The 2024 budget, presented by the newly elected NDP government, brought forward many promises made in the 2023 election, including extending the provincial gasoline sales tax "holiday" implemented earlier in the year, as well as major increases in health care funding.[51]

The Cabinet

Cabinet meets in camera and on a weekly basis.[52] As in other parliamentary systems, government is steered by the premier and those in cabinet, otherwise known as the Executive Council. Decisions and priorities established there determine what takes place in the Legislative Assembly. Paul Vogt, who served as the Clerk of the Executive Council (i.e., the province's most senior public servant) in Gary Doer's NDP government, writes that the cabinet works as "a *deliberative body*, able to maintain a continuous dialogue on the ruling party's core commitments; and as an *executive body*, able to provide clear and detailed direction to government as a whole."⁵³ The premier is usually the dominant player and sets the direction for decisions made in the cabinet. Each premier has his or her own style. Premier Brian Pallister was widely known for running a "tightly controlled government" in which his views in cabinet and caucus prevailed.⁵⁴ The executive council puts forward bills for consideration and spending plans in the annual budget for the assembly's consideration and approval.⁵⁵

In Manitoba, the size of cabinet has varied over the past half-century.⁵⁶ The pattern, especially for PC governments when first elected, has been to operate with a comparatively small cabinet. Typically, "executive creep"⁵⁷ has occurred with increases to the cabinet's size occurring over time. Duff Roblin began governing in 1958 with a cabinet of nine, which grew to fourteen by the time he left provincial politics in 1967.⁵⁸ Gary Doer's NDP government operated with fifteen when it took power in 1999. This grew to sixteen from 2001 to 2003, and then eighteen from 2004 to 2008. Subsequently, upon taking the reins of power in 2009, Greg Selinger's NDP government operated with nineteen cabinet ministers. When Brian Pallister and his PCs took office, he reduced the cabinet to thirteen and put forward the following statement to the media: "The new executive council represents a one-third reduction in the size of Manitoba's cabinet, setting a new tone at the top in conducting government business for Manitobans."⁵⁹ However, despite this intention, the executive council grew every few years, reaching eighteen ministers in 2021, Pallister's final year in office. It remained at eighteen under Kelvin Goertzen's brief reign in 2021 and remained so under Premier Stefanson. Following the 2023 election, Wab Kinew reduced the cabinet's size to fifteen (including himself). Kinew decided to hold onto the Intergovernmental Affairs and International Relations portfolio as well as Indigenous Reconciliation.

Not all cabinet ministers are equal. The most significant position, of course, is the premier. Paul G. Thomas writes that the premier holds many levers of power. Among them are appointing and demoting cabinet ministers, setting policies and priorities for each minister's department as articulated in their mandate letters, setting the agenda for cabinet meetings, determining when cabinet has reached consensus on an important decision, appointing individuals to senior bureaucratic posts, and representing the province in intergovernmental affairs.[60] After the premier, the most significant portfolios are those of Finance, Health, Secondary Education, and Justice (whose minister also serves as attorney general).

Health and Education are significant portfolios for two reasons. First, they make up the lion's share of annual provincial expenditures, with Health being 36 percent and Education at 26 percent in the 2022 provincial budget, thereby making up 62 percent of the total pie.[61] Second, matters relating to health and education touch on the lives of every Manitoban, hence these policy sectors are lightning rods when issues arise.[62] The reorganizing of the hospital emergency wards in Winnipeg during Pallister's first term in government caused much political heat and local protests. With the onslaught of the pandemic in 2020 and afterwards, the government was severely criticized when hospitals began sending patients out of the province. In the field of education, Bill 64, the Education Modernization Act, was introduced by the PC government in November 2020, and was designed to amalgamate school boards under one provincial authority, while also affecting bargaining arrangements with schoolteachers.[63] Before moving into a third reading, it triggered a political firestorm among the electorate, including those among its own supporters in rural areas. With plummeting polling numbers, the bill, which was chosen by the NDP as one of five designated bills for the fall session, was subsequently withdrawn on 6 October 2021 by newly installed Premier Kelvin Goertzen. The third major portfolio mentioned, Justice—which was only 3.1 percent of the pie in *Budget 2024*[64]—receives significant media attention on matters relating to criminal and justice issues.

Conclusion

This chapter has provided a description of the Manitoba legislative system, its history, and how it operates in passing legislation and with government operations led by premiers and their cabinets. While Canadian municipalities and northern territories may vary in their government structures and how laws are created,[65] it is striking how all provinces in Canada are governed using the Westminster model, with Manitoba being no exception. Since its entry into Confederation, it has operated with an executive and legislative branch. Furthermore, procedures by which laws are made, from bills in their first to third readings followed by Royal Assent, the Manitoba system of government reflects in many ways our national parliamentary system based on the British Westminster model.

Notes

1. I thank Patricia Chaychuk, Gordon Mackintosh, and Paul G. Thomas for their helpful comments on earlier versions of this chapter. Any errors remaining are mine.
2. Christopher Dunn, *The Institutionalized Cabinet: Governing the Western Provinces* (Montreal: McGill-Queen's University Press, 1995).
3. Jean Friesen, "The Manitoba Legislature: A Personal Reflection," in *Manitoba Politics and Government: Issues, Institutions, Traditions*, ed. Paul G. Thomas and Curtis Brown (Winnipeg: University of Manitoba Press, 2010), 205–17; Paul Vogt, "The Manitoba Cabinet," in *Manitoba Politics and Government: Issues, Institutions, Traditions*, ed. Paul G. Thomas and Curtis Brown (Winnipeg: University of Manitoba Press, 2010), 181–204.
4. Christopher Adams, *Politics in Manitoba: Parties, Leaders, and Voters* (Winnipeg: University of Manitoba Press, 2008).
5. Jonathan Malloy, *The Paradox of Parliament* (Toronto: University of Toronto Press, 2023), 23.
6. This is similar in Ottawa with a shift in power from the cabinet to the prime minister; see Donald J. Savoie, *Democracy in Canada: The Disintegration of Our Institutions* (Montreal: McGill-Queen's University Press, 2019), Chapter 10.
7. R. MacGregor Dawson, *The Government of Canada* (Toronto: University of Toronto Press, 1947), 165.
8. Robert Jackson and Doreen Jackson, *Politics in Canada* (Toronto: Pearson, 2009), 267.
9. Albert F. Pollard, *The Evolution of Parliament*, 2nd ed., revised (New York: Russell and Russell, 1964), 12.
10. This discussion about Manitoba's bicameral legislature is largely based on David Grebstad, "A Tale of Two Houses: The Rise and Demise of the Legislative Council of Manitoba, 1871–1876," *Manitoba History* 75 (Summer 2014), accessed online 8 February 2025, https://www.mhs.mb.ca/docs/mb_history/75/legislativecouncil.shtml.
11. Boyd is often listed as Manitoba's first "premier," but there was no such thing in the early years of Manitoba. See John L. Finlay, "Boyd, Alfred," in *Dictionary of Canadian Biography*, vol. 13 (Toronto/Laval: University of Toronto/Université Laval, 1994), accessed online 2 January 2025, http://www.biographi.ca/en/bio/boyd_alfred_13E.html; William L. Morton, *Manitoba: A History* (Toronto: University of Toronto Press, 1957), 145.
12. These would have been those people deemed "Half Breeds" (those of Indigenous and English or Scottish descent in the Red River region) as well as those known

as Métis, being of Indigenous and francophone descent. On this, see Gregg Dahl, "A Half-breed's Perspective on Being Métis," in *Métis in Canada*, ed. Christopher Adams et al. (Edmonton: University of Alberta Press, 2013), 93–139.

13   Adams, *Politics in Manitoba*, 9. See also Morton, *Manitoba: A History*, 146. See also Gordon Mackintosh, "The Parliamentary Tradition in Manitoba," *Canadian Parliamentary Review* (Summer 1983): 3.

14   Because Canadian historical data for inflation goes back only to 1914, I based this calculation from an inflation calculator for US dollars, accessed 2 January 2025, (https://www.in2013dollars.com/us/inflation/1876?amount=7000), and then converted the 2022 USD figure to Canadian dollars for 2022.

15   Douglas Kemp, "From Postage Stamp to Keystone," *Manitoba Pageant* (April 1956), http://www.mhs.mb.ca/docs/pageant/01/boundaries.shtml.

16   John L. Holmes, "Factors Affecting Politics in Manitoba" (Master's thesis, University of Manitoba, 1936), 1. The results for the first election of 1871 are reported on pages 7–8.

17   Gerald Friesen, "Homeland to Hinterland: Political Transition in Manitoba, 1870 to 1879," *Historical Papers* 14, no. 1 (1979): 36. Maps for the electoral divisions of 1871, 1873, and 1874 are provided by Holmes, "Factors Affecting Politics," in page inserts following pages 10, 11, and 14.

18   Holmes, "Factors Affecting Politics," 38–40; Adams, *Politics in Manitoba*, 2–3. On the topic of early party politics in Manitoba, Murray Donnelly refers to the Norquay government of 1878 as a "Conservative" government, and the opposition as "Liberal." Murray Donnelly, *The Government of Manitoba* (Toronto: University of Toronto Press, 1963), 46. Tom Peterson also refers to the 1878 government as "Conservative." Tom Peterson, "Ethnic and Class Politics in Manitoba," *Canadian Provincial Politics: Party Systems of the Ten Provinces*, ed. Martin Robin (Scarborough: Prentice-Hall, 1972), 71.

19   BBC, "A History of the World: Pontefract's Secret Ballot Box, 1872," accessed 2 January 2025, https://www.bbc.com/ahistoryoftheworld/objects/WryVwsknTr-aa4IQ-ID9iQ.

20   Jackson and Jackson, *Politics in Canada*, 439; Elections Canada, "Chapter 2: Uneven Progress 1867–1919," *A History of the Vote in Canada*, accessed 2 January 2025, https://www.elections.ca/content.aspx?section=res&dir=his&document=index&lang=e.

21   For a colourful account of how what were called "treats," such as drams of whiskey, were used to buy votes, see Friesen, "Homeland to Hinterland," 37.

22   Elections Canada, *History of the Vote*. For the life story of Cameron, see Donald Swainson, "Cameron, John Hillyard," in *Dictionary of Canadian Biography*, vol. 10 (Toronto/Laval: University of Toronto/Université Laval, 1972), accessed online 2 January 2025, https://www.biographi.ca/en/bio/cameron_john_hillyard_10E.html.

23   Elections Manitoba, *Summary of Significant Legislative Change 1870 to 2019*, 2020 [Report], accessed 2 January 2025, https://electionsmanitoba.ca/downloads/Final_Summary_Legislative_Change_2020_EN.pdf, 8.

24   Kemp, "From Postage Stamp."

25   Sandy Cushon, "Legislative Building," in *Encyclopedia of Manitoba*, ed. Ingeborg Boyens (Winnipeg: Great Plains Publications, 2007), 390–91; Mackintosh, "Parliamentary Tradition," 3–4.

26 Christopher Adams, "Christopher Adams' 10 Scandals That Rocked Manitoba Politics," in *Everything Manitoba: The Ultimate Book of Lists*, ed. Christine Hanlon (Lunenburg, NS: MacIntyre Purcell Publishing, 2019), 139–40.

27 Readers should note that before it was made into "Unicity" in 1971, the City of Winnipeg did not include eleven of its current neighbourhoods, including St. Boniface, St. James, Charleswood, and Transcona.

28 When I interviewed Edward Schreyer (7 September 2006), he agreed that his party probably would not have won the 1969 provincial election if this redistribution had not happened. For a summary of the changing electoral system and the election of MLAs, see Christopher Adams, "Electoral System," in *Encyclopedia of Manitoba*, ed. Ingeborg Boyens (Winnipeg: Great Plains Publications, 2007), 197–99.

29 Election results for the 2019 campaign, as well as for those years prior, can be found at the Elections Manitoba website, accessed 2 January 2025, https://electionsmanitoba.ca/en/Results/Elections/2019.

30 This discussion is chiefly based on Legislative Assembly of Manitoba, "Outline of Procedure" (Winnipeg: Clerk's Office, Manitoba Legislative Assembly, 1986–), 4–5; and email correspondence with Patricia Claychuk, Clerk of the Legislative Assembly, 16 May 2022.

31 The reason for delaying this until just prior to the fall session is so that the legislature can deal with unexpected issues and crises between the two sessions. Legislative Assembly of Manitoba, "Outline of Procedure," 3.

32 For a discussion of the Speaker's role and duties in the House of Commons, see Rand Dyck, *Canadian Politics: Critical Approaches* (Scarborough: Nelson Canada, 1993), 483–84.

33 A list of past Speakers in Manitoba is provided by the Manitoba Historical Society, "Memorable Manitobans: Government of Manitoba: Speakers of the Manitoba Legislature," accessed 24 January 2025, http://www.mhs.mb.ca/docs/people/manitobaspeakers.shtml.

34 Regarding party whips and their role in the House of Commons, see Alex Marland, *Whipped: Party Discipline in Canada* (Vancouver: UBC Press, 2020).

35 Regarding party discipline in the House of Commons, see Savoie, *Democracy in Canada*, 179–84.

36 For more about this puzzling episode, and how it is viewed from different perspectives, see Adams, *Politics in Manitoba*, 125; Howard Pawley, *Keep True: A Life in Politics* (Winnipeg: University of Manitoba Press, 2011); Ian Stewart, *Just One Vote: From Jim Walding's Nomination to Constitutional Defeat* (Winnipeg: University of Manitoba Press, 2009), 150–56, 251–54; Gary Filmon, *Yes We Did: Leading in Turbulent Times* (Winnipeg: Heartland Associates, 2021), 69.

37 *CBC News*, "Manitoba Revolt: 5 Ministers Resign from Premier Selinger's Cabinet," 3 November 2014, https://www.cbc.ca/news/canada/manitoba/manitoba-revolt-5-ministers-resign-from-premier-greg-selinger-s-cabinet-1.2821632.

38 Caitlyn Gowriluk, "Manitoba Indigenous Relations Minister Resigns from Cabinet after Premier's Comments on Colonial History," *CBC News*, 14 July 2021, https://www.cbc.ca/news/canada/manitoba/eileen-clarke-resigns-cabinet-pallister-indigenous-1.6102299.

39 See, for example, the following statement, accessed 2 January 2025: https://twitter.com/MarkWasyliw/status/1237393922587947014.

40 This discussion on how a bill becomes law is based on Legislative Assembly Manitoba, "Fact Sheet No. 4: How Laws Are Made," Office of the Clerk of the Legislative Assembly, accessed 24 January 2025, https://www.gov.mb.ca/legislature/about/faq/fact4.pdf. It was provided by the Clerk's office to Kelly Saunders, 16 March 2022.
41 For how bills move through the House of Commons, see Jackson and Jackson, *Politics in Canada*, 317–21.
42 Legislative Assembly of Manitoba, "Outline of Procedure," 48–50.
43 For details about how the standing committees operate, see Legislative Assembly Manitoba, "Fact Sheet No. 5: How Standing Committees Operate," Office of the Clerk of the Legislative Assembly, accessed 24 January 2025, https://www.gov.mb.ca/legislature/about/faq/fact5.pdf.
44 Dyck, *Canadian Politics*, 477.
45 Friesen, "Manitoba Legislature," 211–12.
46 Legislative Assembly of Manitoba, "Outline of Procedure," 40–41.
47 Ian Froese, "Premier Apologizes for Boasting of Son's Hockey Success When Asked About Patient's Death," *CBC News*, 17 March 2022, https://www.cbc.ca/news/canada/manitoba/manitoba-premier-hockey-accomplishment-patient-transfer-death-1.6389008.
48 Friesen, "Manitoba Legislature," 209–10.
49 I thank Paul Thomas for discussing with me these points about shadow cabinets.
50 Danielle Da Silva, "Surgery Backlog, St. Boniface ER Big-Ticket Items in Health Budget," *Winnipeg Free Press*, 13 April 2022, https://www.winnipegfreepress.com/breakingnews/2022/04/12/surgery-backlog-st-boniface-er-big-ticket-items-in-health-budget, B1.
51 Paul Thomas, "Budget Season in Manitoba," *Winnipeg Free Press*, 6 April 2024, https://www.winnipegfreepress.com/opinion/analysis/2024/04/06/budget-season-in-manitoba, A9.
52 One NDP cabinet minister who served under Ed Schreyer and Howard Pawley in the 1970s and 1980s titled his book on these weekly meetings. Russell Doern, *Wednesdays Are Cabinet Days: A Personal Account of the Schreyer Administration* (Winnipeg: Queenston House, 1981).
53 Vogt, "Manitoba Cabinet," 183.
54 Paul G. Thomas, "Centralized Power in the Pallister Government," Backgrounder # 2-2021, Manitoba Organization of Faculty Associations, 15 July 2021, https://mofa-fapum.mb.ca/wp-content/uploads/2021/07/Brief2_2021_CentralizedPower-2.pdf, 2.
55 Legislative Assembly of Manitoba, "Outline of Procedure," 2.
56 These numbers are derived from the provincial government's website and by using the digital archive "Wayback Machine" (wayback.archive.org) in conjunction with postings from www.gov.mb.ca/minister/index.html for the years from 2000 to 2022.
57 Paul E.J. Thomas and J.P. Lewis, "Executive Creep in Canadian Provincial Legislatures," *Canadian Journal of Political Science* 52, no. 2 (2019): 363–83.
58 The composition of the provincial cabinets from 1958 to 2007 is provided in Vogt, "Manitoba Cabinet," 195–204.
59 Government of Manitoba, "Pallister Administration Sworn In," 3 May 2016, News Release, https://news.gov.mb.ca/news/index.html?item=37791.

60 Thomas, "Centralized Power," 2.
61 References to the 2022 provincial budget are from Government of Manitoba, *Recover Together: Strengthen. Invest. Build. Budget 2022*, https://manitoba.ca/asset_library/en/budget2022/speech-budget2022.pdf, 14.
62 Regarding how education issues percolate onto the political scene, and how the NDP government dealt with this, see Benjamin Levin, *Governing Education* (Toronto: University of Toronto Press, 2015).
63 Government of Manitoba, Education Modernization Act, Bill 64, https://web2.gov.mb.ca/bills/42-3/b064e.php.
64 Government of Manitoba, Department of Finance, *One Future. One People. One Manitoba. Budget 2024, Estimates of Expenditure for the Fiscal Year Ending March 31, 2025*, https://www.gov.mb.ca/asset_library/en/budget2024/estimates_budget2024.pdf, 11.
65 For example, regarding the Northwest Territories, see David M. Brock and Alan Cash, "Is There a Confidence Convention in Consensus Government?" *Canadian Parliamentary Review* 37, no. 3 (2014): 10–16.

CHAPTER 5

Still Politicized? The Partial Evolution of Manitoba's Crown Corporations

MALCOLM G. BIRD

Manitoba's Crown corporations are important policy actors. Manitoba Hydro, Manitoba Public Insurance (MPI), and Manitoba Liquor and Lotteries (MLL) are the largest and most significant publicly owned and operated firms in the province. These three companies are embedded deeply in Manitoba's political economy and contribute to its distinctive prairie culture and society. Like other state-owned enterprises (SOEs) throughout Canada and the world, these three businesses have modernized their internal operations, improved their efficiency and effectiveness, and reformed their governance regimes and how they relate to the Manitoba government, the public, and other stakeholders. Despite these efforts, Manitoba's Crowns are unable to fully decouple themselves from their state owner's (P)political interests and their ideological and partisan influences, and as such their relationship to the government is distinctive since they operate with less autonomy as compared with other Canadian Crowns. These challenges persist, regardless of the partisan stripe of the government, and it is not entirely clear why this is the case.

This chapter sets out to analyze the organizational and governance evolution of these three provincial Crowns over the last fifty or so years. In doing so, it aims to fill a void in the Canadian public policy literature regarding the province's Crowns and the character of their institutional life cycles. It will examine their internal operations and relevant organizational and governance evolutions, and assess how they relate to the Manitoba government, citizens, and other stakeholders. Its core contribution is to provide a description of the formal and informal political dynamics that shape both their operations and external interactions. Its central premise is that while these three Crowns have reformed their internal operations as well as their governance relationships, they continue to be shaped by considerable problematic interference from the political sphere. Both the New Democratic Party (NDP) and Progressive Conservative (PC) governments engage in this behaviour, albeit for different reasons and with divergent effects, but the net result is the same: the relationship between Manitoba's Crowns and their partisan masters is closer than in other places. It is not entirely clear why this is the case, but likely is due to the province's small size, have-not status, and partly parochial "middle" political culture. It could also be that Manitoba's Crowns are simply behind their contemporaries in the evolution of their governance regimes. Despite this, these Crowns serve the province and its citizens well by providing high-value goods and services and revenues to the state, and aid governments in meeting other vital policy goals. They successfully balance diverse and, in some cases, contradictory demands from their owner, numerous stakeholders, and others. Privatization, then, is unlikely as they are deeply embedded in the province's political economy and culture, and ownership changes would require enormous effort on behalf of the government and would yield marginal gains. Institutional path dependencies here, as always, play an essential role.

In its analysis, the chapter will describe SOEs and their growth in Canada and internationally. It will also briefly explain the 1996 privatization of Manitoba Telecom Services (MTS) and will show the exceptional nature of this policy outcome. Next, it will offer a case-by-case analysis of each firm's operations and the raw political dynamics they must manage. The chapter will then provide insights into the governance relationship between these firms and the Manitoba government. Some concluding thoughts on the character and future of Manitoba's Crowns round out the essay.

State-Owned Enterprises: Definition and Evolutions in Canada and Beyond

Crown corporations, or SOEs, are firms owned by states. Their value is derived from being able to link the strategic needs of governments and the importance of public accountability with the dynamism, initiative, and autonomy of a corporate business enterprise.[1] This hybrid character means that these firms must balance commercial operational considerations, on one hand, with their owner's policy demands along with other variables associated with being owned by the public, on the other. In the absence of the unifying profit maximization drive that guides private firms, SOEs are subject to numerous and diverse demands that emanate from multiple sources, ranging from their state owners and regulators to influential stakeholders, as well as their citizen customers. Their large size and dominant market positions (often monopoly-like or nearly so) combined with public ownership mean that they must also manage "contests" between groups over the allocation of scarce resources—from workers and customers to industry players and various components of the state. Public ownership itself brings about intense scrutiny ranging from freedom-of-information requests to criticisms from the media, stakeholder groups, and Opposition parties, among others. Corporate mistakes and employee errors of all sizes often end up as front-page news. SOEs, then, have fluid organizational objectives and operate in contested political terrain. They must be obedient to their owner's demands but at the same time must also delineate between "problematic" interference in their operations for partisan, electoral, or personal gain (political patronage and favourable procurement contracts, for instance) and more "legitimate" demands to meet long-term policy needs of states (economic development or regional employment goals, for example). Clearly delineating between different types of demands is not clear-cut and is an ongoing dynamic within Manitoba's Crown sector.

The use and value of SOEs have oscillated considerably in the postwar period. In Canada and the developed world, SOEs were crucial postwar policy tools of governments during an era that witnessed unprecedented economic growth along with the expansion of the welfare state. State intervention into markets and other aspects of society was viewed in a positive light, and, according to Pier Angelo Toninelli, this period became known as "the great age of public enterprise."[2] By the 1970s, support for strong state intervention started to wane as economic turmoil, slower growth, high government debt levels, and an appreciation as to the limits of the Keynesian welfare state paradigm began to emerge in academic, political, and policy worlds.[3] Many developed Western nations embraced market-oriented policies as they grew skeptical of interventionist efforts. Further emboldened by the collapse of the Eastern Bloc in the late 1980s, some academics suggested that liberalized markets and political systems would become globally ubiquitous.[4] As a result of this shift, states unloaded their SOEs, and between 1977 and 1999 just under 2,500 firms worth $1.1 trillion were sold, reducing their share of global GDP from 9 percent to 6 percent.[5] Outcomes in terms of improved performance were mixed, but many behemoths did undergo significant institutional reforms.

Since 2000, the pendulum has swung back towards the public sector. Acute events, like the 2001 terrorist attack and the 2008 financial collapse, showcased the need for the state to protect citizens and regulate markets. In academia, more people recognized the importance of institutions,[6] and the symbiotic and embedded relationship between public and private domains boosted empirical attention towards the public sphere.[7] But most crucial is the spectacular economic rise of China starting in the late 1970s, where SOEs play a central role in its state-led economic system, and its success illustrates the value of highly structured markets and extensive state interventions.[8] The 2020 global pandemic further cemented the value of the state to protect citizens from harm. Throughout this time, interest in and research on SOEs have grown, and many of the studies are less fixated on privatization questions and rather focus on governance and operational resiliency.[9] Noteworthy is the importance of Sovereign Wealth Funds (SWFs). These enormous, state-owned pools of capital collectively own 15 percent of equities worldwide, and are used by states for strategic and financial gains.[10] Despite several high-profile privatizations (Air Canada and Canadian National Railway, for instance), Canada bucked the trend seen throughout other Anglo nations and did not sell its SOEs en masse as was the case in the United Kingdom.[11] SOEs continue to be vital policy tools in Canada.[12]

The 1996 MTS privatization is significant for Manitoba's Crowns. By the early 1990s MTS became a political problem for the Manitoba government of Gary Filmon. Unlike Manitoba Hydro, which pays water fees to the provincial coffers, MTS remitted little money to the treasury. By the 1990s, MTS was carrying a considerable amount of debt and required significant capital outlays to stay competitive and modernize its infrastructure, particularly regarding cellphone and fibre optic investments. With new firms entering the cellphone market due to deregulation, MTS was unable to substantially raise its revenues, since it faced strong opposition to any rate increases from voters. Yet, despite the shift to cellphones, it was still required to invest in and maintain a province-wide landline system, particularly for the province's rural and small-town residents, and the government feared future obligations to maintain what would become stranded asset infrastructure: its condition and future circumstances would likely expose the provincial government to considerable financial liabilities. Inevitable political interference in its business decisions, especially in terms of capital investments, as well as cabinet's inability to effectively oversee such a large and complex organization, meant the provincial government was keen to eliminate these risks. Ideological factors played a smaller role than these practical, acute variables, and it was this same PC government that approved the purchase of Centra Gas by Manitoba Hydro in 1999. The privatization of MTS was a reasonable response to a context- and time-specific set of factors. However, opponents argue that the loss of a fourth major telecom service provider in the province (public or privately owned) has reduced competition, leading to increased prices. These opponents draw on the experience of Saskatchewan and its publicly owned SaskTel to illustrate the value of regional service providers in promoting market competition with resultant benefits to consumers.[13]

Manitoba Hydro: King of the Crowns

Manitoba Hydro is the most important Crown corporation in Manitoba. In a small province, it is an economic, financial, and technical behemoth. It is a regulated monopoly that distributes natural gas and is a fully integrated electricity provider. It is also entirely owned by the Manitoba government. Formally created in 1961 as the central component of state electrification efforts, it owns electricity production facilities (most hydroelectric dams), and the entire grid, including all transmission infrastructure and end-user systems. It does not produce natural gas, but it owns the transmission and end-user distribution system. Its core founding purpose was to provide low-cost, reliable electricity to the entire province, especially farms and rural and remote communities. A publicly owned monopoly provider was the ideal means to resolve this key policy challenge as the efficiency gains of unitary provision could be shared by all of the province's citizens. In 2023, it earned revenues of $2.6 billion, had a net income of $655 million, held just under $25 billion in debt, and had 5,100 employees.[14] It is a worldwide leader in hydroelectricity production and distribution, and in shared resource-management practices, and its baseload, low-carbon electricity, and high-wage jobs mean that Manitobans and their governments are proud of this firm's accomplishments. Noteworthy are the variation and composition of Hydro's revenues and its contribution to the provincial coffers. Record high 2023 export revenues of $1.13 billion, a 93 percent year-over-year increase, augmented its $450 million return to the government, but such remittances were projected to shrink to $88 million for the next year.[15] Such oscillations are due to changes in water levels (affecting hydro-generation capacity) as well as decisions by its owner, deciding in 2022 to reduce by half both its water rental rates and debt guarantee fees, reducing transfers to the government by $190 million for the year.[16] More generally, allocation of Hydro's revenues towards capital expenditures, state coffers, and the amount of corporate debt it holds is made in conjunction with its owner to meet political objectives of the Manitoba government; similar politically informed financial decisions and dynamics are an enduring characteristic of all firms owned by governments.

Manitoba Hydro is expected to fulfill several critical functions. First, it is to maintain a reliable electrical power source for all residents, regardless of where they live. System reliability takes on extra political importance given Manitoba's relatively sparce population and cold winter climate. Second, it is to provide low-cost electricity. Manitoba's electricity is relatively cheap (second only to Quebec's),[17] and is viewed as an ingrained right of all Manitobans. Any increase in prices is met with firm, organized resistance from a host of groups. Minimal carbon production and low-cost electricity are key components of the province's strategic business advantages.[18] Third, it is to earn revenues for the provincial coffers. Fourth, it is to encourage northern development in partnership with Indigenous peoples to create jobs, support businesses, and contribute to the economic vibrancy of the province. Fifth, it is to reduce power consumption, and it shares this role with Efficiency Manitoba.[19] These directives are broad and at times are in conflict, yet, overall, Hydro succeeds in meeting these demands.

Manitoba Liquor and Lotteries: Retailing Sin, Mitigating Harms, and Earning Money

Manitoba Liquor and Lotteries (MLL) is a purveyor of "sinful" indulgences. It has three core functions. First, it is the dominant provider of beverage alcohol in the province, operating both a monopoly wholesale system and its own sixty-three liquor mart retail outlets. It wholesales products to liquor mart agency stores (usually grocery stores specially licensed to sell MLL products), duty-free and private wine stores, and commercial licensees (bars and restaurants). Second, it is responsible for much of the legalized gaming in the province and operates two casinos (and oversees the others), video lottery terminals, lotteries, and online gaming. Lastly, MLL is the sole wholesaler of cannabis in the province to retailers. Formed in 1923 and named the Government Liquor Control Commission, its creation marked the end of the province's seven-year temperance experiment. This new government entity was responsible for both the distribution and regulation of beverage alcohol in the province. In 2014 it merged with Manitoba Lotteries to form the MLL and its regulatory functions were divested to the Liquor and Gaming Authority of Manitoba.[20] Its head office is in Winnipeg, and it employs approximately 3,000 people.

To fully understand its political value in returning revenues to the provincial coffers, some important context is required. First, the revenues from the MLL are significant. As of March 2023, its $741 million contribution (roughly 3.4 percent of government revenues) is acquired with relatively limited political cost since few people understand how much the price of alcohol and gaming (gambling) is actually an excise tax on these indulgences. Revenues from alcohol comprise 43 percent of its remittances ($319.1 million), cannabis sales contribute 4.3 percent ($31.9 million), and gambling income makes up the remaining 52.7 percent ($390.6 million)—noteworthy is that 26.1 percent of its total earnings comes from video lottery terminals.[21] In terms of political directives, the MLL is to earn revenues for the provincial state but is to be socially responsible and take measures to address the harmful effects of its products since the Manitoba government is concerned about the damages they cause. It is also to provide beverage alcohol throughout the entire province at uniform prices and to support locally produced alcohol products.

The costs these indulgences impose on society influence the behaviour of this Crown. This is because gambling and consuming alcohol and cannabis have considerable health, social, and economic costs, which are borne by governments, firms, individuals, and their families. When these costs are added up, they are far greater than the revenues earned from their sales. Alcohol consumption, for instance, is particularly destructive. While total government revenues from alcohol in Canada in 2018 totalled $10.45 billion, the aggregated costs it imposed were $14.64 billion.[22] Similar differences occur in the gaming and cannabis sectors, although in the latter there is less research to date. The negative features of gambling are considerable and motivate, to some degree, state-run operations to mitigate its destructive effects. For instance, a substantial component of Ontario's gaming revenues, between 30 and 40 percent, by one estimate, is derived from addicted individuals.[23] For alcohol, the MLL, like its other provincially owned counterparts, takes measures to alleviate the damage its products cause, and this alters its corporate behaviour. Mitigation efforts include limited operational hours, specialized employee training programs, and public educational campaigns, among other means, and are a part of a general corporate ethos to hold back from maximizing the volume of alcohol sales. The promotion of high-value products, for instance, in beautiful retail outlets with knowledgeable staff is an attempt to increase revenues earned from sales without a corresponding increase in the volume of alcohol sold, since higher value products yield fatter profit margins. This is a key part of an overall marketing effort to show that moderate alcohol consumption, often of exclusive foreign products, is a normal part of a healthy, middle-class lifestyle. These are corporate responses to calls from governments to increase remittances but not to do so by selling more beverage alcohol. Another key aim is to subtly shift culpability for responsibly consuming alcohol away from the producers and retailers and towards individual consumers; the calls for citizens to "Drink Responsibly" implies that "You"—the individual—have agency and thus an obligation to limit your consumption.[24]

Manitoba Public Insurance: Keeping Vehicles Affordable

Manitoba Public Insurance (MPI) provides comprehensive universal vehicle insurance in the province of Manitoba. It is also responsible for car and driver licensing and training services, and road safety initiatives, and is a source of provincially controlled capital investment. It manages the physical repairs to damaged vehicles as well as the legal and financial liabilities connected to claims; the province is a "no fault" jurisdiction where auto-related damages are not overseen by the courts. As of March 2023, it issued just under 1.48 million policies, had revenues of $1.52 billion, and a small profit of $4.2 million[25]—but rebated policy holders over $300 million in two tranches in the previous two years.[26] It has assets of $4.3 billion, comprised mostly of public and corporate bonds.[27] In 1971, Edward Schreyer's New Democratic Party (NDP) government overcame stern opposition and near defeat[28] and pushed the legislation through to resolve automobile insurance problems including high rates, inadequate coverage, and poor treatment of accident victims and their families by insurers.[29] Headquartered in Winnipeg, MPI has 1,900 employees.

Manitoba Public Insurance also serves other key policy and political functions. Its core purpose is to provide comprehensive auto insurance to all personal and commercial vehicles in the province of Manitoba. It does so at insurance prices that cover its payouts plus its administrative costs, and at rates that are markedly lower than in other provinces with private firms operating in a competitive market. It is worth noting that MPI assesses all drivers and vehicles in a uniform manner, and does not engage in demographic price discrimination (age, gender, and the like), which is used elsewhere throughout the auto insurance industry. Such a system means that average overall insurance rates are cheaper, but some demographic groups (such as older drivers) will pay more than in a private system since they have lower than average claims rates, and private systems base premiums on individual risk assessments. Also, MPI provides vehicle registration and driver licensing and training services throughout the province, as well as collects licensing and other fee revenues on behalf of the province. As of March 2023, MPI received $40.5 million (an increase from $30.3 million the prior year) to offset these costs, but this is only partial compensation for provision, and it had to divert $113 million in 2021 to cover capital investments in driver license and vehicle registration infrastructure.[30] It also invested $12.2 million in road safety initiatives in 2022.[31]

Always in the Spotlight: Crowns, Transparency, and Accountability

All Manitoba Crown corporations are under intense public scrutiny. Such intense surveillance has profound operational and political implications. Mistakes, errors, oversights, shortfalls, and any failings are often the subject of media attention and public outcry. An example from MLL illustrates well how public ownership and heightened public scrutiny, combined with a strong desire to maintain a low profile, will profoundly shape how the corporation functions and resolves operational challenges. Shoplifting at MLL stores was a serious issue prior to the pandemic. In response and due to safety concerns, MLL staff were directed to not interfere or prevent these criminal acts and were instead to contact the police. Over time, these criminal events became more frequent and were occasionally accompanied by violent acts against MLL staff; such open larceny, not surprisingly, caused consternation amongst staff members and patrons. The MLL's passive approach and its non-interference directives to staff, despite mounting losses, ostensibly did not make sense since other retailers went about implementing a range of counter measures, including additional security agents empowered to deal directly with culprits. But, as an instrument of the Crown, the MLL is highly averse to any negative public attention, and when a person is managing a shoplifting incident, a potential confrontation (and injury) to either staff (or agents acting on MLL's behalf) or culprits is likely. The ubiquity of smart phones means altercation images are often publicized on media platforms, making headline news and bringing unwanted attention to the board and the Manitoba government.

In this context, the MLL's solution to install controlled entrances, including its earlier non-interference directive, makes more sense. The MLL outfitted many stores with controlled, double-door entrances, where customers enter an interior space, present identification (and their information is temporarily stored), and then, once approved, are permitted to enter.[32] The MLL's solution has reduced thefts but is a drastic, intrusive, and expensive response to this problem and shows how public ownership and elevated levels of scrutiny shape its corporate behaviour. Other examples of elevated scrutiny abound. Media coverage of cost overruns, delays on MPI's new informational technology system, and an embarrassing incident, where an African Canadian woman's dark skin tone was deemed "unnatural" by MPI imaging equipment, again illustrate how errors and other operational challenges often make public headlines.[33] This reality makes Crowns highly risk-adverse, oftentimes to the detriment of embracing creative business solutions and other organizational innovations.

Governing the Crowns in Manitoba: Not Quite There Yet or Ever?

Over the last thirty years, Canadian Crowns have undergone significant operational and governance reforms.[34] Operationally, these firms pay closer attention to their finances, scrutinizing revenues, costs, and capital expenditures, and all are expected to be financially self-sufficient. Other reforms targeted internal logistics, communications, human resources (especially professionalizing their workforces), and the like, and these reforms often mimic corporate shifts derived from the private sector and are implemented by executives who have experience outside of the public domain. Problematic political interference in their business, such as patronage or procurement favouritism, for instance, has largely disappeared. Overall, Canadian Crowns seek to provide high consumer and stakeholder value. While their core businesses are frequently insulated from competitive markets (yet many of their submarkets are not), they nonetheless recognize the competitive political context in which they operate—a context where perpetual scrutiny from the public, media, the Opposition, other stakeholders, and the government itself is the norm and forces them to be accountable. These three Manitoba Crowns have reformed their operations in a similar manner to that of their Canadian counterparts.

To a large degree, Manitoba's Crowns have also adopted new governance models. Ideally, effective governance of a Crown corporation would have two key components. The first component is a strong "framework governance," whereby governments establish a robust governance structure that includes a clear public purpose, its operating authority and powers, and its financial relationship to the state, and authorizes a particular ministry to oversee its operations. This framework would be transparent and encoded in relevant legislative, regulatory, and other public documents. Second, an effective "specific governance" regime would implement this framework, and would focus on the role, purpose, and selection of key executives such as the chief executive officer and the board chair, as well as the board itself. Regular written correspondence between the Crown, its board, and the government would ensure adherence to the stated framework goals. Mandate letters and policy guidance documents emanating from the government would ensure clear and consistent direction for the firm, and annual reports, business plans (with relevant corporate metrics), and adequate financial and borrowing data would illustrate how the Crown is (or is not) meeting the demands of its political superior. Regular external audits would provide an additional, and disinterested, check on both parties and the functioning of the overall governance regime. More specific directives from either government or cabinet are acceptable so long as they are stated publicly.[35]

The general thrust of an effective governance regime is to have an open and transparent set of directives made by governments to Crowns, and to have active accountability systems to oversee these relations. Governments can, and in fact must, provide clear and consistent policy direction to these firms but at the same time cannot interfere in their day-to-day operations for overtly partisan, (P)political, or personal gains. This conjecture, however, assumes that policy direction from governments to their Crown appendages can be provided relatively free from government-specific partisan interests, and takes on a "common good" character. While these three Crowns and the Manitoba government have modernized their interactions, and, when compared with years past, these firms operate with elevated accountability levels and public transparency, the province has yet to reach a point where there is a "common understanding" amongst NDP and PC governments as to "ideal" policy functions of these firms. Speaking generally, the partisan stripes of governments in other jurisdictions at both federal and provincial levels do not significantly influence the demands made on their Crown appendages. These firms exist to fulfill structural policy voids that are relatively consistent over time, and thus their policy directions from ruling governments are consistent and separate from their partisan stripes. There are differences in the rhetoric used and policy areas to be emphasized, with, for example, left-of-centre governments more concerned with organized labour and equity issues, and right-of-centre governments more responsive to business community needs and efficiency demands. But despite slight differences, when it comes to core demands made by governments to their Crown appendages throughout Canada, they are relatively uniform from government to government.

This is not the case in Manitoba. In this province, there are challenges within the specific governance realm, particularly the operation and composition of Crown boards, that point to larger, structural problems within their framework governance set-up. These structural dynamics persist (albeit in different iterations) regardless of whether they are applied to NDP or PC governments. The best illustration of this problem is that incoming governments replace all board members of these three Crowns. As well, both parties often appoint board members with strong interest-group affiliations such as organized labour (NDP) and business (PC), raising governance issues regarding their ability to fulfill their fiduciary duties to the Crown while being detached from any vested representative interests. The practice of replacing the entire slate of board members is almost unique to Manitoba: rarely do other federal and provincial governments change all board members of their Crowns upon gaining office but, rather, gradually replace them with appointees as their terms come due. Manitoba's governments do this because they have divergent goals for the Crowns and these demands are incompatible with those of the previous administration. In the case of our three Crowns, Brian Pallister's PC government replaced the boards partly because it did not agree with the use of the Crowns as economic development vehicles, and it felt the Crowns had exceeded their mandates. For example, the MLL's efforts to revitalize downtown Winnipeg with a new large, flagship store and new head office (to be built in a renovated building) were, in the eyes of the Tories, not reasonable investments for this Crown to make, and the newly installed board cancelled both projects immediately.

Far more significant are the divergent perspectives on the role of Manitoba Hydro. Under the earlier NDP government (1999 to 2016), Manitoba Hydro embarked on two massive projects: Bipole III transmission line ($5.04 billion) and Keeyask generating station ($8.7 billion). Both developments were delayed and exceeded their initial cost estimates, though not extensively, given their large and complex character. For the NDP, these were long-term visionary projects that safeguarded future low-carbon energy supplies and ensured systemic reliability,[36] but for the PCs, they were viewed as superfluous ventures that lacked adequate oversight and exposed the province to excessive risk and expense—roughly half of Hydro's debt is attributed to these projects.[37] While both perspectives hold merit and there is evidence in support of both views, they are irreconcilable in terms of the ideal vision for, and function of, this Crown corporation. (Manitoba Hydro's elegant and energy-efficient downtown head office building is an example of a bold and expensive NDP-approved project that was completed on time and on budget, but, like all construction projects, it exposed Hydro and the government to considerable risks.) Such divergent views between the NDP and PCs regarding the purpose of this Crown, and its role to be an activist agent for regional and economic development goals, are in conflict. Not surprisingly, the incoming PC government replaced Hydro's entire board upon assuming power in 2016.

These divergent perspectives on Hydro's role continued when Wabanakwut "Wab" Kinew's newly elected NDP government replaced Hydro's board after its 2023 electoral victory, and soon after that its chief executive officer, Jay Grewal, departed. Details are limited, but Ms. Grewal left the position after publicly stating that private investment would play a role in expanding green energy projects, and that the utility would reach generating capacity limits sooner than anticipated; Adrien Sala, its overseeing minister, immediately asserted that all new power projects would be publicly owned.[38] More generally, it is unclear how Hydro will be able to meet increasing residential and commercial energy demands, many brought about by commitments to a green energy transition, without significant expansion of generating (and transmission) capacity in the form of new large-scale energy projects.[39] Such expansions, and upfront capital financing, are made more difficult by Hydro's, and the province's, considerable debt levels.

Further, both PC and NDP governments regularly appoint MLAs (Members of the Legislative Assembly) as board members. This is problematic from a governance perspective because of the potential conflict of interest between an MLA's loyalties to the government (usually the premier) and their fiduciary duty to act in the best interests of the Crown as a board member. The conflict between these two sets of obligations can compromise both its operational integrity and, more importantly, the Crown's strategic efforts as it manages the demands made by stakeholders and the government itself. One of the key roles for the members of a Crown's board is to restrict and further insulate its operations from undue interference from the government, its owner. Further complicating this dynamic is the practice of the government, rather than the board itself, of selecting its chair. Given the central role of the chair of the board as the key conduit between the Crown and its owner, the process of their selection—and the loyalties that follow from that selection process—has a critical impact on how the Crown is governed. Both PC and NDP governments regularly appoint board chairs with close connections to the parties or individuals within it. This practice, some argue, creates a potential conflict as to whether the chairs represent the interests of the government, often short-term in nature, or the needs of the firm itself, where a longer-term perspective is imperative.[40] Other examples of problematic interference were evident when MPI was directed by the PC government to stop hiring staff and was prohibited from seeking untendered contracts,[41] undermining, to some extent, its executive leadership and its board. Regularly, sitting governments will vet Crowns' news and press releases prior to distribution, indicative of the close control exerted over these firms.

No Privatization: Crowns Are Here to Stay

These three Crowns fulfill vital roles in Manitoban society. Operating in a peripheral region within Canada's political economy, they provide critical jobs, services, and revenues, and are key policy tools for the provincial government, regardless of the partisan stripe of the party in power, as they strive to support economic stability and growth for the province's citizenry. And, while they have modernized their operations and their governance regimes, the relationship between these three Crowns and their political master is unlike those in other jurisdictions. This could be partly due to the nature of their evolutions, and because they have not reached the point in their life cycles where their strategic directions are acceptable to both NDP or PC governments. If this is the case, in time, we should see a convergence with how these Crowns interface with their owners when compared with other Canadian Crowns. But this phenomenon could also be an artifact of Manitoba and its unique political culture and economy, whereby each party has a radically different ideal as to what Manitoba's Crowns should, and should not, be doing. If the latter is true, then how Manitoba governs its Crown appendages will continue to be an outlier and is yet another unique factor in how the "middle" province's governments interact with their publicly owned firms. Regardless of the reasons, the leaders of these Crowns must be prepared to please any government when they gain office. This means they must, somehow, compromise between the divergent demands imposed by both PC or NDP governments if they are to be successful over the long term.

Notes

1. Charles A. Ashley and Reginald G.H. Smails, *Canadian Crown Corporations: Some Aspects of Their Administration and Control* (Toronto: Macmillan Company, 1965), 3–4.
2. Pier Angelo Toninelli, *The Rise and Fall of State-Owned Enterprise in the Western World* (New York: Cambridge University Press, 2000), 18.
3. Peter A. Hall, "Policy Paradigms, Social Learning and the State: The Case of Economic Policy Making in Britain," *Comparative Politics* 25, no. 3 (1993): 275–96.
4. Francis Fukuyama, *The End of History and the Last Man* (New York: Free Press, 1992).
5. Bernardo Bortolotti, Marcella Fantini, and Domenico Siniscalco, "Privatisation around the World: Evidence from Panel Data," *Journal of Public Economics* 88, nos. 1–2 (2003): 305–32, 306.
6. Douglass C. North, *Institutions, Institutional Change and Economic Performance* (New York: Cambridge University Press, 1990).
7. Peter A. Hall and David Soskice, "An Introduction to Varieties of Capitalism," in *Varieties of Capitalism: The Institutional Foundations of Comparative Advantage*, ed. Peter A. Hall and David Soskice (New York: Oxford University Press, 2001), 1–68.
8. Karen Jingrong Lin, Xiaoyan Lu, Junsheng Zhang, and Ying Zheng, "State-Owned Enterprises in China: A Review of 40 Years of Research and Practice," *China Journal of Accounting Research* 13, no. 1 (2020): 31–55.
9. Aldo Musacchio and Sergio G. Lazzarini, *Reinventing State Capitalism: Leviathan in Business, Brazil and Beyond* (Cambridge: Harvard University Press, 2014), 15–16.
10. Richard W. Carney, Travers B. Child, Wai-Man Liu, and Phong T.H. Ngo, "The Dynamism of Partially State-Owned Enterprises in East Asia," *Journal of Corporate Finance* 68 (2021): 1–20.
11. Massimo Florio, *The Great Divestiture: Evaluating the Welfare Impact of British Privatizations 1979–1997* (Cambridge, MA: MIT Press, 2004).
12. Malcolm G. Bird, "State-Owned Enterprises in Canada: New Era, New Research Agenda," New Frontiers in Public Policy Series, *Canadian Public Administration* 65 (2022): 729–34.
13. Doug Smith, "The Price of Privatization at MTS—Higher Prices, Fewer Jobs," *Fast Facts*, 30 December 2020, Canadian Centre for Policy Alternatives, https://policyalternatives.ca/publications/commentary/fast-facts-price-privatization-mts-higher-prices-fewer-jobs.

14 Manitoba Hydro, *Manitoba Hydro-Electric Board 72nd Annual Report: Energy for Life, 2022–23*, 2023, https://www.hydro.mb.ca/docs/corporate/annual_report_2022_23.pdf, 19.

15 Government of Manitoba, Department of Finance, *One Future. One People. One Manitoba, Budget 2024, Estimates of Expenditure for the Fiscal Year Ending March 31, 2025*, https://www.gov.mb.ca/asset_library/en/budget2024/budget2024.pdf, 10. 2. (The change in remittances to the province is from *Budget 23/24* to *Budget 24/25*.)

16 Ibid., 25.

17 Manitoba Hydro, *Manitoba Hydro-Electric Board 72nd Annual Report*, 2023, 41.

18 Government of Manitoba, *Manitoba's Strategic Advantages*, 24 February 2023, accessed 2 January 2025, https://www.gov.mb.ca/jec/mbadvantage/index.html.

19 Manitoba Hydro, *Manitoba Hydro-Electric Board 72nd Annual Report*, 2023, 29.

20 Manitoba Liquor Control Commission, *Annual Report 2013–14*, https://www.mbll.ca/content/mlcc-annual-report-2013-14, 6.

21 Manitoba Liquor and Lotteries, *Annual Report 2022–23*, 2023, https://www.mbll.ca/sites/mbll-ca/files/2023-09/0034_MBLL_Annual%20Report_20222023_WR_Sep25.pdf, 10.

22 Malcolm G. Bird, Patrice Dutil, and Christopher Stoney, "Taxing the Tempted: Personal Addictions, Sustainable Revenues and the Public Good," *Canadian Public Administration* 62, no. 4 (2019): 674–96; see especially page 688.

23 Steve Barnes, *The Real Cost of Casinos: A Health Equity Impact Assessment* (Toronto: Wellesley Institute, 2013), https://www.wellesleyinstitute.com/wp-content/uploads/2013/01/Real-Cost-of-a-Casino_Wellesley-Institute_2013.pdf, 2.

24 Malcolm G. Bird, "Radical Change at a Crown Corporation: The Liquor Control Board of Ontario, 1985–2010," *Canadian Political Science Review* 4, nos. 2–3 (2010): 1–17; see especially page 7.

25 Manitoba Public Insurance, *2022 Annual Report*, 2023, https://www.mpi.mb.ca/wp-content/uploads/2022-annual-report.pdf, 12, 29.

26 Manitoba Public Insurance, *2022 Annual Report*, 2023, https://www.mpi.mb.ca/wp-content/uploads/2022-annual-report.pdf, 68.

27 Manitoba Public Insurance, *2022 Annual Report*, 2023, 28.

28 Christopher Adams, *Politics in Manitoba: Parties, Leaders, and Voters* (Winnipeg: University of Manitoba Press, 2008), 119–20.

29 Malcolm G. Bird, "The Insuring Crown: Western Canada's Public Auto Insurers," *BC Studies* (Spring 2013): 127–45; see especially page 132.

30 Kevin Rollason, "MPI Boss Defends Both Cash Diversion for Driver and Vehicle Licensing Upgrades, Threatening Free Press," *Winnipeg Free Press*, 10 January 2022, https://www.winnipegfreepress.com/breakingnews/2022/01/10/mpi-boss-defends-both-cash-diversion-for-driver-and-vehicle-licensing-upgrades-threatening-free-press; and Manitoba Public Insurance, *2022 Annual Report*, 2023, 67.

31 Manitoba Public Insurance, *2022 Annual Report*, 2023, 12.

32 Manitoba Liquor and Lotteries, "Media Advisory Regarding Liquor Mart Controlled Entrances," Media Advisory, 27 November 2019, accessed 2 January 2025, https://www.mbll.ca/content/media-advisory-regarding-liquor-mart-controlled-entrances.

33 Carol Sanders, "Cost of MPI Upgrade Balloons to $290M," *Winnipeg Free Press*, 7 October 2022, https://www.winnipegfreepress.com/breakingnews/2022/10/06/

cost-of-mpi-upgrade-balloons-to-290m; Bryce Hoye, "MPI Computer System Glitch Tells African Canadian Woman Getting Licence Photo Her Skin Tone Is 'Unnatural,'" *CBC News*, 25 June 2022, https://www.cbc.ca/news/canada/manitoba/manitoba-public-insurance-unnatural-skin-tone-complaint-1.6501490.

34 Malcolm G. Bird, "Canadian State-Owned Enterprises: A Framework for Analyzing the Evolving Crowns," *Policy Studies* 36, no. 2 (2015): 133–56.

35 Glen Hodgson, "Finding Jewels Among the Crowns: Optimal Governance Principles for Canada's State-Owned Enterprises," 27 May 2021, C.D. Howe Institute Commentary No. 602, https://papers.ssrn.com/sol3/papers.cfm?abstract_id=4094524.

36 Gary Doer, "Hydro Projects Built for the Future," *Winnipeg Free Press*, 1 March 2021, https://www.winnipegfreepress.com/featured/2021/03/01/hydro-projects-built-for-the-future.

37 Brad Wall, *Economic Review of Bipole III and Keeyask,* Economic Review of Bipole III and Keeyask Commission, November 2020, report, https://www.manitoba.ca/asset_library/en/proactive/2020_2021/ERBK-Report-Volume6.pdf.

38 Bartley Kives, "Manitoba Hydro Punts CEO 2 Weeks after Criticism from NDP Minister," *CBC News*, 13 February 2024, https://www.cbc.ca/news/canada/manitoba/manitoba-hydro-ceo-departure-1.7113855.

39 Bartley Kives, "Confidential Briefing Note Warns Manitoba Hydro Can't Service New 'Energy Intensive' Customers," *CBC News*, 29 September 2023, https://www.cbc.ca/news/canada/manitoba/hydro-electricity-briefing-note-1.6981719.

40 Paul Thomas, "Dual Role for Crown Corporation Board Chairs," *Winnipeg Free Press*, 2 July 2022, https://www.winnipegfreepress.com/opinion/analysis/2022/07/02/dual-role-for-crown-corporation-board-chairs.

41 Dan Lett, "Heavy Is the Head That Watches over the Crown Corporation," *Winnipeg Free Press*, 23 February 2023, https://www.winnipegfreepress.com/local/2023/02/22/heavy-is-the-head-that-watches-over-the-crown-corporation.

CHAPTER 6

Manitoba's Public Service under the Pallister/Stefanson Government and Beyond

ANDREA ROUNCE AND KARINE LEVASSEUR

Introduction

Manitoba's public service delivers democracy to citizens. While elected officials make public policy and governance decisions, it is the public service (and the broader public sector) that provides advice, develops and delivers programs, and ensures that services are accessible to Manitobans, whether through direct delivery or in partnership with community-based organizations and the private sector. New legislation in place since 2021, the Public Service Act, makes two critical changes that affect how we think about the public service. First, it changes the name of the core civil service to the "public" service. Second, it expands the scope of the public service to include the broader public sector. While this will be discussed further throughout this chapter, these significant changes make it essential to examine the state of both the public service—the core group of people employed by the Government of Manitoba—and the broader public sector, which includes the core plus workers located in universities, health authorities, Crown corporations, and many more organizations. Publicly funded services account for approximately 25 percent of Manitoba's economy,[1] meaning the broader public sector has a substantial impact. To that end, while we focus primarily on the core public service in this chapter, we will also address the impact of this broader public sector in Manitoba. We outline the key elements, governance structures, and actors in the public service, then highlight some of the changes in the sector under the Pallister/Stefanson governments and the ongoing challenges the public sector—and the core public service—faces. With the election of the Kinew government in October 2023, we briefly unpack the key issues his government must face with respect to the public service.

Government in a Westminster-style system, like that of Manitoba's, contains three branches: the executive branch, the legislative branch, and the judiciary (see Adams's chapter, present volume, for more detail). The executive branch includes the premier and cabinet, as well as the administrative arm of government—the civil service (a.k.a. the public service). This includes regular government departments (like the departments of Health, Agriculture, Families, and Advanced Education and Training), central agencies (like the Public Service Commission, Justice, and Treasury Board), and other administrative units like regulatory agencies and Crown corporations. It also includes a workforce of just over 12,000 public servants as of March 2023.[2] Ultimately, we can think of the civil service as being the body of organizations and people that, as the government description of the role indicates, "helps the government of the day to develop and deliver policies and programs," and "works in many different areas: from policy to program delivery, legal services to accounting."[3] Its activities are governed by legislation: as of 2021, it is governed by the Public Service Act.

When we think of how the public service is organized in Manitoba, we can think about the leadership of the public service overall, the leader(s) for individual departments and agencies, and the department that establishes guidelines and supports the day-to-day management of the public service. The Clerk of the Executive Council and Cabinet Secretary is the head of Manitoba's public service. As the most senior public servant, the Clerk is the "deputy of deputies." They serve as secretary to the cabinet (or executive council) and the permanent head of the office of the executive council. They are directly responsible to the premier. They meet regularly with all deputy ministers, and their office is often the source and manager of whole-of-government reform, such as the Transformation Strategy. In Manitoba, the Clerk has often been a partisan appointment: the premier appoints a person to fill this role who fits ideologically with the governing party and is trusted by the premier.[4] They may or may not have had direct public service experience, but they are appointed into this role because they have a particular skill set relevant to the public service.

Deputy ministers are the most senior public servants in each department or organization. They have responsibilities to their elected ministers, to their departments, to the premier, and to the Clerk, and are accountable to their minister, the premier, and the Clerk for the operations of their departments.[5] They must manage day-to-day operations for their departments, and work with other deputy ministers on initiatives that cross government departments (whole-of-government). As the administrative head of the department, they have a dual responsibility to work with the minister (who is the political head for the department) and also with the public servants in the department. Most deputy ministers in Manitoba are career public servants, although the premier may also appoint deputy ministers who come from outside government.

The Public Service Commission (PSC; and, before 2021, known as the Civil Service Commission, CSC) is a department of government tasked with leading human resource and labour relations management in government, while ensuring, according to the minister's briefing document of 2021, that "recruitment and selection of civil servants is based on merit, equity and fairness and that the candidates selected meet the government's requirements for service delivery."[6] The 2021–22 report for the civil service commission states that it provides "strategic human resources advice and direct human resources services to all Manitoba government departments."[7]

One of the key areas that the Public Service Commission manages is the range of training and educational programs offered to public servants. These include courses in values and ethics, reconciliation with Indigenous peoples, and many others. The PSC also manages the Learning Fund, which provides funding to individual public servants and to groups who want to take part in particular professional development opportunities.[8]

The public service (or the former civil service) provides advice to elected government, develops new public policy based on the ministers'/ cabinet's direction, implements programs, and delivers government services. It can be thought of as providing "frank and fearless advice" to elected officials, as well as "loyally implementing" decisions and public policies created by the elected officials. It is expected to remain politically neutral and non-partisan: it acts in the public's interest, within the limits of the law. "Public interest" can be a challenging concept to define, but we can think of it as a combination of what should be done and how it should be done to be in the public's best interest: public servants provide input into this decision-making process, but ultimately it is up to elected and publicly accountable officials to make the final decisions.

The Westminster-style system requires a distinction between the non-partisan work done by public servants (or the core public service) and by partisan or political staff (now known as the "allied" public service). Public servants are politically neutral, supporting elected governments from different parties equally. In addition, the Westminster-style system prescribes particular arrangements for the relationships between public servants (the core public service) and elected officials. These arrangements make up the public service "bargain," which requires public servants to provide frank and fearless, neutral and non-partisan advice to decision makers, and then to loyally implement the decisions made by elected officials—whether they agree with the decisions or not. Public servants remain anonymous, which allows them to provide the advice that elected officials need without being challenged publicly. In return, elected officials take responsibility for decisions made and implemented by their departments/agencies. They are accountable to the citizens of Manitoba through the legislature. These relationships are taken seriously, and when challenges arise, they may be addressed by the public service and its unions, by elected officials, or by agents of the legislature like the Manitoba Ombudsman.

An ongoing consideration for the public service has been supporting ethical conduct and behaviour among public servants, and identifying what constitutes these conducts and behaviours. Manitoba has had established codes of values and ethics for the core public service, as well as for elected officials and ministerial staff, since 2003.[9] These have evolved over time to reflect a growing understanding of the key ethics, values, and behaviours that public servants ought to have. These were updated in the Public Service Act of 2021, which outlines values both for an ethical public service (respect for others, integrity, accountability, skill, and dedication) and for an effective public service (service, collaboration, innovation, and sustainability).[10] These values apply to all component parts of the public service, and, as stated in the Public

Service Act, are meant to "guide the public service in serving the public in an ethical manner."[11] In terms of the core public service, the new Act emphasizes, "The code of conduct focuses on the expected behaviours of core public service employees in a parliamentary democracy based on the Westminster-style tradition. The code of conduct informs the commitment of the public service to implementing the decisions of the government of the day, to providing non-partisan advice, and to upholding the law, institutions of government and democratic principles."[12]

The new legislation identifies four key principles that underlie management of the core public service writ large: diversity and inclusion, fairness, merit, and mobility.[13] "Merit" is often a challenging principle to define, but we can think of it as including educational preparation, relevant experience (which includes work experience but also broader experiences), and accomplishment.[14] These principles are meant to be reflected in the management of all public sector organizations, although the legislation leaves it up to the organizations themselves to determine how they might be implemented.

In their July 2021 report, the ombudsman raised concerns about Progressive Conservative (PC) talking points being included in non-partisan news releases, which could threaten the neutrality of the civil service.[15] While this type of language would be customary in communications provided by the allied public service, it would have no place in communications coming from the core public service. The report concluded, "It is important that the separation between the non-partisan civil service and the political realm remain intact."[16]

One of the tensions between public servants (especially the core public service) and elected officials is related to political activities. While public servants have the right to engage in political activities (such as campaigning for a political party, having a lawn sign, or seeking nomination or running in an election), there are acknowledged limits that depend on the type and profile of the work that public servants do in their jobs. This allows for the balance between political activities and the principle of political impartiality/non-partisanship in the core public service. The new Public Service Act (PSA) contains an extensive section addressing political activities, outlining the types of activities that public servants might take on. The PSA more clearly unpacks and guides the political activities for the core public sector than did the previous legislation.

The Civil Service under Former Premier Pallister: Creating a Smaller, Leaner Service

Manitoba's PC government, led by Premier Brian Pallister, took office in April 2016 after Manitoba had experienced an unprecedented seventeen years of New Democratic Party (NDP) government. The PC's election campaign focused primarily on Manitoba's economy, debt, deficit, taxation, and the regulatory regime of the province. With the goal of becoming "Canada's Most Improved Province," the Pallister government's first year in office reduced cabinet (and accompanying departments) by one-third, launched a red tape reduction review, reduced senior management positions across the public sector, and hired a for-profit firm, KPMG, to undertake performance and value-for-money reviews.

As part of the discussion about the government's financial situation within the first year, a series of announcements about public sector employment and unions hinted at coming cuts while also emphasizing that front-line workers would be protected. Its first Speech from the Throne in November 2016[17] included references to cutting management positions, contracting Manitoba Hydro's workforce, revamping the health authorities, etc.[18] In meetings with union representatives, government representatives floated possibilities for shrinking public sector costs such as unpaid days off (implemented in the 1990s and known as "Filmon Fridays"), wage freezes, and reduced pension benefits.[19]

Commissioning a series of reports from industry consulting firm KPMG to identify areas where the government could cut back and restrain expenditures, the government acted on the recommendations quickly. In early October 2017, the Pallister government identified a target of 1,200 positions (8 percent) for civil service reductions in order, as the KPMG report stated, to create a "more efficient civil service."[20] These reductions would take place over three years and be done mainly by attrition. Premier Pallister publicly signalled his approach to public sector unions in 2017 by saying that "[t]rying to get as much co-operation as we can from public-sector leaders who've had it fairly good for quite a while and (have) basically run the government is challenging."[21] Approximately one-third (33.4 percent) of Manitoba's workforce is unionized,[22] and most unionized employees are in the public sector.[23] Thus, any discussion of public sector spending and management has to include a discussion of labour relations. Cutting spending in the public sector was a key part of the Pallister government's way to balance the province's books from the beginning of its first term. Throughout the first year in office, the government consistently reported civil service employment numbers that exceeded those reported by the Civil Service Commission when pointing to why cuts had to be made. Critics asked about whether there would be a trade-off between the number of employees and negative impacts on government services, but the emphasis on cuts and the identified need for austerity won out.[24]

Debates about the appropriate size of government—and expenditures on the public sector—are not new in Manitoba politics. Under Premier Gary Filmon, Manitoba's PC government introduced legislation that froze public sector wages and introduced "Filmon Fridays," the mandatory unpaid days off for public sector workers. In fact, these unpaid days were generally well received by public servants and were followed in 2002 by the creation of the "Voluntary Reduced Work Week" (VRW) days, where public servants could choose to take unpaid days off as part of their regular schedules.[25] While it is common to attribute proposed cuts to public sector employment (and wages) to conservative governments, NDP governments are not exempt from this practice. In February 2010, NDP Finance Minister Rosann Wowchuk announced that the province wanted public sector workers to take a two-year wage freeze.[26] These actions targeted what is now called the "core" public service: those civil servants employed directly by the Government of Manitoba.

Cuts to the civil service are evidenced in Table 6.1. Under Pallister/Stefanson, the core public service decreased by 2,822 regular, term, technical, and other positions from 2016 to 2023. Despite the slight increase in the core public service between 2020–21 and 2021–22, it is clear there is a downward trend.

The Manitoba Public Service has also identified particular groups of people who are traditionally under-represented within the ranks of the public service, including four designated employment equity groups: women, persons with disabilities, Indigenous peoples, and visible minorities. Government has identified a focus on building an inclusive and representative public service, stating, "Manitobans are best served by a public service that is inclusive and representative of the diverse population of Manitoba, at all levels of the organization, including senior management."[27] New benchmark performance measures include

Table 6.1. Smaller Bureaucracy: Composition of the Manitoba Civil Service.

	2015	2016	2017	2018	2019	2020	2021	2022	2023
Regular, Term, Technical and Departmental	14,238	14,318	13,723	13,337	12,512	12,128	11,988	12,248	11,854
Casual	439	537	420	366	309	220	220	242	172
Contract	24	21	19	18	18	21	24	24	28
TOTAL	14,701	14,876	14,162	13,721	12,839	12,371	12,232	12,514	12,054

Note: This table illustrates the total number of active civil service employees, not including extended employees (i.e., employees of a Crown corporation; employees of a regional health authority, etc.).

Sources: *Manitoba Public Service Commission Annual Report for the Year Ended March 31, 2023*, https://www.gov.mb.ca/csc/publications/annrpt/pdf/2022-23_annualrpt_en-fr.pdf, 4; *2017–18 Manitoba Civil Service Commission Annual Report*, https://www.gov.mb.ca/csc/publications/annrpt/pdf/2017-18_annualrpt_en-fr.pdf, 5.

assessments of retention for these groups, as well as the numbers present throughout the core public service and at the senior management level.[28] Data from the most recent Public Service Commission annual report show that goals are being met in terms of recruiting and retaining women and visible minorities, but not yet with Indigenous peoples and persons with disabilities.[29]

Government Reform and Transformation in the Public Service

After focusing on costs associated with the civil service and the broader public sector for the first years of its first term, Pallister's government shifted gears to spearhead "transformation" in the civil service. Launched by the finance minister (responsible for the civil service), the premier, and the clerk of the executive council (the most senior civil servant), the new Transformation Strategy was designed to modernize the public service, and, according to its news release, contained two plans: "one to transform the work of the public service and a second focused on building a culture that is forward thinking, creative, and outcomes driven."[30]

The first component of the Transformation Strategy was called "Transforming our work" and included three commitments: the introduction of balanced scorecards, increased public reporting on government priorities and outcomes, and the design of a centralized citizen engagement portal. The second component, "Transforming our culture," included a focus on the client: to consider what clients truly need from government, harness public servants' talent, establish new mechanisms to mobilize talent and bring people into the public service, and foster innovation: coach, not manage; experiment, not shut down ideas.[31]

The Transformation Strategy was intended to signal a changing and professionally oriented public service in Manitoba. It laid the groundwork for significant legislative changes that would follow in the new Public Service Act as well as in other legislation concerning the public sector. Establishing new performance measures as part of the balanced scorecard process was intended to help make government activity more transparent and to facilitate accountability. These also recognize the value that public servants bring, and measures were developed to capture how public servants themselves felt about their working conditions and what they were able to achieve.

While this new approach was meant to be separate from discussions of wage negotiations and labour relations, the timing of the changes raised some concerns, given that they were happening at the same time as extended discussion about the cost of the public service.[32] In addition, the public service would soon be challenged by an unanticipated circumstance: the COVID-19 pandemic. If ever there would be a test of how quickly the public service could "transform," it would be the pandemic. This will be discussed later in the chapter.

Public Service under PCs: Expanding the Scope of the Public Service

Another significant change to the public service under the PC government is the change to the name of the civil service to the "Public Service," and to expand the definition of the public service to include the broader public sector. The Public Services Sustainability Act of 2017 defines the public sector as containing the following groups of people, essentially expanding the definition to include any employees who receive a portion of their salary from public funds:

> Application to employees 7(1). This Part applies to persons who are employed in or by (a) the government; (b) a government agency; (c) a health organization; (d) an organization prescribed as a reporting organization under The Financial Administration Act; (e) an authority as defined in The Child and Family Services Authorities Act; (f) an agency as defined in The Child and Family Services Act; (g) The University of Manitoba, The University of Winnipeg, Brandon University, Université de Saint-Boniface, University College of the North, or Manitoba Institute of Trades and Technology; (h) the office of the Auditor General, the office of the Chief Electoral Officer, the office of the Ombudsman, the office of the Children's Advocate, the office of the Conflict of Interest Commissioner or the office of the registrar appointed under The Lobbyists Registration Act; (i) the Legislative Assembly; (j) a school district or school division, as defined in The Public Schools Act; (k) any other employer that is designated by regulation, or that belongs to a class of employers designated by regulation.[33]

While municipalities, academic institutions including universities and schools, and hospitals have been reporting on their financial information and have been covered by the so-called sunshine laws (requiring a public reporting of salaries) for years,[34] this new legislation and way of defining the public sector was clearly intended to expand the government's reach.

This understanding of the public sector as being within the control of the government also continued in the PSA, introduced as Bill 3 in December 2019 and then reintroduced in October 2020. This legislation replaces the Civil Service Act and, according to the *Civil Service Commission Annual Report*, establishes "a legislative framework, including principles and values, for an ethical and effective public service in Manitoba."[35] It was argued that this Act would help to modernize Manitoba's public service, including updating the language of the oath of office.[36] One of the most critical things this new Act does is to replace the "civil" service with the "public" service and changes the definition of the public service to be the same as the public sector. The public service is now deemed to include the following groups: the core public service, the allied public service, and the broader public service.

The Act covers the *entire public service*, which is categorized as follows:

- **core public service**—government department employees and senior leadership;
- **broader public service**—Crown corporations, health organizations, post-secondary institutions, school districts and divisions, and other organizations included in the government's financial reports; and
- **allied public service**—staff for the Assembly offices and the constituency offices of members of the Assembly, staff for the officers of the Legislature and political staff.[37]

While the previous Civil Service Act defined civil servants as employees appointed to or employed in positions with the government or agency of the government,[38] limiting the government's reach as employer to these groups, the new PSA includes three categories of public sector employees and creates a governing and values framework that applies to all of the sector. The Government of Manitoba may not be considered the direct employer for the whole sector, but it is clear that this legislation identifies a distinct set of roles for the government in setting employment parameters for the sector. Educational services (including teachers), public administration, and health care and social assistance categories of workers have the highest proportion of unionization rates and are also most commonly in the public sector.[39] This reality means that there is a role for government in these areas. The Civil Service Commission briefings describe the impact of this legislation in the following ways: "Going beyond core government by including the broader and allied public sector, the PSA provides a framework for leading, defining and organizing the public service in an integrated and responsive way.... The Manitoba government has taken a number of steps to ensure partners in the broader public sector are aligned with the principles and priorities of core government. The PSA advances this work by supporting a whole-of-government approach."[40]

Manitoba government has also referred to the broader public service as "not just for staff in core government, but for everyone who serves the Manitoba taxpayer."[41] However, the public is not necessarily the key audience or "client" for the "broader" public service. While the values outlined in the Act seem universal, thinking through their application, evaluation, and enforcement raises more questions about organizational autonomy and the government's reach.

Stefanson: Repairing Broken Relationships(?)

Heather Stefanson was selected as new leader of the PC Party of Manitoba and premier on 30 October 2021, upon the retirement of Brian Pallister. Some of her pledges included repairing the many broken relationships under Brian Pallister and a more collegial approach to governing.[42]

Her cabinet appointments reveal a move towards repairing broken relationships. For example, she appointed a new minister of Labour. This may seem insignificant, but there had not been a minister of Labour since 2016. Stefanson repealed the wage freeze bill that kept wages low across the public sector.[43] But was this promise just rhetoric? In 2022, Stefanson stood in the legislature and spoke about her son's hockey team in response to a question from the Opposition about a woman who died during a failed airlift transfer to a hospital in Ontario from Brandon, Manitoba, during the height of the third wave of the pandemic.[44] The lack of compassion garnered media attention across the country and raised doubt about her sincerity and values as a relationship builder. Stefanson had a short window to rebuild relationships since she had become premier in November 2021 with an impending election in October 2023. Her short tenure prevented meaningful changes to relationships with the public sector.

Ongoing Challenges Facing the Manitoba Public Sector

Manitoba's public sector is facing significant challenges. The list of challenges is so numerous that it is not possible to review them all. Below are some challenges that emerged under the Pallister/Stefanson government that the new Kinew government must address.

Significant Restructuring of Big Policy

Pallister constructed adversarial relationships with a growing number of groups. On the surface, this might not seem to involve the public sector, in part because public servants are politically neutral, but this antagonism makes the job of public servants much more challenging.

The deteriorating relationship this government had with the Manitoba Métis Federation (MMF) is just one example. In 2017, Pallister commented on the issue of night hunting and warned that night hunting was "becoming a race war."[45] Pallister noted: "Young Indigenous guys going out and shooting a bunch of moose because they can. . . . This is a poor practice, a dumb practice."[46] This racist rhetoric causes unnecessary division especially since the province has no jurisdiction related to Indigenous hunting rights.

The challenge is that public servants work with Métis people and the MMF on a variety of policy files. Elected officials come and go, but public servants are permanent and must continue to work with groups like the MMF. Public servants must build relationships with Indigenous organizations and governments because of growing interdependence between actors to resolve persistent public policy problems but also for reconciliation. Yet, the efforts of public servants were continuously undermined by the Pallister government and only served to promote distrust, making their jobs much harder. The actions and dangerous rhetoric of the Pallister government framed anyone who cares about Métis rights as being self-interested or harmful to the public good.[47] Indeed, the relationship between the MMF and Pallister's provincial government was the worst on record, according to Kelly Saunders, a Métis governance specialist.[48]

Bill 64, the Education Modernization Act, is another example. The Bill sought to replace elected school boards with one provincial authority to oversee amalgamated school divisions. The antagonistic nature of the Pallister government played out here, too, when former minister of Education Cliff Cullen accused school trustees, the Manitoba Teachers' Society, and other advocates of deliberately misrepresenting Bill 64. Cullen minimized the opposition, referring to it as nothing more than "a vocal minority." Public servants must work with these stakeholders, but with so much political animosity, their tasks become increasingly difficult because of a loss of trust.[49] Public servants are saddled with high expectations to support large public policy change, but to do so requires good relationships with stakeholders.

Antagonistic Relationships with Unions

Pallister's heavy-handed nature was evident in the passing of the Health Sector Bargaining Unit Review Act in 2018, which decreased the number of health care unions from 190 to 36. This legislation claimed to improve patient care and create a more efficient collective bargaining process, but critics claimed instead that this had more to do with decreasing the power of unions than with patient care.[50]

Moreover, the Public Services Sustainability Act (PSSA, also known as Bill 28) that was introduced in early 2017 had the goal of freezing public service wages for two years, and then instituting a maximum wage cap in the following two years of .75 percent (year three) and 1 percent (year four).[51] Despite not being proclaimed in law, Bill 28 was used to freeze wages, thus preventing meaningful collective bargaining from occurring.[52] The leader of the Opposition at the time, Wabanakwut "Wab" Kinew, responded, "I think what you're seeing is the premier start to lay out the true agenda, which is focused on austerity...on the backs of public-sector employees."[53]

In response, a coalition of twenty-eight unions representing approximately 110,000 public sector workers, led by the Manitoba Federation of Labour, sued the government.[54] Initially, Bill 28—and its impact on the University of Manitoba's Faculty Association (UMFA)—was judged to be a violation of the Charter of Rights and Freedoms in a Queen's Bench ruling by Justice Joan McKelvey. The Manitoba Court of Appeal ruled that the wage freeze bill did not violate section 2(d) of the Charter that protects workers' rights to bargain collectively, which triggered the coalition's seeking leave from the Supreme Court of Canada to appeal the Manitoba Court of Appeal's decision.[55] The Supreme Court of Canada ruled against hearing the case in late 2022,[56] but the Manitoba Court of Appeal ruled in 2023 that the original decision finding in favour of UMFA should be upheld, awarding damages. Despite continued disagreement on the constitutionality of Bill 28, the damage was done by souring the relationship between the Pallister government and public sector unions.

Low Morale, High Turnover

In 2023, the Government of Manitoba released its Employee Perspectives Program Survey. With a sample of 45.9 percent[57] of government employees, this survey shows low morale within the provincial bureaucracy. When given statements, employees answered either in agreement, disagreement, or neutral. While the survey reveals some areas of agreement ("The Manitoba government provides access to respectful workplace resources and supports," 80.9 percent agreement), the results are concerning. When asked to comment on, "I am proud to tell people I work for the Manitoba government," only 56.1 percent of employees agreed. In 2021, however, 62.2 percent of respondents had agreed with this same statement, so in just two years, this represented a real decline in morale.

With workers expressing low levels of feeling valued as employees, it is no surprise that the employee turnover rate steadily increased over the lifespan of the Pallister government. Table 6.2 shows that the employee turnover rate increased from 8.1 percent under the previous year of the NDP government (2015–16) to 13.4 percent[58] under the Stefanson government in 2022–23.[59] There might have been other variables at play: March 2020 was the start of the COVID pandemic so this might, in part, have explained the higher turnover rate in 2020–21, but it should be noted that just one year prior (2019–20), the rate held constant at 9.6 percent, so the pandemic may not have had a significant influence on employees' decisions to leave. Of notable interest is the increase in turnover from 2016–17 (7.5 percent) to 2017–18 (8.4 percent) and then 2018–19 (9.3 percent). In 2017, Pallister introduced Bill 28 (the Public Services Sustainability Act) to freeze wages. While never proclaimed into law, Bill 28 prioritized fiscal sustainability at the expense of collective bargaining, and, when coupled with job losses, it is reasonable that employees looked for opportunities elsewhere. The seismic increase from 2021–22 (9 percent) to 2022–23 (13.4 percent) may have had to do with the election, where employees, uncertain of how the election would unfold, opted for other opportunities. As the turnover rate increases, institutional memory of long-serving public servants is jeopardized and imposes greater costs to hire/train new employees.[60]

Table 6.2. Employee Turnover Rate.

	2014–2015	2015–2016	2016–2017	2017–2018	2018–2019	2019–2020	2020–2021	2021–2022	2022–2023
Employee Turnover Rate	7.6%	8.1%	7.5%	8.4%	9.3%	9.6%	9.7%	9%	13.4%

Sources: Manitoba Civil Service Commission Annual Reports, available at https://www.gov.mb.ca/csc/.[61]

A Modern and Flexible Public Sector

The workforce in Canada is evolving quickly. This evolution started prior to the COVID-19 pandemic whereby advances in technology could support remote/flexible work arrangements and thus achieve better work-life balance and better effectiveness at delivering democracy. Prior to the pandemic, some public servants enjoyed flexible workplace arrangements, especially those public servants who regularly conducted on-site visits, since it made little sense to come into the office each day only to leave to begin on-site visits or attend virtual meetings.

The pandemic was the catalyst that rapidly pushed the implementation of remote/flexible work arrangements within Manitoba's public sector and elsewhere. With the pandemic, much of the public sector began working from home except for those in positions that could be performed only in person (i.e., law enforcement). Once vaccinations were available, the Government of Manitoba turned its attention back to this issue.

On 28 June 2021, the Public Service Commission issued the Flexible Workplace Arrangements Policy.[62] This policy is designed to help management respond to requests from employees for flexible work arrangements, whether that be working from home or adjusting work hours. This policy "set[s] the tone for how [public servants] return to the office" but there is a clear emphasis placed on managers to use their discretion when responding to requests.[63]

In 2022, however, there was an unexpected shift when the Clerk of the Executive Council announced that public servants must return in person to the office a minimum of three days per week. The remaining two days could become flexible work under certain conditions. This move was arbitrary because there was no fulsome review of the positions to conclude which positions absolutely required in-person attendance. If the goal is to support work-life balance and adapt to workforce needs, this arbitrary decision undermines the pursuit of this goal. At a time where labour shortages are high, the government will struggle to recruit/retain public servants with this decision.

Reconciliation

The Truth and Reconciliation Commission of Canada (TRC) advanced a series of calls to action in order to move towards meaningful reconciliation. Call to Action #57 is one that relates directly to the public sector. This call to action requires every level of government to develop and implement training for all public servants related to Indigenous history, culture, treaties, and rights. Given that 18 percent of the population in Manitoba is Indigenous,[64] coupled with the harms that colonization imposed on Indigenous peoples, the Government of Manitoba must make reconciliation a top priority.

In spring 2016, the Government of Manitoba passed the Path to Reconciliation Act in response to the calls to action outlined in the TRC. The Civil Service Commission, which has responsibility for the entire public sector, worked with government departments to provide Indigenous-led workshops to public servants.

Minister of Indigenous Reconciliation and Northern Relations Eileen Clarke was responsible at the time for leading reconciliation efforts, but resigned in 2021, stating, "I made the decision to step down from Cabinet where I felt my voice and others are not heard." Eileen Clarke was perhaps the strongest cabinet minister under the Pallister government and worked hard to build relationships. Indeed, after her resignation, First Nations leaders publicly supported

Clarke's commitment to advancing reconciliation.[65] Speculation ensued as to why she was not heard. It may have been due to Pallister's tight command of cabinet that prevented meaningful discussion. Or, it may have been due to Pallister's inability to advance reconciliation.

In July 2021, Premier Pallister chastised individuals who destroyed the statue of Queen Victoria located on the legislative grounds.[66] Pallister noted: "We need to respect our heritage just as we need to respect one another. . . . Not to find fault, not to tear down, not to highlight every failure, but rather to realize that we're a complex country as we are made up of complex people."[67] Pallister's language denied the genocide intended by the colonization project. He was not the only member to employ this dangerous rhetoric. It was concerning that the new minister of Indigenous and Northern Affairs following Clarke's resignation, Alan Lagimodiere, soon had to apologize for his remarks, made shortly after being sworn into his position, that mimicked Pallister's comments that colonization was not intended to be harmful.[68] Shortly after these two events, there were visible cracks in the allegiance of Progressive Conservative caucus members to Pallister.

Manitoba's auditor general conducted a review of how the Government of Manitoba implemented the Path to Reconciliation Act. The auditor general's report, released in April 2022, concludes that the Government of Manitoba had not fulfilled its goals outlined in the Path to Reconciliation Act. Specifically, the auditor general concluded, there were several areas of concern:

1. there was no real strategy for reconciliation;
2. the minister tried to lead efforts for reconciliation but was not heard in government;
3. there was poor cross-government coordination of reconciliation efforts; and
4. annual reporting on reconciliation efforts was not timely.[69]

What we saw here was leadership not fully respecting or understanding Indigenous peoples, which are important parts of the Path to Reconciliation Act. It is perhaps no surprise that efforts towards reconciliation have been underwhelming when political leaders use such language to undermine reconciliation. Following the auditor general's report, Minister Lagimodiere pledged that the Civil Service Commission would now require mandatory Indigenous training for all public servants. He also announced funding to support Indigenous language services.[70] The new Kinew government has emphasized reconciliation as a priority so it will be important to see how reconciliation with (and within) the public service unfolds moving forward.

Conclusions: Dark Days for the Public Sector but Is There Hope?

Although the editors of this collection speak of moderation in their introductory chapter, readers may feel that our chapter on the public service does not fit well within that theme. To be sure, the public service has undergone tremendous change since 2016, but there has also been a push for moderation. If we think back to Bill 64, as an example, moderation ensued. However, it is evident that the public service has been the focus of much change over the past decade, as well as being an important institution to help support needed change and government responsiveness to Manitoban's needs. In sum, there has been significant challenge and change, but there is also continuity.

While Westminster-style government conventions like the public service bargain, the permanence of the public service, and ministerial accountability remain, there have been challenges to these core practices as well. The core public service for Manitoba continues to provide fearless and frank advice and loyal implementation, but it has been faced with a decline in the size of the public service, an increase in the demands placed on public servants, and significant changes in the economic, labour-relations, and political environments.

In 2023, a general election was held in Manitoba with the NDP elected into government. The Kinew government faces monumental challenges related to the morale of the Manitoba public sector. The new government must establish a plan to recognize the value of the public sector. This started with the Speech from the Throne that publicly thanked public servants and promised an era of collaboration. The tone of the Kinew government is softer, collaborative, and welcoming overall. That said, recognition and tone alone are insufficient.

The government must forge a pathway to pay the public sector fairly in light of the austerity reforms enacted by Pallister and continued under Stefanson. More so, it must better support the needs of the public sector and review the arbitrary recall of staff into the office for a minimum of three days per week. On this issue, the Kinew government has already misstepped. At a forum with members of the Downtown BIZ, Kinew hinted at his aversion to hybrid work models.[71] Public servants were blindsided by his remarks, given that this issue is essential to recruitment and retention, and were confused as to why members of the Downtown BIZ would hear this news first, rather than public servants. Given the dramatic increase in employee turnover in 2022–23 (13.4 percent), vacancy rates are high, so off-the-cuff comments like this are not reassuring. Moreover, the public service commissioner is still in an acting position as of May 2024. It is essential that the Kinew government appoint a public service commissioner permanently who has the trust of public servants, and who has a vision for the commission and is not narrowly focused on human resources matters. As of October 2024, only one cabinet minister has previous cabinet experience in the Kinew government, which means there will be considerable learning to be done about the needs (and value) of the public service.

Paul G. Thomas has observed that "if it [public service] once operated in relatively calm waters, recently it has faced continuous white water of numerous disruptions and challenges."[72] If the Kinew government can listen and engage meaningfully, there may be a ray of hope for the Manitoba public sector. If not, we will witness further erosion of the public sector, longer delays, more stress, poor morale, and weakening democracy.

Notes

1 Government of Manitoba, Civil Service Commission, *Civil Service Commission Minister's Briefing: 2021 Premier Transition* [Winnipeg], 2021, https://gov.mb.ca/asset_library/en/proactive/briefings/november2021/csc_binder.pdf.

2 Government of Manitoba, Civil Service Commission, *Manitoba Public Service Commission Annual Report for the Year Ended March 31, 2023* [Winnipeg], 2023, https://www.gov.mb.ca/csc/publications/annrpt/pdf/2022-23_annualrpt_en-fr.pdf.

3 Government of Manitoba, "Clerk of the Executive Council and Cabinet Secretary," accessed 17 February 2023, https://www.gov.mb.ca/clerk/index.html.

4 Paul G. Thomas, with Curtis Brown, "The Past, Present, and Future of Manitoba's Civil Service," in *Manitoba Politics and Government: Issues, Institutions, Traditions*, ed. Paul G. Thomas and Curtis Brown (Winnipeg: University of Manitoba Press, 2010), 227–56.

5   Government of Manitoba, "Clerk of the Executive Council."
6   Government of Manitoba, Civil Service Commission, *Civil Service Commission Minister's Briefing.*
7   Government of Manitoba, Manitoba Civil Service Commission, *Civil Service Commission Annual Report, 2021–22* [Winnipeg], 2022, https://www.manitoba.ca/csc/publications/annrpt/pdf/2021-22_annualrpt_en-fr.pdf.
8   Ibid.
9   Government of Manitoba, "Manitoba Government Code of Conduct" (Winnipeg: Government of Manitoba, 2022), revised 3 May 2024, https://www.gov.mb.ca/csc/conduct/pdf/manitoba_government-code_of_conduct.pdf.
10 Public Service Act, 2021, https://web2.gov.mb.ca/bills/42-2/b019e.php#:~:text=The%20code%20of%20conduct%20focuses,in%20the%20core%20public%20service, part 2, ss. 4 and 5.
11 Ibid., part 2, s. 4.
12 Ibid., part 3, Core Public Service.
13 Ibid., part 3, s. 8.
14 Luc Juillet and Ken Rasmussen, *Defending a Contested Ideal: Merit and the Public Service Commission 1908–2008* (Ottawa: University of Ottawa Press, 2008); Sanghee Park and Jiaqi Liang, "Merit, Diversity, and Performance: Does Diversity Management Moderate the Effect of Merit Principles on Governmental Performance?" *Public Personnel Management* 49, no. 1 (2019): 83–110, doi: 10.1177/0091026019848459.
15 Dylan Robinson, "Tories Warned against Politicizing Civil Service: Ombudsman Says Citizens Should Not Foot Bill for Partisan Messaging," *Winnipeg Free Press,* 22 July 2021, https://www.winnipegfreepress.com/local/2021/07/22/tories-warned-against-politicizing-civil-service.
16 Manitoba Ombudsman, *Manitoba Ombudsman Act Investigation Report Case 2019-0404: Manitoba Finance, Communication Services Manitoba* [Winnipeg], 2021, updated May 2022, https://www.ombudsman.mb.ca/uploads/document/files/case-2019-0404-updated-en.pdf.
17 Government of Manitoba, *Speech from the Throne at the Opening of the Second Session of the 41st Legislature* [Winnipeg], 2016, https://www.gov.mb.ca/thronespeech/thronespeech_2016.html.
18 Ibid.
19 Katie Dangerfield, "Province to Introduce Bills That May Freeze Public-Sector Wages, Hike University Tuition," *Global News,* 20 March 2017, https://globalnews.ca/news/3321233/province-to-introduce-bills-that-may-freeze-public-sector-wages-hike-university-tuition/.
20 KPMG, *Manitoba Fiscal Performance Review: Phase 2 Report Summary* [Winnipeg], 2017, https://www.manitoba.ca/asset_library/en/proactive/fpr-phase-2-1.pdf.
21 As cited in Nick Martin, "Tories Ready for Legal Action from Unions," *Winnipeg Free Press,* 17 March 2017, https://www.winnipegfreepress.com/breakingnews/2017/03/17/pallister-to-public-sector-union-leaders-youre-no-longer-running-the-government.
22 Government of Manitoba, Business, Mining, Trade and Job Creation, "'Job Tenure and Union Coverage,' Manitoba's Strategic Advantages: People and the Workforce, Economic Development, Investment and Trade," accessed 17 February 2023, https://www.gov.mb.ca/jec/mbadvantage/people_tenure_union.html.

23 Statistics Canada, *Trade Union Density Rate, 1997 to 2021*, accessed 17 February 2023, https://www150.statcan.gc.ca/n1/pub/14-28-0001/2020001/article/00016-eng.htm.
24 See commentary by Dan Lett, "A Diet of Deception Helps No One," *Winnipeg Free Press*, 8 October 2016, https://www.winnipegfreepress.com/opinion/analysis/2016/10/08/use-with-mug-please.
25 Michelle Gawronsky, "What You Didn't Know about the Original 'Filmon Fridays,'" *Union Bug: The MGEU Blog* (blog), 7 March 2017, https://www.unionbug.ca/read,article/1533/what-you-didn-t-know-about-the-original-filmon-fridays#sthash.4xn7whvg.dpbs.
26 Bruce Owen, "Province Wants to Freeze Wages," *Winnipeg Free Press*, 16 February 2010, https://www.winnipegfreepress.com/breakingnews/2010/02/16/province-freezes-wages.
27 Government of Manitoba, Civil Service Commission, *Manitoba Public Service Commission Annual Report, 2021–22*.
28 Ibid. See Performance Measures section.
29 Government of Manitoba, Civil Service Commission, *Manitoba Public Service Commission Annual Report for the Year Ended March 31, 2023*.
30 Government of Manitoba, "Province Announces Vision for the Future of Manitoba's Public Service, News Release, 28 February 2018, https://news.gov.mb.ca/news/index.html?item=43217&posted=2018-02-28.
31 Clerk of the Executive Council Fred Meier spoke as part of the announcement of the new Transformation Strategy, which can be seen here: Manitoba Government, "Building a Highly Engaged Public Service that Embraces Challenges," 28 February 2018, YouTube video, https://www.youtube.com/watch?v=CPaip9hj3GQ&t=1553s. The full documents (press release and Transformation Strategy) can be found here: Government of Manitoba, "Province Announces Vision," News Release, 28 February 2018; and Government of Manitoba, *Transforming the Manitoba Public Service* [Winnipeg], 2018, https://www.gov.mb.ca/asset_library/en/proactive/transformation_2018.pdf.
32 When asked by a journalist in the press conference launching the Transformation Strategy about whether there were actions that could be taken to improve working conditions for civil servants, Premier Pallister responded by saying, "No one can perform to their utmost unless they find joy in their job. Part of finding joy in your job is knowing you have some security there. There's really relatively little security in a company that's leaking a billion dollars a year." A press release from the premier's office, released shortly after the press conference, specified, "Transformation is definitively not connected to wage negotiations." The press release was cited in Dan Lett, "A Relationship on the Rocks: Seems Unlikely Rift between Tory Government and Civil Service Can Be Mended," *Winnipeg Free Press*, 3 March 2018, https://www.winnipegfreepress.com/local/2018/03/03/a-relationship-on-the-rocks.
33 Government of Manitoba. The Public Service Act. 2021. https://web2.gov.mb.ca/laws/statutes/archive/p271(2022-05-31)e.php#3(3).
34 Auditor General of Manitoba, *Audit of the Public Accounts for the year ended March 31, 2008* [Winnipeg], 2009, https://www.poltext.org/sites/poltext.org/files/rapportsVerificateurGeneralNouveau/MB/MB_VG_2008_1.pdf. The Manitoba auditor general said in a 2008 report that universities must be part of

the government's financial statements since the government established parameters regarding tuition fees.
35 Government of Manitoba, Manitoba Public Service Commission, *Civil Service Commission Annual Report, 2021–22*.
36 Government of Manitoba, "Manitoba Government Proclaims New Public Service Act," Media Bulletin, 22 April 2022, https://news.gov.mb.ca/news/index.html?item=54274&posted=2022-04-22.
37 Government of Manitoba, Bill 19, Explanatory Note, https://web2.gov.mb.ca/bills/42-2/pdf/b019.pdf, 2. Bolding and italics added.
38 Government of Manitoba, The Civil Service Act, not in force since 26 February 2022, https://www.canlii.org/en/mb/laws/stat/ccsm-c-c110/latest/ccsm-c-c110.html.
39 Statistics Canada, *Trade Union Density Rate, 1997 to 2021*, accessed 17 February 2023, https://www150.statcan.gc.ca/n1/pub/14-28-0001/2020001/article/00016-eng.htm.
40 Government of Manitoba, Civil Service Commission, *Civil Service Commission Minister's Briefing: 2021 Premier Transition*.
41 Government of Manitoba, "Manitoba Government Proclaims."
42 Sam Thompson, "Manitoba Premier Focused on Fresh Start, Repairing Relationships," *Global News*, 25 November 2021, https://globalnews.ca/news/8402161/manitoba-premier-heather-stefanson-fresh-start-repairing-relationships/.
43 The Canadian Press, "Heather Stefanson Undoes Another Initiative of Her Predecessor, Plans to Repeal Wage-freeze Bill," *CBC News*, 24 November 2021, https://www.cbc.ca/news/canada/manitoba/manitoba-wage-freeze-bill-1.6260671.
44 Ryan Stelter, "Stefanson's Latest Gaffe Could Only Prove to Worsen Approval Rating," *Winnipeg Sun*, 18 March 2022, https://winnipegsun.com/opinion/columnists/stelter-stefansons-latest-gaffe-could-only-prove-to-worsen-approval-rating.
45 Dylan Robertson, "Clash of the Titans: Chartrand vs. Pallister," *Winnipeg Free Press*, 19 October 2020, https://www.winnipegfreepress.com/local/clash-of-the-titans-chartrand-vs-pallister-572791782.html.
46 *CBC News Manitoba*, "Night Hunting 'Becoming a Race War,' Says Premier Brian Pallister," 20 January 2017, https://www.cbc.ca/news/canada/manitoba/night-hunting-brian-pallister-race-war-1.3944949.
47 Scott Billeck, "MMF to File Court Challenge against Gov't, Pallister over Hydro Payment," *Winnipeg Sun*, 1 June 2018, https://winnipegsun.com/news/provincial/mmf-to-file-court-challenge-against-govt-pallister-over-hydro-payment.
48 Dylan Robertson, "Clash of the Titans." See also Will Goodon and Kelly Saunders, "Leading in a Time of Crisis: The Manitoba Metis Federation's COVID-19 Response Plan," in *COVID-19 in Manitoba: Public Policy Responses to the First Wave*, ed. Andrea Rounce and Karine Levasseur (Winnipeg: University of Manitoba Press, 2020), 129–34. See https://uofmpress.ca/books/detail/covid-19-in-manitoba, accessed 4 January 2025.
49 Karine Levasseur and Andrea Rounce, "Declining Morale a Growing Concern in Public Service," *Winnipeg Free Press*, 14 June 2021, A7.

50 *CBC News Manitoba*, "Unions Blast Manitoba Government's Move to Merge Health Sector Bargaining Units," 24 January 2019, https://www.cbc.ca/news/canada/manitoba/mgeu-new-health-sector-bargaining-units-1.4991917.

51 Legislative Assembly of Manitoba, Bill 28, s. 12(1), https://web2.gov.mb.ca/bills/41-2/b028e.php.

52 Julie Guard, "Austerity Politics and Anti-union Animus: Organized Labour in the Pandemic," in *COVID-19 in Manitoba: Public Policy Responses to the First Wave*, ed. Andrea Rounce and Karine Levasseur (Winnipeg: University of Manitoba Press, 2020), 62–71; Dylan Robertson, "Clash of the Titans."

53 As cited in Larry Kusch and Nick Martin, "Premier Promises 'Manitoba Miracle': Pallister Targets Health-care Unions, Vows to Rebuild Economy During State-of-the-Province Address," *Winnipeg Free Press*, 8 December 2016, https://www.winnipegfreepress.com/breakingnews/2016/12/08/pallister-names-all-star-panel-to-work-on-jobs-economic-development.

54 Manitoba Federation of Labour, *MFL Fact Sheet: Public Services Sustainability Act* (Winnipeg: Manitoba Federation of Labour, 2019), accessed 17 February 2023, https://www.umfa.ca/images/pdfs/PDPS_FactSheet_MFL_Nov2019.pdf.

55 Harminder Mundi and Paniz Khosrashahy, "Manitoba Court of Appeal Finds That Legislation Temporarily Preventing Collective Bargaining on Wages Is Constitutional," in *Koskie Minsky: Justice Matters* (blog), 22 November 2021, accessed 17 February 2023, https://kmlaw.ca/manitoba-court-of-appeal-upholds-wage-restraint-legislation/.

56 Steve Lambert, "Unions Lose Bid to Appeal Manitoba's Wage-freeze Law to Supreme Court," *CBC News Manitoba*, 27 October 2022, https://www.cbc.ca/news/canada/manitoba/manitoba-wage-freeze-law-appeal-supreme-court-1.6631468.

57 Government of Manitoba, Engage MB, *Winter 2022 Employee Perspectives Program Survey: Manitoba Government Report on Overall Results*, https://www.gov.mb.ca/asset_library/en/proactive/20222023/employee-perspectives-survey-results-winter-2022.pdf.

58 This represents a total of 1,4284 employees who left the civil service.

59 Government of Manitoba, Civil Service Commission, *2020–2021 Manitoba Civil Service Commission Annual Report* [Winnipeg], 2021, https://www.manitoba.ca/csc/publications/annrpt/pdf/2020-21_annualrpt_en-fr.pdf.

60 Mehmet Akif Demircioglu and Evan Berman, "Effects of the Innovation Climate on Turnover Intention in the Australian Public Service," *The American Review of Public Administration* 49, no. 5 (2019): 614–28.

61 Government of Manitoba, Public Service Commission, *Annual Report for the Year Ended March 31, 2023*; Government of Manitoba, Civil Service Commission, *2020–2021 Manitoba Civil Service Commission Annual Report*; Government of Manitoba, Civil Service Commission, *Manitoba Civil Service Commission Annual Report 2019–20* [Winnipeg], 2020, https://www.gov.mb.ca/csc/publications/annrpt/pdf/2019-20_annualrpt_en-fr.pdf; Government of Manitoba, Civil Service Commission, *Manitoba Civil Service Commission Annual Report 2018–19* [Winnipeg], 2019, https://www.gov.mb.ca/csc/publications/annrpt/pdf/2018-19_annualrpt_en-fr.pdf; Government of Manitoba, Civil Service Commission, *Manitoba Civil Service Commission Annual Report 2016–17* [Winnipeg], 2017, https://www.gov.mb.ca/csc/publications/annrpt/pdf/2016-17_annualrpt_en-fr.pdf; Government of Manitoba,

Civil Service Commission, *Manitoba Civil Service Commission Annual Report 2015–16* [Winnipeg], 2016, https://www.gov.mb.ca/csc/publications/annrpt/pdf/2015-16_annualrpt_en-fr.pdf.

Note that there is a discrepancy in the annual reports for 2020–21 and 2021–22 for reporting employee turnover. For 2021–22, the authors manually calculated the employee turnover rate (12,514 employees; 1,395 employees leaving).

62 Government of Manitoba, "1.2.4 Flexible Work Arrangements," Public Service Commission Policies, accessed 17 February 2023, https://www.gov.mb.ca/csc/policyman/flex_work.html#:~:text=resources%20and%20tools.-,Employees,any%20challenges%20that%20are%20anticipated.

63 Dylan Robertson, "Return to Office a Work in Progress for Manitoba Civil Servants," *Winnipeg Free Press*, 26 July 2021, https://www.winnipegfreepress.com/breakingnews/2021/07/26/return-to-office-a-work-in-progress-for-manitoba-civil-servants.

64 Auditor General of Manitoba, *Report to the Legislative Assembly: Manitoba's Implementation of The Path to Reconciliation Act*, April 2022, https://www.oag.mb.ca/audit-reports/manitoba's-implementation-of-the-path-to-reconciliation-act-2022#.

65 Ibid.

66 Caitlyn Gowriluk, "Manitoba's Indigenous Relations Minister Resigns from Cabinet after Premier's Comments on Colonial History," *CBC News Manitoba*, 14 July 2021, https://www.cbc.ca/news/canada/manitoba/eileen-clarke-resigns-cabinet-pallister-indigenous-1.6102299.

67 Ibid.

68 *CBC News Manitoba*, "Manitoba Indigenous Reconciliation Minister Offers 'Sincerest Apologies' Over Residential Schools Remarks," 16 July 2021, https://www.cbc.ca/news/canada/manitoba/lagimodiere-apology-manitoba-1.6106459.

69 Auditor General of Manitoba, *Report to the Legislative Assembly: Manitoba's Implementation of the Path to Reconciliation Act*.

70 Carol Sanders, "Manitoba Fails to Keep Reconciliation Promise: AG," *Winnipeg Free Press*, 21 April 2022, https://www.winnipegfreepress.com/breakingnews/2022/04/21/manitoba-fails-to-keep-reconciliation-promise-ag.

71 Danielle Da Silva, "Kinew No Fan of Hybrid Work; Wants More Public-sector Employees Back in City's Core," *Winnipeg Free Press*, 19 January 2024, https://www.winnipegfreepress.com/breakingnews/2024/01/19/kinew-no-fan-of-hybrid-work-wants-more-public-sector-employees-in-citys-core.

72 Paul G. Thomas, "Employee Surveys and the Health of Manitoba's Public Service," *Winnipeg Free Press*, 4 May 2024, https://www.winnipegfreepress.com/breakingnews/2024/05/04/employee-surveys-and-the-health-of-manitobas-public-service.

CHAPTER 7

The News Media and Public Opinion in Manitoba

CURTIS BROWN AND MARY AGNES WELCH

When things are working well, the news media plays a critical role in keeping Manitobans informed about the decisions made on their behalf by their elected officials. In tandem with this, public opinion research serves as a key gauge—one of the only ones—of how citizens feel about their government and the big policy issues of the day.

In Manitoba, like elsewhere in Canada, news outlets and public opinion research companies work closely together to measure which political parties Manitobans plan to vote for, how they feel about the big issues making headlines, and how these views shift over time. Broadly speaking, this is a symbiotic relationship. Polling by public opinion researchers generates content for media outlets, helps calibrate coverage, and provides context to "streeters" (or "man-on-the-street" interviews) that reporters still rely on in a limited way to offer colour and reaction to the news of the day. Meanwhile, stories based on polls provide exposure to the research firm conducting the polling and helps the firm build credibility and visibility among potential clients and the broader public, including potential survey respondents.

However, this symbiotic relationship between the media and polling firms has evolved significantly over time and continues to change, including in Manitoba. Broader technological and market forces have changed the nature of media coverage of public opinion polls as well as the way these two entities work together.

This chapter provides an overview of the news media in Manitoba in the early 2020s, including a discussion of the major media outlets and how they cover politics and government in this province. It also examines how public opinion polling is used by media outlets in their coverage of Manitoba's political scene, including specifically how polling has been presented in recent provincial election campaigns. While this is not the primary focus of the chapter, it also examines the extent to which social media fits into this relationship, as an increasing proportion of Manitobans get their news from this channel as traditional media outlets' audiences shrink.

The Media in Manitoba

Since the days of legendary *Winnipeg Free Press* editor and columnist John Dafoe,[1] Manitobans have been comparatively well served by a wide array of print and broadcast media outlets. These range from large and influential outlets with sufficient resources to staff political bureaus and to tackle long-form investigative journalism, to smaller outlets focusing on their local towns and regions or specific ethnocultural communities. The role and influence of these outlets—and the specific means by which Manitobans consume information about the world around them—have shifted rapidly during the past fifteen years, as more citizens turn to such sources as online discussion boards, community Facebook pages, Twitter, Instagram, and TikTok to learn about and debate political issues.

Given its size and demographic dominance within Manitoba—more than two-thirds of Manitobans live in Winnipeg and the surrounding capital region[2]—Winnipeg-based media outlets have the widest reach and offer the most comprehensive coverage of provincial politics. Among newspapers, the independently owned *Winnipeg Free Press* is the largest and most influential. The *Free Press* publishes a print edition six days per week, and a significant portion of its readership now comes from its website, which, like many newspapers in today's market, requires a digital subscription to access. First published in 1872—two years after Manitoba joined Confederation and one year before Winnipeg became a city—the *Free Press* has always played a prominent role in covering provincial affairs. Until recently, the *Free Press* had the largest contingent of full-time reporters (two) dedicated to covering the Manitoba legislature from an office within the legislative building, with one correspondent also covering municipal politics at Winnipeg City Hall full time. Until 2022, the *Free Press* had a dedicated correspondent in Ottawa covering the federal government from a Manitoba perspective. He was one of only two parliamentary correspondents working for regional newspapers. In addition to its news coverage, the *Free Press* publishes extensive commentary on the provincial issues of the day, including via two regular political columnists whose work focuses mainly on provincial issues, as well as through its editorial pages, which include unsigned editorials and op-ed submissions by regular and intermittent contributors, many of whom are local.

The other daily newspaper in the provincial capital is the *Winnipeg Sun*. The *Sun*'s coverage of provincial politics has been scaled back in recent years due to significant staff cuts. The newspaper no longer has a permanent reporter stationed at the Manitoba legislative building or the city hall. Compared to the *Winnipeg Free Press*, the *Sun*'s circulation is significantly smaller.[3] The most recently available public data, from 2015, show the *Free Press* with a total average weekly circulation of 101,229, compared with the *Sun* with 48,767. In May 2024, this newspaper, which had been owned by Postmedia for many years, was sold to a group of local owners fronted by former *Sun* publisher and former Progressive Conservative (PC) cabinet minister Kevin Klein. Time will tell if this shift to local ownership leads to enhanced coverage of provincial affairs.

The Canadian Press (CP) national news wire service is a private, not-for-profit cooperative that is owned by member newspapers throughout the country. Both the *Free Press* and *Sun*—as well as the websites of local broadcast outlets—also run articles by this wire service, which has had at least one reporter in the press gallery for decades and whose local office is currently based in the legislative building. Indeed, for the last decade or so, Manitoba has been very well served by CP's coverage of provincial politics.

The parent company that owns the *Free Press*, FP Newspapers Inc., also owns two other newspapers that serve important regional audiences. The *Brandon Sun* publishes five days a week and serves the province's second-largest city and rural southwestern Manitoba, and the *Steinbach Carillon* publishes weekly and focuses on southeastern Manitoba. The Postmedia national media chain has also owned several other weekly community newspapers serving regional hubs in different parts of the province, including the *Interlake Spectator* (based in Gimli) and the *Portage Graphic* (formerly a daily newspaper). The *Portage Graphic*, it should be noted, was part of the same deal in May 2024 between Postmedia and the Klein Group. It is worth observing, however, that in recent years Postmedia has shuttered many small-town papers across Canada and the remaining papers are unable to provide robust news coverage for their readers.

In west-central Manitoba, WCMB News publishes weekly newspapers serving larger communities such as Dauphin (the *Herald*), Swan River (the *Times & Star*), and The Pas (*Opasquia Times*). In northern Manitoba, the *Thompson Citizen* provides news and information to those living in the North's largest centre, and the *Flin Flon Reminder* covers that city. Both these newspapers are owned by Glacier Media Group.

While these regional newspapers do not have reporters permanently covering the Manitoba legislature, they do provide their readers with news coverage and commentary on provincial issues from a regional and community perspective. Much of the interaction between provincial officials and news reporters occurs at the legislative building—from formal news conferences to impromptu hallway scrums after the question period—but elected officials interact regularly with these regional media outlets at events in these communities, as well as via conference calls on specific issues and via press releases.

Turning to broadcasters, one of the major players when it comes to provincial affairs is the publicly owned Canadian Broadcasting Corporation (CBC). Its English-language service provides reasonably extensive coverage of public affairs in the province via radio, television, and its website. Until the spring of 2022, CBC Radio One had the largest audience share in the Winnipeg market. Privately owned talk radio station 680 CJOB, which covers provincial and civic politics extensively on several of its programs throughout the day, has historically had the largest audience share among radio stations in the Winnipeg market.[4] Corus Entertainment owns 680 CJOB, and also owns the Global Television affiliate in the city. Global, CTV, CBC, and City-TV all cover the provincial legislature to some degree on their evening newscasts and their websites, and both CTV and Global have local morning shows that feature longer interviews with politicians, pundits, and advocacy groups about important political topics. Of these three television broadcasters, CTV has historically had the largest audience for its evening newscast, and CTV has had a veteran television reporter dedicated to city and provincial politics for some time.[5] Although CBC's television broadcast audience is relatively small, it attracts a significant audience to its website, and also typically has at least one reporter dedicated to provincial politics and one at the city hall.

There are also several significant and long-standing media outlets that cater specifically to ethnocultural communities in the province. *La Liberté*, a French-language weekly newspaper, serves Manitoba's historically important francophone community, as does publicly funded Radio-Canada through radio, television, and the Web. There are several specific print newspapers and websites that cater to the Filipino, Mennonite, Indo-Canadian, Ukrainian, and Jewish communities in the province, though none offer leading coverage of politics. For Manitoba's First Nations and Métis populations, there are several smaller publications, but the drivers of news are Native Communications Inc.'s NCI-FM radio station as well as the television network APTN, which is based in Winnipeg and offers daily news and strong investigative coverage of politics and policy issues affecting Indigenous peoples.

During the past decade, both print and broadcast outlets in Manitoba have experienced additional competition from community-based websites/discussion forums—and, increasingly, Facebook community groups. Brandon, for example, has two local, independently owned websites that are conduits for civic information (ebrandon.ca and bdnmb.ca), and Pembina Valley Online (which is owned by Golden West Radio) plays a key role in delivering news and information in the growing Morden-Winkler-Altona region of south-central Manitoba. The reach of community Facebook groups also continues to spread. To offer just one example, the *Dauphin Herald* newspaper has a weekly circulation of just under 6,000,[6] whereas a community Facebook group called "Dauphin Talk" has nearly 10,000 active users. While these community groups are not explicitly focused on provincial politics and do not produce journalism in the same manner as other traditional media outlets, they are a public sphere for discussing events and issues and illuminating public views.

Overall, although the legacy print and broadcast media outlets in Manitoba do not have the same audience reach that they did twenty or thirty years ago, they remain influential conduits shaping how Manitobans learn and think about the province's major issues.

Social Media and Provincial Politics

As traditional media audiences shrink, the role of social media in disseminating information about provincial politics has increased in Manitoba. However, social media usage is quite diffuse, with different platforms being used to communicate with specific audiences.

To greater and lesser degrees, provincial politicians have embraced these new tools to communicate directly with voters rather than go through intermediaries working for news outlets. The New Democratic Party (NDP) Premier Wabanakwut "Wab" Kinew, for example, has a relatively large audience with more than 229,000 followers on Instagram[7] and 110,900 followers on X/Twitter,[8] and more than 235,000 followers on TikTok.[9] To reflect the increasing importance of social media in government communications, when the Kinew administration came to power in October 2023, it created a communications position within the premier's office solely focused on digital engagement.[10] Kinew's social media is a blend of political messaging and fun—one Instagram video showing outtakes of him shooting baskets at a Winnipeg community centre for an election-day video, for example, had more than 12,000 likes.[11] Other Manitoba politicians have had relatively modest audiences and presences on social media—former Progressive Conservative premier Heather Stefanson, for example, had only about 10,000 followers on Twitter and 3,600 on Instagram at the time of the 2023 election, while as of March 2025 PC leadership candidate and Fort Whyte MLA Obby Khan had slightly more than 5,500 followers.[12]

When X (previously known as Twitter) was in its heyday, conversation about Manitoba political issues coalesced around the #mbpoli hashtag, as this was used by journalists, provincial politicians, and citizens to share posts about provincial issues. During the COVID-19 pandemic, Twitter and Instagram also became a place where information and even blow-by-blow live tweeting of daily pandemic briefing became highly prized.

How Media Outlets Cover Provincial Politics

Manitoba's centrist political culture does not lend itself to the kind of political drama that often seizes the media's interest in Alberta or British Columbia. As noted, although media coverage of provincial politics and elections has been fairly consistent in Manitoba during the past few decades, there are relatively few reporters covering provincial politics full time.

Day-to-day coverage of provincial politics varies and is driven by the top-of-mind issues of the day (including new polling), the government's press release or announcement agenda, and the sophistication of the relationships and sources journalists have cultivated within the government, the Opposition, and, to a lesser degree, the civil service. When the legislature is sitting, the small cadre of journalists working in the building or visiting tend to build their day around the question period—not so much for the debate that happens in the house as for the informal scrums that occur in the hallway afterwards. Although this practice has fallen out of fashion somewhat in recent years, the post-question period scrums have traditionally given journalists and columnists relatively unfettered access to ministers and MLAs (Members of the Legislative Assembly), as well as the chance to chat informally with political staff. This organic and unscripted access remains a reliable element of political coverage in the province, as it allows journalists to explore stories beyond the government's agenda.

When the house is not sitting, access can be a challenge. Both NDP and PC governments have significantly reduced the number of direct interactions with journalists, preferring to rely on press releases or emailed statements (which, many reporters note, fail to answer basic questions). The previous Progressive Conservative government had not been as accessible to reporters as past governments, with the premier and cabinet ministers conducting fewer interviews or formal press availabilities, and at times having a tense relationship with reporters. This phenomenon is not unique to Manitoba's Progressive Conservative government, however, as it has been occurring to a greater degree at the national level and in other provincial capitals as government spokespeople have sought to limit opportunities for reporters to question cabinet ministers and key government decision makers.[13] Although the new NDP administration appears to have a less testy relationship with the news media than did its predecessors, the new government relies extensively on canned statements to respond to stories rather than making ministers available for interviews with journalists.

The somewhat controlled and "on-message" interactions between reporters and politicians change to some extent at election time.

Additional journalists are typically assigned to the election beat during a provincial campaign period, offering profiles of swing ridings as well as coverage of each day's campaign promises. However, few (if any) reporters travel with party leaders around the province during campaigns. Manitoba, given its size and the limited budgets of both parties and media outlets, does not have a modern tradition of campaign buses that ferry the leader, political staff, and reporters to announcements around the province. However, leaders usually make two or three short campaign swings through rural and northern Manitoba, and occasionally one reporter stationed at the legislature follows these short tours. More often, though, the announcements made during election campaigns that take place outside the Perimeter Highway are covered only by representatives of local media outlets. However, a campaign typically offers local political and beat reporters the chance to interact less formally—in other words, the valuable "face time" that helps build relationships, trust, and sources.

Election night results in Manitoba receive more thorough coverage from the different media outlets in the province, with reporters stationed at each of the campaign headquarters or election night celebrations. All three major broadcasters in Manitoba—CTV, CBC, and Corus (Global/CJOB)—carry live coverage that includes in-studio analysis and riding-by-riding results, along with correspondents offering live hits and reaction from each party's event. Journalists also feed live online coverage by tweeting into live blogs and filing online stories from swing ridings.

The Role of Public Opinion Research in Political Coverage

For several years, public opinion research has been commissioned by— and, increasingly, provided freely to—Manitoba media outlets. These data give Manitobans a regular barometer of the public mood: how they feel about the current party in power at the legislative building on Broadway Avenue in Winnipeg and insights into views on specific issues in the zeitgeist.

The longest-standing relationship in this regard is a partnership between Manitoba-based public opinion research firm Probe Research and the *Winnipeg Free Press*. Since 1998, Probe Research has conducted a quarterly omnibus poll that includes a series of questions measuring provincial party support, with the results published in the *Free Press* and often picked up by other Manitoba media outlets. Typically, this poll also includes questions gauging Manitobans' views on specific policy issues making headlines at the time. For instance, in June 2022, Probe Research asked Manitobans whether private-sector providers should be contracted to help deal with diagnostic and surgical backlogs in the health care system.[14] In December 2021, Probe Research gauged the preferences of Winnipeggers regarding the City of Winnipeg's sidewalk snow-clearing policy.[15]

The Probe Research–*Winnipeg Free Press* quarterly provincial politics numbers are highly anticipated by the news media and those who closely follow politics in the province, including political staff. In a way, they are used as a framing mechanism by reporters, columnists, and pundits, providing context that helps explain government decision making and setting the stage for upcoming provincial election campaigns. They are also a data repository that tracks the changing views of Manitobans, and of subsets of Manitobans such as women, rural residents, and new Canadians.

Manitoba has always played an outsized role in the public opinion research industry. It is the birthplace of the Angus Reid Group, which grew into a significant national firm in the 1980s and 1990s and was purchased by multinational market research firm Ipsos in 2001. In addition to Probe, the key local players in the Manitoba market have been Prairie Research Associates (PRA), Viewpoints Research, and Western Opinion Research/Nordic Research Group (which was purchased by Leger, a large national firm, in 2019). Viewpoints has had a long-standing connection to the Manitoba NDP and labour, while historically Western Opinion Research/Nordic Research Group has had a close relationship with the PC Party of Manitoba. Probe and PRA, meanwhile, are officially non-partisan. Both firms—as well as Leger—conduct public opinion research on behalf of provincial government departments and Crown corporations under standing offer agreements.

During the past two decades, the traditional barriers to conducting public opinion research have fallen, allowing new players to enter the market and conduct surveys relatively inexpensively, with little in the way of fixed overhead costs. Public opinion surveys traditionally conducted by live telephone interviewers have given way to a proliferation of surveys conducted either online with pre-recruited respondents who have agreed to take part in surveys sent to them via email, or via

Interactive Voice Response (IVR) messaging that involves dialling telephone numbers and asking respondents to press digits on their keypad in response to questions asked by an automated voice. Compared with surveys with live interviewers, online panel surveys and IVR polls are much cheaper to conduct, and large numbers of interviews can be conducted relatively quickly. These new technological options appear to have led to an increase in the number of public opinion polls released during Manitoba provincial election campaigns, mirroring a trend at the national level and in other provinces. For instance, there were only four public opinion polls released during the 2011 Manitoba provincial election campaign.[16] Five years later, there were ten polls released by five different public opinion research firms during the 2016 campaign period.[17] Interestingly, though, there were only seven polls released publicly during the 2019 election campaign. This is likely because, unlike the 2016 election when a change in government was expected, most pre-election polling suggested the governing Progressive Conservatives would easily win a second term. During the 2019 election campaign, five companies released separate surveys during the writ period: Probe Research, Mainstreet Research, Research Co., Forum Research, and Converso.

Generally, election-time polling in Manitoba has been reasonably accurate, avoiding some of the more serious misses that sparked debates in provinces such as British Columbia, Alberta, and Quebec about the value and methodology of election polling. However, the 2019 race saw one notable miss, which highlighted some of the more technical aspects of public opinion research not often explored by media and political watchers.

Converso, which specializes in conducting online and telephone public engagement (such as telephone town halls) and had not yet conducted formal election polling, released a poll during the campaign that initially showed a close race between the governing Progressive Conservatives and the New Democrats. This contradicted polling from Probe and other firms leading up to the campaign that showed the PCs firmly in the lead. Although many media outlets chose not to report on this survey when it was initially released, in the end Converso had to retract its initial numbers, confessing that the data from this IVR survey was not statistically weighted correctly, overweighting northern Manitoba's population and thus giving the NDP a higher level of hypothetical support.[18] While this incident raised eyebrows among political watchers, ultimately the surveys released closer to election day proved to be largely accurate—showing the PCs would easily win a second majority government, as the following Table 7.1 shows.

Table 7.1. List of Public Opinion Polls Conducted in the 2019 Manitoba Election.

Polling firm	Last date of polling	Method	PC	NDP	Liberal	Green	Other
Forum Research*	Sept. 9	IVR	43%	29%	17%	10%	1%
Research Co.**	Sept. 9	Online panel	44%	31%	16%	7%	1%
Mainstreet Research***	Sept. 4	IVR	43%	34%	15%	6%	1%
Probe Research****	Aug. 24	Online panel	40%	29%	18%	10%	3%
Election result			46.8%	31.6%	14.6%	6.7%	0.3%

Sources: *Forum Research, The Forum Poll, "Manitoba Election," 10 September 2019, http://poll.forumresearch.com/post/3027/manitoba-election/; **Research Co., "Progressive Conservatives Remain Ahead of NDP in Manitoba," 9 September 2019, https://researchco.ca/2019/09/09/its-my-turn-the-circle-game-has-brought-me-here/;***Mainstreet Research, "Manitoba PC Government Most Likely Outcome," 6 September 2019, https://www.scribd.com/document/424759944/Mainstreet-Mb-06september2019; and ****Probe Research, "PCs Maintain Province-Wide Lead, Although Race Remains Deadlocked in Winnipeg," 31 August 2019, https://probe-research.com/polls/pcs-maintain-province-wide-lead-although-race-remains-deadlocked-winnipeg.

One of the things that sets these new entrants to the Manitoba market apart—and which mirrors a trend that has been occurring nationally for the past several years—is that increasingly these election polls (and polls conducted prior to elections) are distributed for all media outlets to use rather than as part of a specific partnership between media outlet and research company. While Probe Research continues to partner with the *Winnipeg Free Press* and sometimes CTV and CBC, this type of symbiotic relationship is less common today as more public opinion research companies enter the field and newsroom budgets shrink.

Despite Manitoba's outsized number of polling firms and the easy availability of public opinion data, media outlets do not always use polling to maximum advantage. Coverage of polling is largely passive. Most outlets do not use new polling figures as an excuse to speak directly with voters or to explore the nuances of public opinion research or the views of critical subsets of voters such as women or rural residents. Media outlets will report on the latest survey if poll results are provided to them but rarely commission their own custom polls with comprehensive questions on specific topics that inform a deeper look into the views and habits of Manitobans. There are two notable exceptions to this, however. First, in a municipal as opposed to a provincial context, CBC commissioned a poll to understand the views of Winnipeggers in advance of a high-profile plebiscite on reopening the Portage Avenue and Main Street intersection to pedestrians.[19] And, leading up to the 2023 election, CBC commissioned Probe Research to conduct three focus groups with swing voters living in Winnipeg and rural Manitoba to explore their perceptions of the parties, leaders, and issues.[20]

It is fair to say that while news media outlets work with a relatively thin level of public opinion research, other civil society groups, particularly labour unions and advocacy organizations, frequently commission more in-depth public opinion polling on key issues such as health care funding and education reform as part of their advocacy work. In some cases, these organizations will release the results to the media as a way of positively framing their particular issues.

Manitoba's media are generally conscientious when reporting on polling data and tend to follow the advice outlined by the Canadian Research Insights Council on what to disclose when reporting on a poll.[21] Most major outlets typically follow best practices such as reproducing the full question, and noting the sample size, methodology, margin of error (if one can be ascribed), and which organization paid for or conducted the survey. Most outlets also post the full poll report, including data tables, online for readers and viewers to see. Local CBC reporters must vet all polls through the CBC's research office in Toronto to ensure only high-quality and methodologically rigorous surveys are reported on—a process that, while occasionally slow, is very valuable.

Conclusion

Political coverage in Manitoba—still strong but shrinking—will continue to evolve with the times, as governments and civil society groups find new ways to communicate and listen to the public, including through polling and social media. The use of public opinion polling has been a long-standing gauge of how citizens feel about their government and its decision making at any given time, and has offered needed context for reporters who rely on survey data more and more as their reach shrinks. There is no doubt that public opinion researchers and local media outlets will continue to collaborate to better understand the electorate during and between future elections.

Notes

1. Manitoba Historical Society, Centennial Business, *Manitoba Free Press/Winnipeg Free Press*, accessed 4 January 2025, http://www.mhs.mb.ca/docs/business/freepress.shtml, 1. The *Winnipeg Free Press* was founded as the *Manitoba Free Press* in 1872 and changed its name to the *Winnipeg Free Press* in 1931.
2. Manitoba's capital region includes the municipalities of East St. Paul, Selkirk, Cartier, Headingley, Macdonald, Ritchot, Rockwood, Rosser, Springfield, St. Andrews, St. Clements, St. François Xavier, Tache, and West St. Paul, as well as Niverville, Stonewall, and Dunnottar. Collectively, 124,683 people live in these communities in addition to the 749,607 in Winnipeg. Statistics Canada, *Census Profile: 2021 Census of Population*, https://www12.statcan.gc.ca/census-recensement/2021/dp-pd/prof/index.cfm?Lang=E.
3. News Media Canada, Daily Newspaper Circulation Data, 2015, "Daily Newspaper Circulation Report by Title," spreadsheet, https://nmc-mic.ca/wp-content/uploads/2016/06/2015-Daily-Newspaper-Circulation-Report-by-Title-SPREADSHEET_FINAL.xlsx. News Media Canada circulation data are publicly available only up to 2015. For paid subscriptions only, the divide is even larger—an average of 67,503/day for the *Winnipeg Free Press* and 14,055 for the *Winnipeg Sun*.
4. ChrisD.ca, "680 CJOB, CBC Rule Radio Dial in Winnipeg," 3 June 2022, Enews. https://www.chrisd.ca/2022/06/03/winnipeg-numeris-spring-2022-radio-ratings/.
5. *Winnipeg Sun*, "CTV Winnipeg's Newscast Continues to Dominate in Ratings," 7 May 2016, https://winnipegsun.com/2016/05/07/ctv-winnipegs-newscast-continues-to-dominate-in-ratings. Specific statistics for local television affiliates are no longer released publicly, but as of 2016, CTV Winnipeg's 6:00 p.m. newscast had a higher audience share than that of Global and CBC combined.
6. Sources, *Dauphin Herald*, accessed 4 January 2025, https://www.sources.com/MNN/Subscribers2/Me201.htm.
7. As of 7 March 2025, https://www.instagram.com/wabber/.
8. As of 7 March 2025, https://x.com/WabKinew.
9. As of 7 March 2025, https://www.tiktok.com/@wabkinew.
10. Steve Lambert, "Manitoba Premier Says He Follows Security Precautions on Social Media App," *CTV News*, Canadian Press, 29 December 2023, https://winnipeg.ctvnews.ca/manitoba-premier-says-he-follows-security-precautions-on-social-media-app-1.6704263.

11   Video can be found at https://www.instagram.com/p/CyEG7wGgY_k/, 6 October 2023.
12   https://www.instagram.com/obbykhan60/.
13   Les Whittington, *Spinning History: A Witness to Harper's Canada and 21st Century Choices* (Ottawa: Hill Times Publishing, 2015). Although this book focuses on how more tightly controlled media relations practices were implemented during Conservative prime minister Stephen Harper's tenure in Ottawa, many of these practices have been used by governments of all partisan stripes throughout Canada during the past decade.
14   Tom Brodbeck, "Manitobans Open to Private Help to Clear Backlogs: Poll," *Winnipeg Free Press*, 24 June 2022, https://www.winnipegfreepress.com/arts-and-life/life/health/manitobans-open-to-private-help-to-clear-backlogs-poll-576620382.html.
15   Probe Research, "Views on Snow Clearing in Winnipeg," 28 December 2021, https://probe-research.com/polls/views-snow-clearing-winnipeg.
16   Wikipedia, List of 2011 Manitoba general election opinion polls, 2011, accessed 4 January 2025, https://en.wikipedia.org/wiki/2011_Manitoba_general_election#Opinion_polls. These include a survey by Viewpoints Research conducted 14–21 September 2011, an online survey conducted by Environics Research (results released 26 September 2011), a Probe Research telephone survey conducted 21–28 September 2011, and one by Angus Reid Public Opinion conducted 30 September–2 October 2011.
17   Wikipedia, List of 2016 Manitoba general election opinion polls, accessed 4 January 2025, https://en.wikipedia.org/wiki/2016_Manitoba_general_election#Opinion_polls. These included four IVR surveys conducted by Mainstreet Research, two online surveys conducted by Insights West, two online surveys conducted by Insightrix Research, one IVR survey conducted by Forum Research, and one telephone survey conducted by Probe Research.
18   Sam Thompson, "Pollster Attributes Inaccurate Election Survey to Weight of Northern Manitoba Numbers," *Global News*, 20 August 2019, https://globalnews.ca/news/5787758/pollster-attributes-inaccurate-election-survey-to-weight-of-northern-manitoba-numbers/.
19   Bartley Kives, "'Deep, Intense Dislike for This Idea' of Opening Portage and Main, Poll Finds," *CBC News*, 11 September 2018, https://www.cbc.ca/news/canada/manitoba/portage-main-probe-poll-1.4818959.
20   Ian Froese, "'Elitist,' 'Relatable' and 'Who?' Swing Riding Voters Have Their Say on 3 Manitoba Political Leaders," *CBC News*, 5 September 2023, https://www.cbc.ca/news/canada/manitoba/manitoba-election-2023-swing-ridings-focus-group-1.6950619. This project was modelled closely on quantitative and qualitative research conducted during Alberta election campaigns for the CBC by Janet Brown Opinion Research, a Calgary-based research firm.
21   Canadian Research Insights Council, "10 Questions Journalists Should Ask Before Publishing the Results of a Survey," accessed 4 January 2025, https://www.canadianresearchinsightscouncil.ca/wp-content/uploads/2019/09/10-questions-journalists-should-ask-before-publishing-results-of-research.pdf.

PART 3
Politics and Communities

CHAPTER 8

Women, Gender, and Legislative Politics in Manitoba

JOAN GRACE

Introduction

It is easy to find where women are in Manitoba politics. Now more than ever, women in the province are taking on the hard and rewarding work of running as party candidates, and, if successful, the duties of lawmakers and constituency representatives. Apart from partisan affiliation, the number of women running as candidates in Manitoba provincial elections has increased over the years. Yet there is a caution. Like in other Canadian jurisdictions, the indicators are clear: in their introduction to *Women, Power and Political Representation*, editors Roosmarijn de Geus, Erin Tolley, Elizabeth Goodyear-Grant, and Peter John Loewen state that "the progression of women in politics cannot be taken for granted. Plateaus, losses, and backlash are just as likely as progress."[1]

In this chapter, I focus on women's participation in Manitoba provincial politics, seeking to assess how they participate in the Legislative Assembly and the degrees of influence they can exert. I begin with a discussion on the argument for women running for elected office, then assess the political context of electoral politics for women in the province, which leads to a discussion of electoral trends over time, along with a current comparison of the number of women elected between provinces and territories. Based on the last two provincial elections, I assess the percentage of women elected to the Manitoba legislature and the expectations those victories will potentially bring to the legislature as MLAs (Members of the Legislative Assembly), Opposition members, and members on legislative committees. The next section considers three offices of executive power and women's leadership: the premiership, cabinet appointments, and the Speaker of the House. The conclusion considers whether it is time for the Manitoba legislature to undergo a gender-sensitive parliamentary audit, which could lead to bolstering women's empowerment and influence.

The time frame for this overview is 2018 into the early portion of 2024, to include the electoral outcomes of the most recent election held on 3 October 2023. This time spans some of the years of Progressive Conservative (PC) governments under the leadership of Brian Pallister, the subsequent election as leader of the PC party to the office of premier by Heather Stefanson on 2 November 2022, and the election of the current New Democratic Party (NDP) government. A portion of my attention is focused on the composition of the Legislative Assembly from November 2022 to 2024, to provide a current descriptive picture of women who now sit in the assembly, representing the two major parties in Manitoba.

Why Run for Elected Office?

The federal House of Commons Standing Committee on the Status of Women published a plethora of research data and witness testimony outlining the experiences of women who ran for election and what happens when they assumed office. Offering fourteen recommendations on how to encourage more women to seek public office, the report begins with the reasons why women feel discouraged to participate in elections.[2] These include the varied gender stereotypes and discrimination women encounter that can shape a woman's lack of confidence to run for elected office, insufficient efforts by political parties to recruit female candidates, and political party practices of nominating female candidates in unwinnable ridings.[3] Women also often have difficulties in financing campaigns, confront organizations that are not gender-sensitive workplaces,[4] and, according to Sylvia Bashevkin, are targets of violence, harassment, and "hostile," "less forgiving and more polarized" gender-biased social media coverage.[5]

In thinking about the numerical outcomes of the 2019 and 2023 provincial elections, and how women legislators can potentially be influential as MLAs, it is helpful to consider representation.[6] Ideally, women legislators will be able to make indelible differences if they are able to exercise substantive representation: that is, standing for women in proposing and advocating for laws, programs, and policies that promote an array of equality outcomes. But, for this to happen, the legislative surround must change to facilitate substantive representation.

It has been long debated in feminist political science that a critical mass of 30 percent of women elected to a legislature could lead to a shift in the political culture of the institution, instigating shifts in legislative behaviour, practices, and outcomes that better attend to the lived realities of many women legislators. There are, however, significant critiques of critical mass theory. This line of argument draws attention to the ideas that what is important is not about *when* women make a difference but it is *how* they do so; and it is not about what women do but what *specific* actors do and how they conduct themselves.[7] Not all elected women support or wish to advance the tenets of substantive representation. In other words, what is important is not just about how many women are elected. Promoting and implementing substantive representation includes critical actors (men and women) as allies.

Sarah Childs and Mona Lena Krook state that critical actors are "legislators who initiate policy proposals on their own and/or embolden others to take steps to promote policies for women, regardless of the numbers of female representatives."[8] Critical actors in concert with substantive representation can be a path forward for progressively promoting gendered legislative debates, if the positions articulated by women in parliamentary settings reflect those advocated by women outside of parliament, are responsive to women in society, and are inclusive of the diversity and range of "women's interests."[9]

Westminster parliaments, like the Manitoba Legislative Assembly, are, according to Marian Sawer, historically rooted and shaped by "masculine styles of politics with the rival teams lined up facing each other."[10] Legislatures are "atypical" workplaces for women.[11] Because of parliamentary realities, confidence cannot be placed solely in the hands of individual legislators to change their ideological perspectives, partisan priorities, or the use of parliamentary privilege to defend questionable behaviour. Indeed, as a representative of the Inter-Parliamentary Union recently stated at a conference gathering, gender mainstreaming in parliaments ought to be thought of as an "institutional responsibility,"[12] and can be implemented with the commitment of the varied institutions and groups within legislatures, such as political parties and party leaders, who are key to promoting reforms to legislative processes.

Women, Diversity, and the Political Context in Manitoba

Yet, when faced with these realities, given the enduring inequalities experienced by a diversity of women in the province, women's participation in electoral politics is important; I argue that it is critical. Women's presence can interject missing voices and perspectives into legislative debates, into public discourses, and into election campaigns. Women sitting in the chamber can also potentially change the tone of legislative debates, and act as important triggers to interrogating gender stereotypes and unconscious bias present within legislatures. Ultimately, women's presence may instigate institutional reforms that could build deliberative, democratic practices.[13]

It strikes me that there are several factors in Manitoba politics that support the argument for a diversity of people elected as MLAs. Provincial politics matters to women, and, critically, to the range of gender experiences and diversities of women. The perceived parochial politics of local jurisdictions distracts from the reality that representation, policy debates, and decision making conducted at this level of government greatly impact the lives of women.[14] First, local politics is closer to the communities of people facilitating the willingness to run for elected office as a career ladder, which is especially true for women who are often the primary caregivers. Second, those who choose to run for office are still able to maintain their local relationships and connections, with their communities being a valuable conduit to legislative politics and a space that keeps them immersed in policy communities and personal networks.

My thoughts speak to the certainty that the Manitoba of today is not the Manitoba of yesterday. Manitoba is now enlivened with multicultural populations and communities who can contribute ideas and experiences to political conversations, advocating, for example, improved settlement programs. Given sustained high levels of child poverty, and vulnerable, marginalized groups spread out across a vast and often remote geographic expanse, it can be difficult for many people to run for elected office, or even to visit the Legislative Assembly. The province's de facto two-party system rather limits, perhaps even polarizes, policy debates to either end of the political spectrum, restricting the interjection of alternative proposals and perspectives. As well, Manitoba's pragmatic political culture tends to prohibit major institutional and political reforms with those in charge preferring instead to maintain the status quo.[15] All of this makes it even more important to focus on the diversities of people in the province and be encouraged by local political parties and partisan networks to participate in public life.

Election of Women – Trends over Time

As a result of the 2007 provincial election, a record eighteen women were elected to the Manitoba legislature—thirteen for the NDP and five for the PC Party—representing 31.5 percent of the legislature.[16] At the time, this was an exceptional result, albeit an anomaly years following.

There was a time when western provinces were leading the way in electing women. Kathy Brock's work draws our attention to this interesting history, when, beginning in the early 1980s, more women were being elected in western provinces such as Manitoba than in eastern provinces.[17] The newness of western provinces' electoral institutions was cited as a possible explanation, as was Manitoba's early history with social activism.[18]

Forward to more recent elections in the province, two trends are obvious in Manitoba electoral politics that, to my mind, continue to build on the history of women's relatively high participation rate in politics in the 1980s.

The first is that Manitoba tends to the middle—not the worst, but not the best—when it comes to the election of women. For example, based on data from 2018, comparing Manitoba with Canada-wide jurisdictions, only five other provinces or territories posted worse electoral results for women: 11 percent in Northwest Territories, 19 percent in Prince Edward Island, 23 percent in Newfoundland and Labrador, and 22 percent in both Nunavut and New Brunswick.[19] Higher percentages in British Columbia (30 percent), Ontario (40 percent), and Quebec (40 percent) likely reflect decisions of key partisan actors to nominate more women for election.

The second trend is that the NDP have for several decades nominated more women as electoral candidates than the PC party although that did not necessarily lead to more women being elected for the NDP.

The higher nomination numbers for the NDP reflect a party policy of working toward equity in nominations between men and women.[20] However, the PC party began to nominate more women over the years, presumably to reach out to a potentially important voting block of conservative or centre-leaning women. This tactic could portray to the electorate that the party is accessible to equity seekers, or perhaps an acknowledgment of socio-demographic shifts over time in the province.

For example, looking to data from the 2011 to 2019 provincial elections, the following Table 8.1 indicates the NDP had far and away nominated more women candidates in 2011 than the PCs. However, while keeping the lead over their main competitor, the gap began to close between the two parties between 2016 and 2019.

Table 8.1. Female Candidates in Manitoba Elections.

	2011	2016	2019
Liberal Party	14	14	19
NDP	22	24	24
PC Party	12	20	22

Source: Joan Grace, "Women and the 2019 Manitoba Election," in *Understanding the Manitoba Election 2019: Campaigns, Participation and Issues*, ed. Royce Koop, Barry Ferguson, Karine Levasseur, and Andrea Rounce (Winnipeg: University of Manitoba Press, 2019), 26.

Electoral Results

As a result of the 2019 election, there was a marginal increase to 28 percent of women elected to the Legislative Assembly,[21] up slightly from the previous 25 percent of members.[22]

According to the website of the Manitoba Legislative Assembly, prior to the recent 2023 election, party standings indicated that out of the thirty-five seats captured by the PC party, eight women were elected or re-elected. As part of the Official Opposition, five women were elected or re-elected in 2019 for the NDP, including one non-binary person, Uzoma Asagwara. For the Liberal party, out of the small caucus of three people, Cindy Lamoureux was the lone woman elected.[23]

At 26 percent of the chamber, women's electoral successes in 2019 certainly weren't the so-called critical mass of 30 percent that some people argue is needed to potentially instigate institutional change toward a more gender/women/progressive legislative chamber.[24] This changed in 2023.

Looking at Table 8.2, based on data collected by Equal Voice, an organization which promotes women's participation in Canadian politics, the results from the 2023 election indicate the "highest recorded" number of women elected—nineteen women or non-binary individuals now form 33 percent of the legislature.[25]

Table 8.2. Number of Men and Women Elected (as of 6 October 2023).

	2003	2007	2012	2015	2019	2023
Men	43	40	41	44	42	38
Women	14	17	16	13	15	19
Percent women (of 57 seats)				22	26	33

Source: Equal Voice, *Election Trackers*, 6 October 2023, https://www.equalvoice.ca/2023_manitoba_election. Percentages for 2015–2023 calculated by the author.

While the percentage of women elected increased in both 2019 and 2023, indicating organizational uptake of equality objectives, certainly on the part of the PC party, a mindful eye is required. Gender- and women-friendly legislative and policy outcomes do not necessarily result from the presence of a high number of women. As discussed above, even with the historic record number of women elected in 2023, critical actors, across all parties, can be key in building alliances and networks to advance legislative initiatives.

The Westminster Legislature

In Westminster legislative assemblies, there typically isn't much room to manoeuvre for MLAs, given party discipline and centralized party-leader decision making. In caucus, however, women legislators can contribute to policy development, should the tone and tenor established by the party leader be open and amenable to varied voices and perspectives.

A potential "parliamentary space" of influence for all women within the chamber are legislative committees,[26] providing opportunities to take on a leadership role such as chair of the committee, or, as a member, the ability to shape the agenda of the committee's work.[27] Influence can especially be available to women if they participate on gender-focused committees that are, as Karen Celis, Sarah Childs, and Jennifer Curtin say, "by design, established to promote women's interests and gender equality,"[28] and which, by their degree and scope, have the power to influence or amend legislation.[29]

Prior to the 2023 election, there were eleven permanent standing committees of the Legislative Assembly: Agriculture and Food, Crown Corporations, Human Resources, Intergovernmental Affairs, Justice, Legislative Affairs, Social and Economic Development, Private Bills, Rules of the House, Statutory Regulations and Orders, and Public Accounts.

Regrettably, there has never been a gender-focused committee in the Manitoba assembly committee system. To the previous PC government's credit, however, they kept in place a two-prong women's policy machinery in the Manitoba bureaucracy—the Status of Women (now called Women and Gender Equity), and the community-based Women's Advisory Council—each housed in the Families ministry. While the women's policy machinery has an important role in public administration, within the legislative committee system (which potentially has political weight and direct influence on laws under debate), gender-based issues and other issues of concern to women and their families too often become spread and fragmented across several committees—either in Families or Justice, for example, or the Social and Economic Development committee.

The standing committee structure and regulations are problematic for another reason. Except for the Public Accounts Committee, the position of chair of each committee is elected at each meeting of the committee. In other words, they are non-permanent rolling chair positions decided at the time of the meeting. This could be beneficial to women MLAs if the composition of the committee is responsive in terms of electing a woman and if the dominant government caucus members (which for several years have been PC members) are open to electing, for example, an Opposition member from the NDP. This process, too, could work against the election of women as chair.

In sum, the point I am making is that it matters where women are situated within the legislature and party structure after election regarding the presence of allies, networks, and their ability to exercise substantive representation. It matters even further whether they are appointed to cabinet or hold other potentially influential leadership positions.

Women and Leadership in the Legislative Assembly

Leadership and decision-making roles in legislative chambers are significant sites of parliamentary power and influence. As a premier, party leader, cabinet minister, or opposition critic, there are opportunities for women to develop the party's policy priorities, guide the direction of the government, exemplify a governance vision to civil society, and, for women legislators, act as role models to future generations.

Mona Lena Krook and Diana O'Brien[30] offer a series of explanations that could help in understanding how to facilitate women's appointment to leadership positions. While their research study focused on cabinet, their insights are instructive for many of the executive-level office appointments in a legislature. The first explanation has to do with the overall institutional regime of the jurisdiction. In Manitoba, the parliamentary structure of legislative politics affords a measure of influence for elected women should their party form a majority government. Equally, women in opposition parties, too, can be influential, not only as defenders of the public good in challenging government decisions and policies, but also as members of the Official Opposition's shadow cabinet. The second explanation refers to a commitment to a gender-equality ethos. This would include, for example, political party commitments to advance women within the ranks. Here we can think about the NDP and their centre-left policy priorities and gender-equity nomination objectives. The third explanation highlights the degree to which women are already present and who participate in the party, and who may, at some point, rise to the top. These individuals are party insiders or party activists who have built up social and political networks and have a public profile.

According to Krook and O'Brien, explanations one and three are the strongest in terms of determinants toward the promotion of women to cabinet. The institutional regime and the presence of women active in party politics work together as relatively strong structural factors that can and have become more effective over time in advancing the electoral success of women in the province. In the end, it is likely that all three of these aspects of legislative politics are important, particularly when they work in tandem to influence the practices of political parties in promoting a diversity of women.

Premiership

It has been a challenge for women to ascend to leadership roles in electoral politics, not the least because of women's low numbers as party caucus members. Research by analysts add important insights on the election of women to elite, executive positions of leadership in Canadian politics. These lines of enquiry point out that women are more likely, in Melanee Thomas's words, to "rise to party leadership when the party is under crisis conditions stemming from either scandal or major electoral failure"—the so-called glass cliff phenomenon.[31] Sharon Carstairs, for example, assumed the leadership of the Liberal Party in Manitoba when the party was in "disarray" and holding no seats in the legislature.[32]

Once in office, women party leaders have shorter tenures than those of their male counterparts,[33] and confront impatience from insider party operatives.[34] This is similar to the experience of Rana Bokhari, who, after assuming leadership of the Manitoba Liberal Party, faced internal criticisms due to a disappointing electoral performance under her tenure.[35] Ms. Bokhari was Liberal Party leader from October 2013 to September 2016.

And it can be the case that political parties sometimes look to women as a "novelty," arguably as a way to portray a new public image.[36] With these arguments in mind, the premiership of Heather Stefanson could be characterized as "imperilled," given she took over leadership after years of low support for the party and what seemed to be the enduring unpopularity of the former premier.[37] A rebranding of the PCs may have led to the election of Heather Stefanson as they ventured closer to the next election. Still, experience and determination may have accounted for why Heather Stefanson ran for leader, knowing full well what the party was confronting. The year 2023 did not bode well for the first woman premier of Manitoba. As noted, the PCs lost the election in 2023. Heather Stefanson resigned as leader of the PCs and eventually resigned as an MLA in April 2024.

Kelly Saunders has reflected that during Brian Pallister's time in office as premier, he appeared to spend considerable time "picking fights with everyone from the mayor of Winnipeg and the Manitoba Metis

Federation to the prime minister."[38] Heather Stefanson appears to have had a different leadership style. While it is still early days for a fulsome analysis of her premiership, her style was, to my mind, rather managerial. This perhaps isn't surprising, given she assumed office during the recovery years of the COVID-19 pandemic, increasing inflation, and financial worries among the electorate.

There have, however, been mishaps and criticisms. There was a stretch of time when the former premier was absent from the legislature and unavailable to the media. And on 17 March 2022, the premier apologized in the legislature for her comment to a question from the leader of the Official Opposition about a First Nation woman's death, at which time the premier instead replied boasting about her son's hockey win.[39]

Still, to my mind, there are indications of Ms. Stefanson governing differently from former Pallister governments. In her first Speech from the Throne as premier, presented in the Legislative Assembly on 23 November 2021, Stefanson spoke of building a "stronger, healthier, and more inclusive province" based on the values of "equality [and] inclusivity."[40] Having the first female premier in Manitoba's history, who possessed extensive ministerial experience since first elected in 2000, had a long-time presence in the legislature, and was a veteran PC party member, seemed to bode well for a refreshed approach to governance and policy focus on policies that broadly benefit Manitobans. It is notable, too, that Heather Stefanson took on the role as chair of the Council of the Federation, an all-premier organization that advances the interests of provinces and territories. And while it is the case that federal funding is critical to Manitoba's financial health, facilitating the premier's ability to smooth the road toward better health care services in preparation for the next provincial election,[41] the premier was a willing signatory to the Canada-wide ten-dollars-a-day child care agreement, and made commitments to bolster early child care learning at post-secondary institutions.[42]

Cabinet Appointments

Research highlights that appointments to cabinet are facilitated in parliamentary systems because they are generalist rather than specialized.[43] In generalist systems like those in Manitoba and across Canada, cabinet ministers are selected from a pool of "political insiders" (that is, from elected members). In specialist systems like the U.S., cabinet appointments are made based on the specific talents or expertise of individuals who are not elected members of Congress. In other words, a generalist system (as is the case in Manitoba) appears to better advance the appointment of women, given that the premier selects from a limited number of *elected* members, a process that receives tremendous media attention and public scrutiny considering who is in or who was left out of the cabinet.

There is also general agreement that there are degrees of prestige in cabinet portfolios and appointments as being either of high, medium, or low status, each measured based on the visibility of the portfolio, the policy control afforded the minister, access to resources, the department's budget, and the department's priority to government.[44] This literature relates, too, that women are typically appointed to "feminine" portfolios, which are considered to hold low to medium prestige, such as departments of Health, Families, Environment, and Status of Women.

Following Brian Pallister's cabinet shuffle announced 23 October 2019, five women were appointed minister, which included the portfolios of the Department of Conservation and Climate, Municipal Relations (along with Francophone Affairs), Families, Status of Women (along with Sport, Culture and Heritage), and Indigenous and Northern Relations.[45] In Heather Stefanson's government, as of 10 November 2022, four women were appointed cabinet minister: Eileen Clarke to Municipal Relations, Rochelle Squires to Families, Sarah Guillemard to Mental Health and Community Wellness, and Audrey Gordon to Health.

With the election of a majority NDP government in October 2023 and Wabanakwut "Wab" Kinew as premier, seven women or non-binary individuals were appointed to cabinet (out of fourteen potential cabinet posts), which was a positive increase from the cabinet composition during PC governments.

Uzoma Asagwara was appointed deputy premier and minister of Health, Seniors and Long-Term Care. Nahanni Fontaine is the minister of Families, Accessibility, and Gender Equity. Bernadette Smith was appointed to Housing, Addictions and Homelessness, as well as Mental Health. Malaya Marcelino is the minister of Labour and Immigration, and is responsible for the Workers Compensation Board. Lisa Naylor is Transportation and Infrastructure minister. Renée Cable is minister of

Advanced Education and Training, and Tracy Schmidt was appointed minister of Education and Early Childhood Learning.[46]

While it is too early to dive into the effectiveness of these relatively new cabinet appointments, there is arguably an expectation that a NDP cabinet will expand its focus on women's and gender-equality initiatives. My assessment, too, is that while it may be early days, the cabinet appointments are quite interesting in that they range from the expected appointments to Families and Gender Equity but also include the deputy premier post and key sectors such as infrastructure, advanced education, and housing.

Official Opposition—NDP to PC

During PC majority governments there has been a vocal and highly visible NDP Official Opposition. Notably, three First Nations women have held various legislative offices and key opposition critic roles of import to women.[47] Nahanni Fontaine, for example, has acted as house leader, Justice critic, Families critic, and Status of Women critic, and has been for some time the NDP's spokesperson on missing and murdered Indigenous girls, women, and two-spirit people. Bernadette Smith has acted as party whip for the NDP, along with critic for the Department of Health, Seniors and Active Living. Ms. Smith has acted as critic for Mental Health and Community Wellness and was caucus chair. Amanda Lathlin has acted as deputy whip, and opposition critic for Indigenous and Northern Affairs, and for the Families portfolio. She currently acts, too, as critic for the Department of Sports, Culture and Heritage. Uzoma Asagwara was the critic for Health and the 2SLGBTTQ+ spokesperson. Lisa Naylor was the deputy caucus chair and critic for Municipal Relations, and Malaya Marcelino acted as critic for Labour and Immigration. These NDP shadow cabinet members represented a diversity of cultures, ethnicities, and genders, all ardent critics of PC government cuts affecting women, notably to health care, with individuals such as Nahanni Fontaine at the forefront, stressing the varied colonial practices impacting Indigenous women, girls, and their families.

As for the current PC party shadow cabinet and Official Opposition, the party is certainly rebuilding following the 2023 election defeat. Of the nineteen PC shadow cabinet members, four are women. Jodie Byram is critic for Labour and Immigration, and Workers

Compensation. Kathleen Cook acts as deputy caucus chair and is critic for Health. Carrie Hiebert was appointed critic for Housing, Addictions and Homelessness, and Lauren Stone, appointed deputy whip, is also critic for Families, Accessibility, and Gender Equity.[48]

Speaker of the House

Myrna Driedger was elected Speaker of the House in the Manitoba Legislative Assembly in 2016, resigning the position after the PC loss in 2023. Among other critical parliamentary roles, the Speaker is the chair of the Legislative Assembly Management Committee (Commission), which oversees the financial management of the chamber and reviews the budgets and administrative policies for assembly offices, along with the budgets of the independent officers of the chamber such as the auditor general and the chief electoral officer.[49] The composition of the commission includes four MLAs from the government caucus and three MLAs from the Official Opposition.

In her role as Speaker, in 2018 Myrna Driedger was key in initiating the review and update to anti-harassment policies in the Manitoba Legislative Assembly.[50] This was a substantive review finally taking place, inspired arguably because of the #MeToo movement and most certainly precipitated due to harassing behaviour of an MLA who was eventually banned from caucus.[51]

Well-documented across jurisdictions, Equal Voice has reported that anti-harassment policies and associated infrastructure are much needed for women in politics, given that women legislators are often the targets of unwanted attention, harassment, sexism, and gendered heckling during legislative debates.[52] Recent research has highlighted how this type of behaviour should be thought of as a form of violence against women in politics. This violence, as described in a report by Tracey Raney, Cheryl N. Collier, Grace Lore, and Andrea Spender, is a "result of historically unequal power relations between men and women in society,"[53] motivated by a politician's political viewpoint and support for certain policies, and because they are women.[54] Violent acts toward women can be physical, psychological, emotional, economic, or symbolic, and are experienced by many individuals involved in electoral politics, such as campaign workers, candidates, scrutineers, election officials, staffers, political party volunteers, and voters.[55]

In Manitoba, to ensure that "interactions between staff, managers, MLAs and the public are conducted appropriately and within the expectations of a modern, respectful workplace," the Legislative Assembly Management Commission approved an updated Respectful Workplace Policy during their 2019–20 meeting. *The Respectful Workplace Policy: Addressing and Preventing Sexual Harassment, Harassment and Bullying* outlines types of harassment and violence, procedures to report inappropriate behaviour, and information on how to submit a formal complaint.[56]

While the update to the policy was an encouraging and important action of the commission, as Equal Voice has highlighted, in order for an anti-harassment policy to work best, members of a legislative assembly must feel that open dialogue is possible, even welcomed; that persons reporting harassment are not viewed as "whiney"; and that reporting will not result in disruptions to career advancements.[57] And vigilance is necessary. There may be a policy in place, but, as Equal Voice has commented, "there is not always the culture, norms, and dialogues necessary to ensure that people who *need* these measures actually feel safe enough to *use* them."[58]

Conclusion: Is it Time for a Gender Audit of the Manitoba Legislature?

In their February 2020 analysis of how legislators can be effective representatives, Equal Voice made several recommendations focusing on how to work toward a gender-sensitive legislature, framed around three "over-arching pillars": Safe and Respectful Workplaces (anti-harassment policies along with an effective, transparent reporting infrastructure); Family Friendly Measures (sitting times and other measures that facilitate a work-life balance); and Modernization (implementation of proxy voting if a member is unable to physically attend the legislature).[59]

A gender-sensitive parliament is defined by the Inter-Parliamentary Union as an institution that "promotes and realizes the equality of men and women in numbers, devises a gender equality policy framework implemented within its own legislative context, mainstreams gender equality and facilitates an 'internal culture that respects women's rights, promotes gender equality and responds to the needs and realities of

MPs—men and women—to balance work and family responsibilities' ensuring too that parliamentary staff are provided the capacity and resources to promote gender equality."[60] With the increasing number of women elected to the Manitoba Legislative Assembly, more women are assuming important legislative leadership roles and are, in their own ways, regendering the assembly. Although Krook and O'Brien remind us that "political elites are drawn from dominant groups,"[61] a gender-sensitive legislative audit would ask key questions of legislative actors to determine how regulations, appointments, and rules of the chamber too often function against the participation of women and other under-represented groups.

A gender audit could highlight, for example, how updated and new procedures could be put in place within the legislative chamber, like those noted above (i.e., proxy voting and substantive anti-harassment procedures). Importantly, measures could target political party practices such as encouraging uptake of voluntary nomination quotas. Lessons could be drawn from a recent example, when, prior to the election in Ontario, the provincial Liberal party made a rule change to bolster gender parity by directing twenty-two ridings to *only* nominate women candidates.[62]

To conclude, organizational transformation is difficult to achieve, especially within institutions rooted in partisan interests and personal ambitions. If transformations do not come about, however, the status quo will serve only to further entrench established and too-often accepted patterns of social behaviour and Westminster politics and practices. While social and political norms have certainly changed in Manitoba over the past decades, it is clear that much more could be done to encourage a wide diversity of women to stand for political office and thus, overall, the hope of fostering better democratic governance.

Notes

1   Roosmarijn de Geus, Erin Tolley, Elizabeth Goodyear-Grant, and Peter John Loewen, "Introduction," in *Women, Power and Political Representation: Canadian and Comparative Perspectives*, ed. Roosmarijn de Geus, Erin Tolley, Elizabeth Goodyear-Grant, and Peter Loewen (Toronto: University of Toronto Press, 2021), 3.

2   House of Commons, *Elect Her: A Roadmap for Improving the Representation of Women in Canadian Politics*, Report of the Standing Committee on the Status of

Women, 1st Session, 42nd Parliament, April 2019, https://www.ourcommons.ca/Content/Committee/421/FEWO/Reports/RP10366034/feworp14/feworp14-e.pdf, 2.

3   Melanee Thomas and Marc Bodet, "Sacrificial Lambs, Women Candidates, and District Competitiveness in Canada," *Electoral Studies* 32, no. 1 (2013): 153–46.
4   Ibid.
5   Sylvia Bashevkin, "New Backlash? New Barriers? Assessing Women's Contemporary Public Engagement," in *Women, Power and Political Representation: Canadian and Comparative Perspectives*, ed. Roosmarijn de Geus, Erin Tolley, Elizabeth Goodyear-Grant, and Peter John Loewen (Toronto: University of Toronto Press, 2021), 167.
6   Roosmarijn de Geus and Peter John Loewen, "Women's Representation in Canadian Federal Cabinets, 1980–2019," in *Women, Power and Political Representation: Canadian and Comparative Perspectives*, ed. Roosmarijn de Geus, Erin Tolley, Elizabeth Goodyear-Grant, and Peter John Loewen (Toronto: University of Toronto Press, 2021), 13–25; Sarah Childs and Mona Lena Krook, "Analysing Women's Substantive Representation: From Critical Mass to Critical Actors," *Government and Opposition* 44, no. 2 (2009): 125–45.
7   Childs and Krook, "Analysing Women's Substantive Representation," 126.
8   Ibid., 138.
9   Karen Celis, Sarah Childs, and Jennifer Curtin, "Specialised Parliamentary Bodies and the Quality of Women's Substantive Representation: A Comparative Analysis of Belgium, United Kingdom and New Zealand," *Parliamentary Affairs* 69, no. 4 (2016): 813.
10 Marian Sawer, "Parliamentary Representation of Women: From Discourses of Justice to Strategies of Accountability," *International Political Science Review* 21, no. 3 (2000): 369.
11 Equal Voice, *Gender-Sensitive Parliaments Report* (Ottawa: Equal Voice, 2020), https://assets.nationbuilder.com/equalvoice/pages/2782/attachments/original/1708545592/Gender_Sensitive_Parliaments_Report.pdf?1708545592, 13.
12 Inter-Parliamentary Union, *One Decade On: How Gender Sensitive Are Our Parliaments Now?* Conference proceedings, 15 March 2022, YouTube video, accessed 5 January 2025, https://youtube.com/watch?v=uwzMtMNqoCQ.
13 Melanee Thomas, "Barriers to Women's Political Participation in Canada," *University of New Brunswick Law Journal* 64 (2013): 218–33.
14 Joan Grace, "Has the Manitoba 'Advantage' Worked for Women?" in *Manitoba Politics and Government: Issues, Institutions, Traditions*, ed. Paul G. Thomas and Curtis Brown (Winnipeg: University of Manitoba Press, 2010), 382–403.
15 Joan Grace, "Regendering the Federal Bargain," in *Handbook on Gender, Diversity and Federalism*, ed. Jill Vickers, Joan Grace, and Cheryl N. Collier (Cheltenham, UK: Edward Elgar Publishing Limited, 2020), 180–93.
16 *CBC News Manitoba*, "Record Number of Female MLAs Elected," 24 May 2007, https://www.cbc.ca/news/canada/manitoba/record-number-of-female-mlas-elected-1.687691.
17 Kathy Brock, "Women and the Manitoba Legislature," in *In the Presence of Women: Representation in Canadian Governments*, ed. Jane Arscott and Linda Trimble (Toronto: Harcourt Brace, 1996), 185.
18 Ibid.

19 House of Commons, *Elect Her*, 18.
20 Brock, "Women and the Manitoba Legislature"; Grace, "Has the Manitoba 'Advantage' Worked?"
21 Equal Voice, *Gender-Sensitive Parliaments Report*, 4.
22 House of Commons, *Elect Her*, 18.
23 Manitoba Legislative Assembly, *MLA Alphabetical Listings*, 22 May 2024, https://www.gov.mb.ca/legislative/members/mla_list_alphabetical.html.
24 Childs and Krook, "Analysing Women's Substantive Representation."
25 Equal Voice, *Election Trackers*, 6 October 2023, https://www.equalvoice.ca/2023_manitoba_election.
26 Joan Grace and Marian Sawer, "Representing Gender Equality: Specialised Parliamentary Bodies," *Parliamentary Affairs* 69, no. 4 (2016): 745–47.
27 Grace and Sawer, "Representing Gender Equality."
28 Celis, Childs, and Curtin, "Specialised Parliamentary Bodies," 813.
29 Sonia Palmieri, *Gender-Sensitive Parliaments: A Global Review of Good Practice* (Geneva: Inter-Parliamentary Union, 2011).
30 Mona Lena Krook and Diana Z. O'Brien, "All the President's Men?" *The Journal of Politics* 74, no. 5 (2012): 840–55.
31 Thomas, "Barriers to Women's Political Participation"; Thomas and Bodet, "Sacrificial Lambs"; Brenda O'Neill and David K. Stewart, "Gender and Political Party Leadership in Canada," *Party Politics* 15, no. 6 (2009): 737–57.
32 Brock, "Women and the Manitoba Legislature," 188.
33 O'Neill and Stewart, "Gender and Political Party Leadership."
34 Bashevkin, "New Backlash?"
35 *CBC News Manitoba*, "Manitoba Liberal Wants Leader Rana Bokhari to Resign at Post-election Meeting," 21 May 2016, https://www.cbc.ca/news/canada/manitoba/rana-bokhari-liberal-manitoba-1.3546489.
36 Linda Trimble and Jane Arscott, *Still Counting: Women in Politics across Canada* (Peterborough: Broadview Press, 2003).
37 Sylvia Bashevkin, ed., *Doing Politics Differently? Women Premiers in Canada's Provinces and Territories* (Vancouver: UBC Press, 2019).
38 Kelly Saunders, "The Progressive Conservatives," in *Understanding the Manitoba Election 2019*, ed. Royce Koop, Barry Ferguson, Karine Levasseur, and Andrea Rounce (Winnipeg: University of Manitoba Press, 2019), 7.
39 Ian Froese, "Premier Apologizes for Boasting of Son's Hockey Success When Asked about Patient's Death," *CBC News*, 17 March 2022, https://www.cbc.ca/news/canada/manitoba-premier-hockey-accomplishment-patient-transfter-death-1.6389008.
40 Manitoba, *Speech from the Throne*, 23 November 2021, https://www.gov.mb.ca/asset_library/en/thronespeech/throne_speech_nov_2021.pdf.
41 Bartley Kives, "More than Other Premiers, Manitoba's Heather Stefanson Needs a Health-Care Deal with Ottawa," *CBC News*, 7 February 2023, https://www.cbc.ca/news/canada/manitoba/premiers-healthcare-meeting-trudeau-1.6738872.
42 *CBC News Manitoba*, "Manitoba's $10-a-Day Child-Care Plan Starts in April—3 Years Ahead of Schedule," 3 March 2023, https://cbc.ca/news/canada/manitoba/prime-minister-justin-trudeau-winnipeg-child-care-1.6766799.

43 de Geus and Loewen, "Women's Representation," 14.
44 Krook and O'Brien, "All the President's Men?"
45 Government of Manitoba, "Premier Brian Pallister's New Administration Sworn In," News Release, 23 October 2016, https://news.gov.mb.ca/news/index.html?item=45987&posted=2019-10-23.
46 NDP Caucus, *Our Team*, 3 June 2025, https://www.yourmanitoba.ca/team.
47 NDP Caucus, *Our Team*, 22 April 2023, https://www.yourmanitoba.ca/team.
48 PC Caucus, *PCs Announce Official Opposition Cabinet*, 24 October 2023, https://pcmbcaucus.com/2023/10/pcs-announce-official-opposition-shadow-cabinet/.
49 Legislative Assembly Management Commission, *Annual Report, April 1, 2021 to March 31, 2022*, 2021/2022, https://www.gov.mb.ca/legislature/about/lamc.html.
50 *CBC News Manitoba*, "Manitoba Legislature Working on 'Strengthened Policy' on Harassment in Wake of #MeToo Movement," 31 January 2018, https://www.cbc.ca/news/canada/manitoba/harassment-policy-manitoba-legislature-1.4511388.
51 Ibid.
52 Equal Voice, *Gender-Sensitive Parliaments Report*.
53 Tracey Raney, Cheryl N. Collier, Grace Lore, and Andrea Spender, *Democracy During #MeToo: Taking Stock of Violence Against Women in Canadian Politics* (Ottawa: Equal Voice, 2019), 7.
54 Gabrielle Bardall, Elin Bjarnegård, and Jennifer M. Piscopo, "How is Political Violence Gendered? Disentangling Motives, Forms, and Impacts," *Political Studies* 68, no. 4 (2019): 916–35.
55 Raney, Collier, Lore, and Spender, *Democracy During #MeToo*.
56 Legislative Assembly Management Commission, *Annual Report, April 1, 2019, to March 31, 2020, Decisions/Recommendations*, 2019/2020, https://www.gov.mb.ca/legislature/about/lamc/annualreport2019_2020.pdf, 4.
57 Equal Voice, *Gender-Sensitive Parliaments Report*, 17–18.
58 Ibid., 17.
59 Ibid., 12–17.
60 Inter-Parliamentary Union, *Plan of Action for Gender-Sensitive Parliaments* (Geneva: Inter-Parliamentary Union, 2017), 17.
61 Krook and O'Brien, "All the President's Men?" 841.
62 Albert Delitala, "Boosting Gender Parity: Ontario Liberals Create Women-Only Candidate Ridings," *Global News*, 26 November 2021, https://globalnews.ca/news/8405943/ont-liberal-women-only-candidate-ridings/.

CHAPTER 9

Where in History? Indigenous Peoples and Rights in Twenty-First-Century Manitoba

JEREMY PATZER

Where in History Is Manitoba?

In 2016, after seventeen years of the New Democratic Party (NDP) governing the province, Manitoba's electoral pendulum swung once again in the other direction and the Progressive Conservative Party (PC)—under the leadership of Brian Pallister—was swept to power with forty of the fifty-seven seats available in the legislature. The victory was touted as the largest electoral majority in the province's history.[1] Pallister was a polarizing figure for much of the five years that he remained at the helm of his party and the province, especially within the context of the relationship between the provincial government and Indigenous peoples. In July 2021, Pallister offered a broadly whitewashed portrait of history that glossed over the dispossession and marginalization of Indigenous peoples, arguing, "The people who came here to this country, before it was a country and since, didn't come here to destroy anything. They came here to build. They came to build better."[2] This, of course, sparked further controversy and raised questions of just how out of date the former premier's vision of Manitoba and Canada was.[3]

Invoking the controversial remarks of a leader as polarizing as Brian Pallister may seem like the analytical equivalent of picking low-hanging fruit—especially given Pallister's precipitous loss of popularity, abrupt mid-term retirement from politics, and replacement by Premier

Heather Stefanson in late 2021. Nevertheless, as noted above, this twenty-first-century manifestation of the Progressive Conservative Party of Manitoba was voted in with the largest majority in the province's history, and the questions raised by such contemporary controversies do help to frame broader and more weighty questions about modern Manitoba and its relationship to Indigenous peoples; primary amongst these: *Where in history is the relationship between Manitoba and Indigenous peoples situated?* In other words, has the province of Manitoba kept up with the times insofar as its conduct toward Indigenous peoples is concerned? Certainly, the Manitoba of today is not the Manitoba of 1870,[4] 1952,[5] or 1967,[6] but the question is nevertheless mindful of a broader, more fundamental transformation sought by Indigenous peoples for generations and either dismissed, dodged, or delayed by many Canadian leaders. Indeed, even with the occurrence of the October 2023 election during the writing and publication process for this volume—in which the pendulum swung once again and Manitoba voted in an NDP government led by Wabanakwut "Wab" Kinew, widely celebrated as Canada's first First Nations premier—questions concerning the place occupied by Indigenous nations within the legal, political, and economic landscapes of the province persist, illustrating the work that lies ahead for any new government. And the fact of the matter is that Manitoba—the province with the largest proportional population of Indigenous peoples, and the sole province ushered into Confederation by an Indigenous leader—has had difficulties keeping attuned to the shift towards reconciliation and Indigenous rights that began in the late twentieth century, to say nothing of leading the way toward the relationship sought by Indigenous nations in the twenty-first century.

A Broad Periodization of the Crown-Indigenous Relationship since 1867

If one were to paint, with broad strokes, an historical timeline of the legal politics of colonialism since the creation of Canada and Manitoba—since settler colonialism is a phenomenon that is *ongoing* and not simply "in the past"[7]—one could draw on Canada's Indigenous/Aboriginal rights[8] turn of the late twentieth century as a primary inflection point. In other words, the Indigenous rights turn that began roughly fifty years ago, and has been developing ever since, can be used to broadly conceive of a "before" and "after" in the law and politics of the Crown-Indigenous relationship.

During the era *before* the Indigenous rights turn, in the nineteenth and early twentieth centuries, the predominant Euro-Canadian vision of the Crown's relationship with Indigenous peoples was one of outright dispossession and assimilation: regardless of whether any inherent or treaty rights were recognized for any particular Indigenous people within any given region, the Crown's general desire for Indigenous peoples was that they not be an impediment to settler acquisition of, access to, and profit from territory. To the extent that Indigeneity was associated with a prior occupation and possession of the land, and also associated with claims to ongoing recognition and resources from the Crown, the goal of many federal and provincial governments was that this Indigeneity eventually disappear. Perhaps not surprisingly, this was also the era when governments instituted highly interventionist, social-engineering forms of assimilation such as forced residential schooling.[9]

Canada's Indigenous rights turn, which will be examined in more detail, consisted largely of a more sympathetic approach to treaty and inherent rights instigated by the higher courts, as well as the affirmation and protection of treaty and inherent rights in the Constitution Act, 1982.[10] In the latter half of the twentieth century, higher courts began to contend with the fact that Indigenous peoples were here to stay, and there were lingering, unresolved questions over their dispossession and their continuing rights within Canada's legal-political landscape. While the courts certainly have not gone so far as to undo the colonial act of dispossession, they have brought to the Canadian political and legal landscape an increasingly rich body of case law that outlines the courts' approach to recognizing and protecting the rights of Indigenous peoples.

To be clear, there are many shortcomings and weaknesses to criticize in the modern courts' approach to Indigenous rights, and I count myself among those voices[11]—although a full critique of Canadian Aboriginal law is beyond the scope of this chapter. Nevertheless, the Indigenous rights turn that began in the late twentieth century has without a doubt made it such that federal, provincial, and territorial governments must acknowledge the multiple and varied rights of the Indigenous peoples whose lands they now occupy. These rights in the contemporary era—many of them land-based—not only have the imprimatur of the highest court in Canada but also the added robustness of constitutional protection.

Yet, if the before and after of the Indigenous rights turn mark two broad stages of the Indigenous-Crown relationship, we can also argue for a third stage: namely, the hope and promise for an Indigenous-Crown relationship that is *yet-to-come*. In effect, the modern Supreme Court of Canada (SCC) approach to Indigenous rights need not, and should not, represent the limits of decolonial justice for Indigenous peoples in Canada. Indigenous nations have long advocated for recognition of their status as self-determining original peoples with a commensurate partnership in Canadian federalism. In addition, self-determination necessitates economic forms of self-sustainability that reflect both the special status of Indigenous peoples as the original possessors of the land and the mutual benefit sought in the original agreements between many Indigenous peoples and the Crown. This is the territory *beyond* the SCC model of rights recognition that Canada is still struggling to find. As suggested above, however, my contention is that contemporary Manitoba has demonstrated difficulties in finding its way out of the dispossessory politics characteristic of the nineteenth and early twentieth centuries and into the era of Indigenous rights, let alone leading the way toward the just relationship yet-to-come envisioned by Indigenous nations themselves.

Indigenous Peoples, Governments, and Organizations in Manitoba

The province of Manitoba exists on the territories of the Dene, the Cree, the Anisininew (Oji-Cree), the Anishinaabe (Ojibway, Saulteaux), the Dakota, and the Métis Nation. While a detailed history of the colonization of Manitoba is beyond the scope of this chapter, it is noteworthy that assimilationist policies and practices of the nineteenth and early twentieth centuries shaped the political and legal landscapes on which these Indigenous peoples would live and struggle for generations to come.

Shortly after Confederation in 1867, Canada began negotiating and signing a series of Numbered Treaties with Indigenous peoples from northern Ontario westward, with the goal of paving the way for the country's westward expansion. The Numbered Treaties whose territories cover portions of what is now Manitoba include Treaty 1, 2, 3, 4, 5, and 9. (Two First Nations from northwestern Manitoba are actually signatories to Treaty 10, despite the fact that Treaty 10 territory is located within Saskatchewan and a small portion of eastern Alberta.) During the same period, however, Canada began building for itself a plenary bureaucratic and legislative power over First Nations with provisions such as the Gradual Enfranchisement Act[12] of 1869 and the first iteration of the Indian Act[13] in 1876—and it imposed this regime over First Nations across Canada regardless of whether they had signed a treaty with the Crown or not. (In Manitoba, five Dakota First Nations in the southwest of the province are not signatory to any historical treaty.)

While the Indian Act has undergone many amendments and an evolution of sorts over a century and a half, such legislation and government policy have time and again broken both the spirit and the letter of treaties with Indigenous peoples. The historical grievances sourced in this period of history are too numerous to outline in detail. To list a few, however, the powers asserted by the Crown included the power to both recognize and take away "Indian status," to accord First Nations only weak self-governing powers over minor municipal-style matters, and to dismantle traditional Indigenous governance structures in order to forcibly impose the chief and band council systems envisioned by the Indian Act. Fundamentally, the spirit of what was negotiated in treaties with Indigenous peoples was betrayed because, as noted by the Royal Commission on Aboriginal Peoples (RCAP), "First Nations were assured orally that their way of life would not change unless they wished it to. They understood that their governing structures and authorities would continue undisturbed by the treaty relationship."[14] In effect, Indigenous leaders and scholars have been asserting for decades that the true intent of what Indigenous peoples negotiated orally in the treaties has not been reflected in the Crown-Indigenous relationship that developed over the nineteenth and twentieth centuries.[15]

The *scale* of Indigenous peoples' self-governance and association has been harmed as well—not only by the artificially imposed provincial, territorial, and international borders that bisect their territories but also by the Indian Act band system that ignored the larger cultural-territorial associations of Indigenous peoples and reduced the scale of their governance to bands delimited to small reserves. According to the RCAP, even in the original Gradual Enfranchisement Act, "[t]here was simply no provision for traditional groupings going beyond the individual band level. In fact, the goal of the measures was specifically to undermine nation-level governance systems and the broader nation-level associations of Indians more generally."[16] The result of this is that contemporary Indigenous peoples have been left to explore, re-form, and develop larger models of association and political mobilization in the wake of Indian Act dispossession.

Within the Manitoban context, this effect can be seen in the modern development of multiple levels of organization for First Nations representation. At base, the bulk of First Nations governance is meant to take place at the band level—and their powers of governance are shaped by Indian Act limitations, or the extent to which they have been able to negotiate their way out of those limitations. (Presently, only two First Nations in the province have *comprehensive* self-government agreements: Sioux Valley Dakota Nation, completed in 2013, and O-Pipon-Na-Piwin Cree Nation, completed in 2005.) Beyond this, however, many bands in Manitoba have joined one of seven First Nations *tribal councils*, which have formed in various regions:

- Dakota Ojibway Tribal Council
- Interlake Reserves Tribal Council
- Island Lake Tribal Council
- Keewatin Tribal Council
- Southeast Resource Development Council
- Swampy Cree Tribal Council
- West Region Tribal Council

In addition, eight Manitoba First Nations have no tribal council affiliation.

While Manitoba First Nations' rights frameworks are rooted primarily in the treaties, and the treaty relationship between First Nations and the Crown is seen as foundational, tribal councils have not typically been formed according to treaty territories. (In Alberta, by contrast, one does find shared treaty history as a principle of association in some tribal councils, such as the Confederacy of Treaty Six First Nations, the Treaty 7 First Nations Chiefs' Association, and Treaty 8 First Nations of Alberta.) In fact, some First Nations advocates have informally observed that the map of tribal councils in Manitoba better reflects the historic distribution of Indian agencies across Manitoba, with their corresponding Indian agents, than it does the borders of shared treaty territories themselves.

On an even broader scale, representing Manitoba along a north-south divide are the two First Nation political advocacy organizations of Manitoba Keewatinowi Okimakanak (MKO) and the Southern Chiefs Organization (SCO). The MKO represents a number of Dene and Cree First Nations across northern Manitoba, while the SCO represents a group of Anishinaabe and Dakota First Nations found in the southern half of the province. At the pan-provincial level, the Assembly of Manitoba Chiefs (AMC) represents sixty-two out of sixty-three First Nations in Manitoba, accounting for over 151,000 First Nation Manitobans and approximately 12 percent of the provincial population.[17] (Sioux Valley Dakota Nation, one of two Manitoba First Nations with a comprehensive self-government agreement that brings it out from under the Indian Act, is not represented by AMC.)

This plurality of First Nation representation, from the individual band level to the pan-provincial, brings with it the potential for complexity, overlap, or tension in organizational mandates and constituencies. Portfolios related to core areas of concern—such as health, Jordan's Principle, child and family services, or education—can be found within the mandate and activities of many organizations. Navigating this complexity requires recognition of the differing activities that organizations may engage in, including governance, service delivery, or simply advocacy. For example, while the band itself is the core unit of governance, service delivery for certain institutions may be delegated to the level of tribal council—or higher. A notable example is child and family services. Following the report of the Aboriginal Justice Inquiry (AJI) and the work of the Aboriginal Justice Inquiry-Child Welfare Initiative in the 1990s, Manitoba's Child and Family Services Authority Act of 2003 provided for the creation of new authorities for the delivery of child and family services in the province. These were, namely, a Northern Authority (managed by MKO), a Southern Authority (managed by SCO), a Métis Authority (managed by Manitoba Métis Federation, MMF), and a General Authority managing child and family services for non-Indigenous Manitobans.

The Métis, for their part, occupy a distinct place within the history and the Indigenous politics of Manitoba. Although the historical record mentions the desire of some First Nations leaders to have their "half-breed" kin included in the treaty process or be offered some other sort of consideration for their Indigenous title,[18] and some Métis did take treaty with their First Nations kin,[19] representatives of the Crown were generally reluctant to admit Métis into the treaty processes and were adamant that there would be another process put in place for them. The resistance of the Métis to Canadian expansionism across the West enabled the negotiation of what would ultimately become the Manitoba Act of 1870. This ushered the Red River Colony into Confederation as the fifth province and secured for the Métis key promises from the Crown—including land grants and other rights—but the long-term result for the Métis was swindled land, abrogated rights, and more than a century of non-recognition by the province and the federal government.

The effect of this history on the contemporary legal-political landscape is that the Métis of Manitoba developed as a separate and distinct political force, represented by the Manitoba Métis Federation, which was formed in 1967—the same year as the Manitoba Indian Brotherhood, the precursor to the Assembly of Manitoba Chiefs. The MMF is subdivided throughout the province into seven regions, each of which is further divided into smaller locals. As of the 2021 census, 96,730 people in Manitoba identified as Métis.[20] Given that enrolment in Métis organizations is not controlled externally by federal statute or registry in the way that Indian status is, obtaining citizenship in the MMF is an affirmative and voluntary endeavour and thus not all Métis in the province have officially obtained citizenship in the MMF. Due to their historic coexistence, the traditional territory of the Manitoba Métis overlays First Nations' treaty territories across much of Manitoba and any inherent Aboriginal rights recognized for the Métis will coexist with the treaty rights and inherent Aboriginal rights of Manitoba First Nations.

The Contemporary Indigenous Rights Landscape

For treaty First Nations in Manitoba, the primary source of rights recognized by the courts and the province will typically be their respective historical treaty signed with the Crown. Included among recognized treaty rights are traditional activities such as hunting, fishing, and trapping—among a variety of other possible rights, depending upon the particular treaty, such as the provision of health care. It was not always the case that governments would respect, or courts would enforce, treaty promises for Indigenous signatories, however. It was only after an extended history of disregarding the treaty promises made to Indigenous peoples that courts, in the latter half of the twentieth century, would begin a tidal change in treaty jurisprudence.[21] This reversal would see them enforce treaty promises to Indigenous peoples and develop a number of legal principles designed to preserve the honour of the Crown in treaty rights disputes and to offer interpretations of treaties that would be more generous and honourable toward the Indigenous signatories.

Indigenous rights can exist independently of treaty agreements, however, and be sourced simply in an Indigenous people's prior occupation of land. Such rights are described as *inherent* because their existence and recognition are not dependent on treaties, legislation, or proclamations from the Crown. When Indigenous nations and colonial governments have disagreements concerning inherent rights, the courts often become the final arbiter to decide on what is or is not recognized as a right. The "test" developed by the SCC for determining whether an activity qualifies as an inherent Aboriginal right,[22] however, garnered a wave of criticism for its restrictive "cultural rights" formula that trades in romanticized stereotypes of traditional Indigenous cultures and employs historical time frames and geographical specificities that narrow the scope of potential rights claims.[23]

The Aboriginal rights case law has played a role in the struggles of Indigenous peoples in Manitoba. While treaty First Nations can, and do, take recourse to the inherent Aboriginal rights jurisprudence for disputes relating to activities that go beyond the scope of what is outlined in their respective treaties, the Métis of Manitoba have been particularly reliant on this avenue of rights assertion.[24] This is due primarily to the fact that the courts have not recognized any historical treaty rights for citizens of the Manitoba Métis Federation.[25] (As I will cover later in the chapter, however, at the time of writing the MMF is on the cusp of signing and having recognized its first *modern* treaty with the federal government.) While First Nations' treaty rights are recognized as applying across the province, then, a mix of two decades of inherent Aboriginal rights court decisions and negotiations have made it such that Manitoba recognizes Métis harvesting rights only in certain regions of the province, essentially excluding a swath of the northeast and far north of the province from Métis harvesters.

While the late twentieth-century switch to recognizing inherent rights for Indigenous peoples marked a tidal shift in Canadian Aboriginal law, the subsequent passage of the Constitution Act, 1982, and the judiciary's interpretation of its protections for inherent and treaty rights have been just as influential. Section 35(1) of the Act states that "the existing aboriginal and treaty rights of the aboriginal peoples of Canada are hereby recognized and affirmed," and section 35(2) specifies that, "In this Act, 'aboriginal peoples of Canada' includes the Indian, Inuit and Métis peoples of Canada."[26] With section 35, then, the varied rights of Indigenous peoples have the added robustness of constitutional protection and can no longer be unilaterally extinguished by the Crown.[27]

Lastly, many of the changes brought about during the Indigenous rights turn that began in the latter half of the twentieth century have been anchored in, and animated by, the doctrinal concept of the *honour of the Crown*. Aboriginal law in Canada thus goes beyond recognizing Indigenous peoples' rights to engage in certain activities and also outlines a number of *Crown obligations* that govern federal and provincial relationships with Indigenous peoples. These include, most significantly, the Crown's duty to consult Indigenous peoples when contemplating activities that might have an adverse effect on rights or title,[28] as well as the obligation of justifying federal and provincial actions and approach when governments do elect to infringe, for compelling public purposes, the constitutionally protected rights and title of Indigenous peoples.[29] This brief sketch of the legal-constitutional framework underlying Indigenous rights therefore offers a sense as to why governments, Crown corporations, extractive industries, and other outside interests must reconcile in some way with Indigenous interests when contemplating activities that could affect constitutionally protected Indigenous rights.

Slow to Change, or Some Things Never Change?

If the modern Indigenous rights turn amounted to a sea change in Canadian law and politics, it is curious at times the extent to which provinces such as Manitoba seem poorly attuned to the new reality. In essence, Indigenous rights related to the land are akin to a *sui generis* form of property rights—interests in land with juridical and constitutional dimensions that are recognized by the courts—and yet, contemporary politics in Manitoba can still demonstrate a persistent hostility to Indigenous peoples' assertions of their rights.

As one example, in 2017 then-premier Brian Pallister accused night hunting among some First Nations treaty hunters as potentially inciting "a race war," seemingly oblivious to the irony that his comments were doing precisely that: inciting hostility to Indigenous rights among many non-Indigenous Manitobans.[30] Months later, both the AMC and MMF asserted that tensions over Indigenous hunting rights continued to rise and were driven, in part, "by racially charged comments from Premier Brian Pallister."[31] The assertions by the MMF and AMC came as two Métis hunters were acquitted of charges of illegal night hunting—an acquittal that was due in large part to allegations that conservation officers provided a forged confession as evidence against the two men.[32]

Similarly, in 2018 Manitoba's former Progressive Conservative government cancelled two deals between Manitoba Hydro and the Manitoba Métis Federation that would offer long-term compensation to the MMF for the effects of hydroelectric projects on their Aboriginal rights,[33] criticizing such agreements as "persuasion money" and "hush money" for a "special interest group."[34] This is despite the fact that the board of directors of the Crown corporation Manitoba Hydro negotiated these agreements with the MMF in recognition of the fact that it was taking up land utilized by Métis rights holders who possessed constitutionally protected, and legally actionable, interests in that land. Subsequent to the cancellation of the first agreement, nine out of ten members of the board of Manitoba Hydro—who had been appointed by the provincial cabinet itself—resigned in protest. In frustration, former board chair Sandy Riley wrote, "For over a year we have attempted to meet with the premier to resolve a number of critical issues related to the finances and governance of Manitoba Hydro, including matters related to Hydro's efforts to further develop its relationship with Indigenous peoples."[35]

Relations in the area of health have not fared much better. An added complication, however, is the issue of jurisdiction: while the provinces administer their own health care systems, section 91(24) of the Constitution Act, 1867, states that the federal government is responsible for "Indians, and Lands reserved for the Indians."[36] The federal government has long translated this jurisdictional responsibility, combined with the mention of health in some historical treaties, into responsibility for health services and benefits for recognized Inuit and persons with Indian status. In practical terms, however, when status First Nations seek services in many off-reserve locations in Manitoba, they are dealing with the provincial health care system. Jurisdictional wrangling between the province and the federal government, in order to reduce their costs for First Nations' health services, has had tragic consequences. Jordan's Principle, in memory of a Cree boy from Manitoba who died in hospital while the province and the federal government argued over who should pay for his home care services, has thus been recognized across Canada, stipulating that the level of government of first contact simply pays for the health service in question, leaving questions of jurisdiction and payment to be resolved afterwards.[37]

Perhaps not surprisingly, the politics of health and Indigeneity found its most recent controversies during the global COVID-19 pandemic. In the uncertain early days of vaccine rollout during the pandemic, the Pallister government pushed the federal government for prioritized access to vaccines for Indigenous people—a policy option that would surely benefit provinces with high Indigenous populations, such as Manitoba. In contrast to a number of other provinces, and despite evidence concerning the social determinants of health making it well known that poorer and underhoused Indigenous people would be at greater risk,[38] Manitoba refused this prioritized access to vaccinations for the Métis and Inuit of the province.[39] In addition, after learning that the prioritized access for First Nations would come out of the general supply of doses coming to the province, and not be sourced as a separate, additional supply for the province, Pallister publicly griped that the vaccine rollout "puts Manitobans at the back of the line," and thus implied, according to the province's largest daily newspaper, that "Indigenous people aren't actually Manitobans."[40]

Moving Forward, with 150-Year-Old Problems?

The issues that we have begun to examine here signal fundamental problems that persist in the Crown-Indigenous relationship. It is true that, with the complexities of Canadian federalism and the division of powers between levels of government, both provincial governments and the federal government are implicated in many of the issues raised by Indigenous peoples. Indeed, the complicated jurisdictionality surrounding Indigenous issues—whereby the Crown's relationship with Indigenous peoples is considered a federal responsibility, but so many of the lands, laws, and services they encounter are under provincial jurisdiction—makes it such that Indigenous peoples have to contend regularly with refusal, unresponsiveness, infringement, and deflection from multiple levels of government. Nevertheless, with the largest urban Indigenous population and the largest proportional Indigenous population amongst all the provinces, Manitoba should be leading the way in responsiveness to Indigenous nations. It is when Indigenous peoples envision and strive to work toward the relationship that should be, however, that it becomes all too apparent to what extent Manitoba is still plagued with century-old problems.

Some of these problems are rooted, quite simply, in the age-old colonial practice of dispossession. A manifestation of this that is quite particular to Manitoba is the legacy of hydroelectric development in Manitoba. It is only within the last couple of decades that Manitoba has begun to reckon with the myriad negative effects that hydroelectric development has had for northern Indigenous communities. Apart from the fact that Indigenous peoples have historically shared little in the profits produced from the damming and flooding of their traditional territories, contemporary advocacy and research have also enumerated a litany of other negative effects: detrimental impacts on traditional activities; the racism, sexism, and harm to Indigenous women from the movement of workers from the South to the North and the establishment of camp culture; and increases in addictions and other related social problems.[41]

If anything speaks to the notion of 150-year-old colonial problems, however, a primary candidate would have to be the treaty promises made by the Crown that remain, to this day, unfulfilled. In his 1995 portrait of the Canada's treaties with Indigenous peoples, D.N. Sprague dedicates a section to the federal-provincial stalemates created by the fact that Canada, after having made promises of land to various treaty First Nations, eventually devolved public lands in Manitoba and other western provinces to provincial jurisdiction without having selected and set aside the necessary amount of land for a number of First Nations.[42] Once public lands were under provincial control, provincial approval was effectively required to fulfill any outstanding treaty promises, and the end result was the persistence of broken promises for generations.

Sprague notes that, in Manitoba, a primary obstacle was the province's insistence on the "retention of riparian, river-bank rights to facilitate hydroelectric development."[43]

The modern process for resolving these land debts has come to be known as the Treaty Land Entitlement (TLE) process and, in 1997, Manitoba signed a Treaty Land Entitlement Framework Agreement with a number of First Nations. While Manitoba and Saskatchewan have had some of the largest numbers of entitlement claims, a 2005 report commissioned by the Southern Chiefs Organization identified Manitoba as a laggard in resolving these outstanding claims and as being, on balance, less efficient and less effective than Saskatchewan in achieving resolution of the average claim.[44] In 2022, the First Nations Treaty Land Entitlement Committee filed a statement of claim in Federal Court, pursuing the federal government for losses stemming from its failure to fulfill treaty land entitlements in a timely fashion.[45]

The 2022 claim was not the first time that a federal or provincial government found itself facing the courts for a TLE issue. The federal government faced a prolonged case after it decommissioned the Kapyong Barracks land in Winnipeg but dismissed the requests of four First Nations to pursue the development of an urban reserve as fulfillment of their treaty land entitlements. In 2015 the Federal Court of Appeal agreed with the First Nations claimants that Canada's failure to consult with them on the potential for the former military lands to fulfill TLE obligations constituted a breach of the federal government's duty to consult.[46] Relatedly, in early 2023, Grand Chief of the Assembly of Manitoba Chiefs Cathy Merrick threatened to sue the provincial government over an auction of agricultural Crown land leases for more than 100 parcels of land across the province, arguing that "auctioning off large swaths of unoccupied Crown lands obstructs the exercise of First Nations' inherent and treaty rights, including the right to hunt and trap," and that "it is also in violation of the land promises made in the framework agreement for treaty land entitlement, which continues to remain unfulfilled to this day."[47]

In addition to dispossession and broken treaty promises, Manitoba's Indigenous peoples are still dealing with the harm suffered to their governance systems. Although it is primarily an issue sourced in federal legislation, the Indian Act model of First Nations government traditionally offered weak municipal-style powers that removed First

Nations' right of self-determination. As alluded to above, the federal government has recognized an inherent right of self-government for Indigenous peoples since 1995. For First Nations, however, getting out from under the Indian Act requires the onerous negotiation of comprehensive self-government agreements. Short of comprehensive self-government agreements, various forms of delegation and devolution agreements can offer recognition of the jurisdiction of Indigenous governments over certain services and institutions and provide funding for their operation. A variety of initiatives and agreements have existed over the years, in particular concerning institutions such as child and family services, adoption, and education.

Typically requiring years of tripartite negotiations with provinces and the federal government, comprehensive self-government agreements for Indigenous governments in Manitoba have been elusive and slow to come. In effect, Manitoba has seen remarkably few milestones thus far. In 1994, the Assembly of Manitoba Chiefs and the federal government signed the Manitoba Framework Agreement Initiative (MFAI) on the Dismantling of the Department of Indian Affairs and Northern Development, the Restoration of Jurisdictions to First Nations Peoples in Manitoba and Recognition of First Nations Governments in Manitoba. By 2007, the initiative had been quietly disbanded with little to show for it and,[48] as mentioned above, only two First Nations in the province have comprehensive self-government agreements.

As for the Métis, after generations of non-recognition, a string of three monumental victories at the Supreme Court of Canada (from 2003 to 2016) pushed the Manitoba Métis Federation leaps and bounds forward.[49] Subsequently, in 2021, the MMF signed the Manitoba Métis Self-Government Recognition and Implementation Agreement with Canada, which set the stage for the negotiations of a modern treaty in relation to its own self-governance.[50] At the time of writing, the MMF is on the cusp of signing the core initial agreement of a multi-stage treaty with the federal government. The content of the treaty was approved by Métis in an extraordinary general assembly in June 2023. Once the MMF and the federal government have signed the treaty, Parliament is meant to pass treaty implementation legislation, giving Manitoba Métis their first legally recognized modern treaty. The strategy of the MMF is to lock in the constitutional recognition and protection of a treaty with core self-government provisions while a Liberal government is still in power at the federal level, leaving a series of "Supplementary Self-Government Arrangements" concerning specific areas of jurisdiction to be negotiated and added to the treaty in the years to come.[51]

Pushing Forward for Mutual Benefit

It may be the twenty-first century, but Manitoba, in many ways, is still adapting to the twentieth-century reality of the Indigenous rights turn. This difficulty adapting is largely emblematic of the age-old settler colonial perception of Indigenous peoples as problematic obstacles to be removed in order to extract wealth from territory. This is evidenced in the perpetual frictions concerning Indigenous rights, the continued stymieing of the Treaty Land Entitlement process, and the glacial progress in recognizing the right of self-government. Despite three decades of Canada's affirming an inherent right of self-government, little progress has been made for Manitoba's Indigenous peoples. As Kiera Ladner has argued forcefully, what is needed in Canada is "a reconciliation of constitutional orders" through which colonial governments come to terms with the *other* constitutional orders that continue to exist within Indigenous nations.[52] This is the necessary precondition for the advent of a treaty federalism, or treaty constitutionalism, that would truly recognize the inherent right of self-government within all Indigenous nations. What remains to be seen is the progress that a new provincial government can make toward the Crown-Indigenous relationship that Indigenous peoples have sought for generations.

And yet, self-government and self-determination are meaningless without the means for *self-sustainability*—in other words, the *mutual benefit* that has always been sought by Indigenous peoples in their agreements with the Crown. Piecemeal devolution and delegation arrangements that allow for Indigenous nations to manage certain services and institutions—as important as they are—often combine anemic funding with high-needs populations, making it difficult for Indigenous governments to maintain robust services and respond to significant levels of need.[53] Such arrangements are a far cry from the sharing in the bounty of the land envisioned by many Indigenous nations in the era of treaty making. The lack of mutual benefit in the treaty relationship becomes more and more apparent as Canada's

Indigenous rights turn reaches new stages of maturity. In effect, the irony of Canada's legal history is that those Indigenous nations who were dispossessed of their lands *without* historical treaties—such as many in British Columbia, the Far North, or eastern Canada—are now able to utilize the SCC's modern Indigenous rights framework to claim an inherent Aboriginal title that was defined in the 1997 *Delgamuukw* decision as *exclusive* occupation of traditional territory with *natural resource rights*.[54] This has created striking contrasts in Canada's Indigenous rights landscape, whereby Indigenous nations in some regions of the country pursue recognition of exclusive title over perhaps tens of thousands of square kilometres, with resource rights, and many people in historic treaty territories are meant to carry on with rights to a few traditional activities, insufficient funding for essential services, and annuities that amount to a handful of dollars per band member per year.

If governments really desire to ameliorate conditions for Indigenous Manitobans, they should actively and expeditiously seek to ensure this mutual benefit exists in the Crown-Indigenous relationship, in order to help Indigenous peoples build the economies they want to sustain—be those economies traditional or modern. Instead, First Nations are employing all avenues to compel that mutual benefit, such as advancing the TLE process or advocating for urban reserves. Relatedly, perhaps inspired in part by a successful treaty annuities case in Ontario,[55] representative claims have recently been launched by claimants for Treaty 1, Treaty 2, Treaty 4, and Treaty 5 First Nations, seeking billions of dollars in damages and interest for the failure to index treaty annuities to inflation over the past 150 years. In essence, treaty First Nations have recognized the need to first return to the nineteenth century in order to bring the Crown-Indigenous relationship into the twenty-first century.

Similarly, while all of the territories and several provinces have instituted government resource revenue-sharing models with Indigenous nations, Manitoba has long counted itself among those who have not[56]—and this despite the fact that the previous NDP government created the Manitoba Mining Advisory Council with some fanfare in 2013, announcing that it would help lead the way to greater partnership and revenue and benefit sharing.[57] In fact, it is only during the writing and publication phase of this volume that the province announced a memorandum of understanding between the provincial government, three First Nations from western Manitoba, and the Louisiana-Pacific Canada logging company that envisages the co-development of a twenty-year forest management plan—a small first step that Premier Kinew refers to as an act of "economic reconciliation."[58]

Nevertheless, it is notable that this agreement, like so many other developments, came on the heels of litigation from the First Nations involved. Time and again, in seeking to assert that right relationship, First Nations and the Métis Nation have the guidance of their modern experience. The lion's share of the Indigenous rights turn in Canada has been initiated by Indigenous litigation and shaped by decisions of the courts. When circumstances require it, it is to the courts that Indigenous peoples return. And yet, as they seek the dual goals of self-determination and mutual benefit, a major vector of future study will be to what extent Indigenous nations are truly able to choose their own distinct paths of development, and to what extent new forms of reconciliation lauded by provinces, federal governments, or outside industries may in fact represent the same old settler interests.[59]

Notes

1 Donna Lee, "Brian Pallister's PCs Win Majority Government in Manitoba," *CBC News*, 20 April 2016, https://www.cbc.ca/news/canada/manitoba/manitoba-election-results-1.3543735.

2 Rachel Bergen, "Pallister '50 Years Out of Date,' Professor Says after Premier's Comments on Colonial History of Manitoba," *CBC News*, 10 July 2021, https://www.cbc.ca/news/canada/manitoba/brian-pallister-manitoba-chiefs-colonialism-first-nations-1.6094834.

3 Ibid.

4 The year 1870 is when Manitoba was created and joined Confederation, but it is also the same year that the Wolseley military expedition drove Louis Riel from Manitoba and instigated what historians have referred to as the "reign of terror" over the Métis. See Fred Shore, "The Emergence of the Metis Nation in Manitoba," in *Metis Legacy: A Metis Historiography and Annotated Bibliography*, ed. Lawrence J. Barkwell, Leah Dorion, and Darren R. Préfontaine (Winnipeg: Pemmican Publications, 2001), 75.

5 The year 1952 marked when status Indians regained the right to vote in Manitoba, having had it taken away not long after Manitoba became a province.

6 Both the Manitoba Indian Brotherhood—the precursor to the Assembly of Manitoba Chiefs—and the Manitoba Métis Federation were formed in 1967.

7 For his key argument that we should see settler colonialism as a *structure*, and not an *event*, see Patrick Wolfe, "Nation and Miscegenation: Discursive Continuity in

the Post-Mabo Era," *Social Analysis: The International Journal of Social and Cultural Practice* 36 (1994): 93–152.

8   While the term "Indigenous" has been supplanting "Aboriginal" in broader societal discourse, there is a subtle and specific distinction commonly recognized when these are used as adjectives modifying the word "law": "Indigenous law" is typically seen as referring to those laws, customs, and norms instituted, recognized, and upheld *by Indigenous peoples* themselves, within their nations. "Aboriginal law," on the other hand, is typically used to describe the body of law *within the Canadian legal system* that deals with the rights of Indigenous peoples and the Crown's relationship with them. I will therefore expressly use the adjective Aboriginal when I am referring specifically to the jurisprudence and legal doctrines of Canadian courts.

9   Jeremy Patzer, "Residential School Harm and Colonial Dispossession: What's the Connection?" in *Colonial Genocide in Indigenous North America*, ed. Andrew Woolford, Jeff Benvenuto, and Alexander Laban Hinton (Durham: Duke University Press, 2014), 166–85.

10 See Constitution Act, 1982, s. 35, being Schedule B to the Canada Act 1982 (UK), 1982, c. 11.

11 See, for example, Jeremy Patzer and Kiera Ladner, "Indigenous Rights and the Constitution Act, 1982: Forty Years on and Still Fishing for Rights," in *Constitutional Crossroads: Reflections on Charter Rights, Reconciliation, and Change*, ed. Kate Puddister and Emmett Macfarlane (Vancouver: UBC Press, 2022), 348–66; Jeremy Patzer and Kiera Ladner, "Charting Unknown Waters: Indigenous Rights and the Charter at Forty," *Review of Constitutional Studies* 26/27, no. 2/1 (2022): 15–38.

12 Canada, Act for the gradual enfranchisement of Indians, the better management of Indian Affairs, and to extend the provisions of the Act 31st Victoria, Chapter 42, SC 1869 (32–33 Vict.), c. 6, s. 6 [Gradual Enfranchisement Act].

13 Canada, An Act to amend and consolidate the laws respecting Indians, SC 1876 (39 Vict.), c. 18 [Indian Act].

14 *Report of the Royal Commission on Aboriginal Peoples*, Volume 1, *Looking Forward, Looking Back* (Ottawa: Supply and Services Canada, 1996), 174 (hereafter *RCAP*, vol. 1). See also Sheldon Krasowski, *No Surrender: The Land Remains Indigenous* (Regina: University of Regina Press, 2019).

15 See, for example, John Borrows, "Wampum at Niagara: The Royal Proclamation, Canadian Legal History, and Self-Government," in *Aboriginal and Treaty Rights in Canada: Essays on Law, Equality, and Respect for Difference*, ed. Michael Asch (Vancouver: UBC Press, 1997), 155–72; Sharon Venne, "Understanding Treaty 6: An Indigenous Perspective," in *Aboriginal and Treaty Rights in Canada: Essays on Law, Equality, and Respect for Difference*, ed. Michael Asch (Vancouver: UBC Press, 1997), 173–207.

16 *RCAP*, vol. 1, 253.

17 Assembly of Manitoba Chiefs, "Representing Manitoba First Nations," Assembly of Manitoba Chiefs, accessed 12 February 2023, https://manitobachiefs.com/about/.

18 See Alexander Morris, *The Treaties of Canada with the Indians of Manitoba and the North-west Territories* (Toronto: Belfords, Clarke and Co., 1880), 16 and 69.

19 Ibid., 41 and 50.

20 Statistics Canada, *Membership in a Métis organization or Settlement: Findings from the 2021 Census of Population*, 21 September 2022, https://www12.statcan.gc.ca/census-recensement/2021/as-sa/98-200-x/2021006/98-200-x2021006-eng.pdf.

21 Earlier court decisions held that the terms of the treaties were mere promises made by Crown representatives and thus were unenforceable in the courts. See *Attorney-General of Ontario v Attorney-General of Canada: Re Indian Claims*, [1897] AC 199 at 213 (PC).
22 *R v Van der Peet*, [1996] 2 SCR 507 at 538 [*Van der Peet*].
23 See, for example, John Borrows, "Frozen Rights in Canada: Constitutional Interpretation and the Trickster," *American Indian Law Review* 22, no. 1 (1998): 37–64; Ronald Niezen, "Culture and the Judiciary: The Meaning of the Culture Concept as a Source of Aboriginal Rights in Canada," *Canadian Journal of Law and Society* 18, no. 2 (2003): 1–26.
24 Jeremy Patzer, "Even When We're Winning, Are We Losing? Métis Rights in Canadian Courts," in *Métis in Canada: History, Identity, Law and Politics*, ed. Chris Adams, Gregg Dahl, and Ian Peach (Edmonton: University of Alberta Press, 2013), 307–36.
25 See Darren O'Toole, "Section 31 of the Manitoba Act, 1870: A Land Claim Agreement," *Manitoba Law Journal* 38, no. 1 (2015): 73–118.
26 Constitution Act, 1982, s. 35.
27 See *R v Van der Peet*, [1996].
28 *Haida Nation v British Columbia (Minister of Forests)* 2004 SCC 73, [2004] 3 SCR 511 [*Haida Nation*].
29 For the outline of the Sparrow test of justification, see *R v Sparrow* [1990] 1 SCR 1075 at 1111–1119. Justified infringement was later spread to the treaty rights jurisprudence in the case of *R. v Badger* [1996] 1 SCR 771.
30 *CBC News*, "Night Hunting 'Becoming a Race War,' Says Premier Brian Pallister," 20 January 2017, https://www.cbc.ca/news/canada/manitoba/night-hunting-brian-pallister-race-war-1.3944949.
31 *CBC News*, "Night Hunting Confession Forged, Allege Indigenous Groups," 4 May 2017, https://www.cbc.ca/news/canada/manitoba/night-hunting-confession-1.4099538.
32 Ibid.
33 Elisha Dacey, "Pallister Using 'Race Card Tactics' Over Agreement with Manitoba Hydro: Manitoba Metis Federation," *CBC News*, 21 March 2018, https://www.cbc.ca/news/canada/manitoba/pallister-race-card-tactics-manitoba-metis-federation-1.4586606; Sean Kavanaugh, "Pallister Comes under Fire after Province Cancels 2nd Agreement with Manitoba Metis Federation," *CBC News*, 31 October 2018, https://www.cbc.ca/news/canada/manitoba/metis-mmf-government-agreement-hydro-manitoba-1.4885479.
34 Dylan Robertson, "'No Reconciliation Whatsoever with Brian Pallister,'" *Winnipeg Free Press*, 9 July 2021, https://www.winnipegfreepress.com/breakingnews/2021/07/09/no-reconciliation-whatsoever-with-brian-pallister.
35 Elisha Dacey, "Premier Says 'Persuasion Money' Reason for Mass Resignation of Manitoba Hydro Board," *CBC News*, 21 March 2018, https://www.cbc.ca/news/canada/manitoba/manitoba-hydro-board-resigns-en-masse-1.4586013.
36 Constitution Act, 1867 (UK), 30 & 31 Vict., c. 3, s. 91, reprinted in RSC 1985, App. II, No. 5.
37 Cindy Blackstock, "Jordan's Principle: Canada's Broken Promise to First Nations Children?" *Paediatrics and Child Health* 17, no. 7 (2012): 368–70.

38 Some of the data on the overrepresentation of BIPOC (Black, Indigenous, and People of Colour) populations in COVID-19 cases and severe outcomes came from provincial institutions themselves. See, for example, Government of Manitoba, *COVID-19 Novel Coronavirus: Race, Ethnicity, Indigeneity (REI) Analysis, Wave Three*, 5 July 2021, https://www.gov.mb.ca/asset_library/en/proactive/20212022/covid19-rei-data-july2021.pdf.

39 Cameron MacLean, "Métis, Inuit in Manitoba Want Similar COVID-19 Vaccine Priority as First Nations," *CBC News*, 24 February 2021, https://www.cbc.ca/news/canada/manitoba/indigenous-manitobans-vaccine-priority-1.5926939.

40 Robertson, "'No Reconciliation.'"

41 See Aimée Craft and Jill Blakley, *In Our Backyard: Keeyask and the Legacy of Hydroelectric Development* (Winnipeg: University of Manitoba Press, 2022); Thibault Martin and Steven M. Hoffman, *Power Struggles: Hydroelectric Development and First Nations in Manitoba and Quebec* (Winnipeg: University of Manitoba Press, 2009).

42 D.N. Sprague, "Canada's Treaties with Aboriginal Peoples," *Manitoba Law Journal* 23 (1995): 341–51.

43 Ibid., 349.

44 Curt J. Pankratz and Bryan A. Hart, *Comparative Analysis of TLE Implementation in Manitoba and Saskatchewan with Focus on Solutions for Manitoba First Nations*, prepared for Southern Chiefs Organization, March 2005, https://scoinc.mb.ca/wp-content/uploads/2014/04/TLE_Comparative_Analysis_Final_Report.pdf.

45 *CBC News*, "First Nations in Manitoba Take Ottawa Back to Court over Failure to Live Up to Land Debt Agreement," 30 June 2022, https://www.cbc.ca/news/canada/manitoba/treaty-land-entitlement-committee-manitoba-suing-federal-government-1.6507467.

46 *Canada v Long Plain First Nation* 2015 FCA 177, 388 DLR (4th) 209.

47 Quoted in Danielle Da Silva, "First Nations Eye Legal Action to Halt Crown Lands Lease Auction," *Winnipeg Free Press*, 6 February 2023, https://www.winnipegfreepress.com/breakingnews/2023/02/06/first-nations-eye-legal-action-to-halt-crown-lands-lease-auction.

48 Frank Larue, "Multi-Million Self-government Initiative Dies in Manitoba," *First Nations Drum*, 3 February 2008, http://www.firstnationsdrum.com/2008/02/multi-million-self-government-initiative-dies-in-manitoba/.

49 *R v Powley* 2003 SCC 43, [2003] 2 SCR 207; *Manitoba Metis Federation Inc v Canada (Attorney General)*, 2013 SCC 14, [2013] 1 SCR 623; *Daniels v Canada (Indian Affairs and Northern Development)*, 2016 SCC 12, [2016] 1 SCR 99.

50 Manitoba Metis Federation Inc., *Manitoba Métis Self-Government Recognition and Implementation Agreement*, 6 July 2021, accessed 4 January 2025, https://www.mmf.mb.ca/wcm-docs/docs/news/manitoba_metis_self_government_recognition_and_implementation_agreement.pdf.

51 Manitoba Metis Federation Inc., "Extraordinary General Assembly: Frequently Asked Questions regarding Treaty," accessed 28 June 2023, https://www.mmf.mb.ca/ega-faqs.

52 Kiera Ladner, "Up the Creek: Fishing for a New Constitutional Order," *Canadian Journal of Political Science* 38, no. 4 (2005): 936.

53 In 2016, the Canadian Human Rights Tribunal ruled that the federal government's underfunding of child and family services on First Nations reserves, as well as

its failure to ensure equitable access to services according to Jordan's Principle, discriminates against First Nations children under the Canadian Human Rights Act. See Cindy Blackstock, "The Complainant: The Canadian Human Rights Case on First Nations Child Welfare," *McGill Law Journal* 62, no. 2 (2016): 285–328.

54 *Delgamuukw v British Columbia* [1997] 3 SCR 1010 at 1086.

55 *Restoule v Canada (Attorney General)* 2021 ONCA 779. The Restoule case concerns the escalation clause within the Robinson Treaties that was meant to embody a Crown promise to raise annuities as Crown revenue from resources increased.

56 Ken S. Coates, *Sharing the Wealth: How Resource Revenue Agreements Can Honour Treaties, Improve Communities, and Facilitate Canadian Development*, January 2015 (Ottawa: Macdonald-Laurier Institute, 2015).

57 Government of Manitoba, "New Mining Advisory Council to Ensure First Nations Benefit from Resource Development," News Release, 8 November 2013, https://news.gov.mb.ca/news/index.html?item=19495.

58 Darren Bernhardt, "3 First Nations, Manitoba Government Sign Deal on 20-Year Forestry Plan," *CBC News*, 28 June 2024, https://www.cbc.ca/news/canada/manitoba/first-nations-manitoba-forestry-plan-duck-mountains-1.7249717.

59 See, for example, Amy Fung, "The Melancholy of Extraction: Settler Sentimentality in Canada's Ahistorical Era of Economic Reconciliation," in *To the Last Drop: Affective Economies of Extraction and Sentimentality*, ed. Axelle Germanaz, Daniela Gutiérrez Fuentes, Sarah Marak, and Heike Paul (Bielefeld: [transcript], 2023), 65–88; Courtney Jung, "Reconciliation: Six Reasons to Worry," in *Reconciliation, Transitional and Indigenous Justice*, ed. Krushil Watene and Eric Palmer (London: Routledge, 2020), 252–65; Andrew Woolford, "Governing through Repair: Historical Injustices and Indigenous Peoples in Canada," in *Facing the Past: Amending Historical Injustices through Instruments of Transitional Justice*, ed. Peter Malcontent (Cambridge: Intersentia, 2016), 303–20.

CHAPTER 10

Municipal Government and Politics in Manitoba

AARON MOORE

Introduction

Although they are not recognized as a level of government in the written constitution of Canada, municipalities are the de facto third level of government in the country, a fact recognized by the Supreme Court of Canada in its decision in *Spraytech v Hudson, 2001*.[1] As the third level of government, municipalities are responsible for most services and infrastructure at the local level, and they have a reasonable degree of autonomy and own revenue sources to pursue these responsibilities. However, despite the growing understanding of the importance of municipalities in Canadian governance, their subordination to provincial governments, institutional structure, limited revenue, and the limited media coverage of municipal politics all play a role in frustrating their ability to meet their many responsibilities.

The nature of municipal politics, which is very distinct from politics at the provincial and federal levels, tends to exacerbate these issues. Local politics tends toward parochialism, which undermines municipalities' capacity to deliver municipal-wide agendas and maintain proper transparency and oversight. While voters may endorse municipal-wide policy in theory, they tend to be reactive and focused on their own neighbourhoods and homes in practice. In addition, while they may support new programs and services, they also fight against any attempt to increase their taxes. As a result, elected officials, particularly municipal councillors, focus on keeping taxes low and addressing the parochial interests of their constituents, while often ignoring more long-term problems.

This chapter provides a brief overview of the history of municipalities in Manitoba, followed by examinations of how municipal responsibilities and fiscal constraints, the structure of municipal elections and oversight, and provincial and municipal relations influence and shape municipal politics and governance in the province of Manitoba. The chapter then concludes by assessing the state of municipal governance and politics in the province, identifying causes for concern and the potential for change. Growing conflict at the municipal level in Manitoba may undermine provincial traditions of accommodation and consensus in politics. However, this conflict could result in better representation, oversight, and accountability among Manitoba municipalities.

History of Municipal Government in Manitoba

The basis for the creation and nature of municipal government in Manitoba, and, ultimately, the basis of much of municipal politics in the province, derives from the same need and principles that shaped local governance throughout the U.S. and Canada. On the one hand, senior governments created municipalities to provide the goods and services necessary for a growing population that were otherwise difficult to administer from afar, whether from England or the provincial capital. This rationale for local governance underpins almost all systems of municipal government throughout the world. On the other hand, the creation of municipal government in Manitoba represents the demands for representative, local self-governance and government in the province. As in the rest of Canada and the United States, these two factors led to the creation of municipalities with a wide range of authority, taxation power, and autonomy, relative to municipal and local government in other parts of the world. Municipal politics in Manitoba, then, is a product of clashes over the municipal government's use of its authority and its capacity to tax residents.

Despite the relative broad authority and autonomy that Manitoba municipalities wield, and although now widely recognized as the third level of government, municipalities in Manitoba, as in the rest of Canada, are still the creation of provincial governments and governed by provincial legislation. Forms of local governance existed in Manitoba prior to the province's founding; however, municipal government in Manitoba emerged only after the province joined Confederation in 1870. In 1873, the new government of Manitoba created the province's first Municipal Act. The Act required that two-thirds of residents in an area vote in favour of incorporating their community as a municipality.[2] Upon creation, the Act permitted municipalities to collect property taxes and pass bylaws (the municipal form of legislation and regulation) and listed several municipal responsibilities. This Act would serve as the foundation of all subsequent municipal Acts in the province. The first municipality incorporated under the Act was the Township or Parish of Springfield and Sunnyside (now the Rural Municipality of Springfield).[3]

In December of 1873, the province passed a separate Act for the creation of the City of Winnipeg, recognizing the city's distinction as the largest urban community in the province and its role as the provincial capital. The province later repealed this separate Act in 1886. From that point to 1902, the Municipal Act governed the City of Winnipeg. In 1902, the province once again created a specific Act for the City of Winnipeg, which would form the basis for the city's current charter. This early flip-flopping on the special status of Winnipeg represents the province's regularly fickle approach to municipal government.

After the creation of the Municipal Act in 1873, the provincial government made several changes to the structure and nature of municipal government in the province. In 1875, the province tried to institute a two-tier county system based on the system in Ontario (with a municipal county serving as an upper tier, and townships serving as smaller lower-tier municipalities). This system proved too cumbersome in Manitoba, leading the province to abolish this two-tier system in 1883.[4] By 1886, the province introduced the current separation of Manitoba municipalities into urban municipalities (cities and towns), rural municipalities, and local government districts—today, only two local government districts remain,[5] effectively leaving two categories of municipalities. Except when multiple municipalities amalgamate, the definition of urban and rural municipalities is based on the population of the municipality (more or fewer than 1,000 residents), and population density (more or fewer than 400 residents per square kilometre).[6]

Responsibilities and Limitations of Municipal Government

Although several provincial statutes and regulations apply or affect municipalities, the Municipal Act is the primary governing legislation for municipalities in Manitoba today,[7] apart from Winnipeg, which has its own enabling legislation, the City of Winnipeg Charter Act (Winnipeg Charter).[8]

Through the Municipal Act, Winnipeg Charter, and other pieces of legislation such as the Planning Act,[9] which governs land use planning in the province, the Province of Manitoba establishes the role and responsibility of municipalities, and determines the extent of municipal authority, what revenue tools are available to municipalities, and the structure of municipal government and elections. While the Municipal Act and Winnipeg Charter include an omnibus provision, the provincial government retains the right to intervene and make changes to the structure of municipal governments, as well as their authority, responsibilities, and revenue sources, as it sees fit.

All municipalities in Manitoba, aside from the City of Winnipeg, share a list of basic responsibilities, or spheres of jurisdictions, as outlined in the Municipal Act. Winnipeg's list of responsibilities, as delineated in the Winnipeg Charter, is longer, as are its respective authority and powers. In addition to the Municipal Act and Winnipeg Charter, other pieces of legislation, including the Planning Act and the Police Services Act, delineate additional responsibilities and powers.

In the past, the Canadian judiciary restricted municipality authority to only those responsibilities listed in the governing legislation. When municipalities attempted to act outside of their prescribed responsibilities, the court would strike down any bylaws as exceeding the authority of the municipality. The result of such decisions was governing legislation that grew longer and longer to accommodate the growing reality and need of municipal intervention into ever-expanding areas. To combat this so-called laundry list legislation, provincial governments, beginning in Alberta, began adding the aforementioned omnibus provisions to legislations. Omnibus provisions are statements within the legislation that governs municipalities that grant municipalities broad authority to pursue whatever actions they deem necessary in order to provide good governance.[10] These provinces intended, through such provisions, to allow municipal government to act in best interests of the municipality.

The Province of Manitoba added omnibus provisions to both the Municipal Act and Winnipeg Charter, thus granting municipalities the authority to enact bylaws on issues that extend beyond their delineated spheres of jurisdiction. While the courts in Canada were initially reluctant to recognize such provisions, in its decision in *Spraytech v Hudson, 2001*,[11] the Supreme Court recognized both the legitimacy of omnibus provisions and municipal governments' growing need for broader authority to tackle emerging challenges.

In practice, smaller municipalities in Manitoba typically confine themselves to the responsibilities explicitly outlined in the Municipal Act. This list is still long, however, and includes such responsibilities as policing, fire services, water and wastewater, solid waste collection, parks and recreation, land-use planning, building codes and building inspections, and roads construction and maintenance. Larger municipalities often find the need to intervene in areas beyond their expressed spheres of jurisdiction. For instance, cities such as Brandon and Selkirk choose to provide transit services to their residents, even though the Municipal Act does not require them to do so. In addition, both the cities of Brandon and Winnipeg devote resources to bolster relations with Indigenous peoples and provide services for the homeless despite the absence of those stipulations in the Municipal Act and Winnipeg Charter.

In the province's cities and large towns, there are constant demands from the public for their municipal governments to address pressing issues such as housing affordability. However, a fiscal straitjacket binds municipalities in Manitoba, despite their relative high level of autonomy and breadth of authority. This straitjacket constrains their ability to expand their support for and coverage of services, and often their ability to meet their basic responsibilities.

Municipalities' Fiscal Straitjacket

Unlike governments at the provincial and federal levels, municipalities cannot run operating deficits. This means that they cannot borrow money to pay for operating expenses in the long run and must balance their budget at the end of each fiscal year. To pay for the various services they provide, municipalities rely on three major sources of revenue: property tax, user fees, and provincial grants/transfers. Municipalities have no control over transfers from the province and are often at the mercy of their provincial governments when it comes to such funding. While user fees are increasingly important sources of revenue for municipalities, a municipal government can spend the revenue only on the specific services that generate them, like water or transit. As a result, user fees are not available as a source of general revenue.[12] This leaves the property tax as the municipal governments' main source of own-source revenue (revenue they collect and control).

Property tax, as the name suggests, is a tax on parcels of property within a municipality. In Manitoba, the property tax process begins with the province, which assesses the value of all property (apart from Winnipeg, which conducts its own assessment) and determines the apportion percentage for different property types (how much of the value of a property municipalities and school divisions can apply the property tax to). Municipalities then set their property tax rates and collect property taxes for themselves and school divisions.[13]

Unlike provincial and federal sales and income tax, the property tax does not fluctuate with the economy. This makes it a very consistent revenue source. However, this fact also means that municipalities must regularly increase the property tax to keep their revenue in line with inflation. This can lead to problematic optics for the municipal government.

The property tax is highly visible to property owners, as they receive a bill from the municipality each year, in contrast to income tax, which the federal government collects every pay cycle, and sales tax, which accrues over the course of a year as we purchase goods and services. As a result, residents tend to get upset when municipalities increase property taxes each year, as they perceive it as a yearly billing increase. This poses a problem for municipally elected officials. If they increase taxes too much or too often, voters may revolt. If they do not increase property tax, then revenue will decline relative to expenses, forcing municipalities to make cuts to services and infrastructure maintenance since they cannot run operating deficits. Municipal governments' heavy reliance on property tax, thus, severely restricts their capacity to respond to inflation and other economic variables beyond their control.

The Cost of Policing

Municipal governments' struggle to contain the cost of police services is a good example of how their limited fiscal resources undermine their capacity to deliver services. Outside of Brandon and Winnipeg,

Manitoba residents are used to seeing the RCMP when they call for police. However, while the RCMP does provide policing throughout most of the province, most of the cost and responsibility for policing falls on municipal government. Unlike many of the other prescribed responsibilities of municipal government, a specific Act, called the Police Services Act, governs municipal policing in the province.[14] The Act requires all municipalities with 750 or more residents to provide local policing. Municipalities may create their own police force, as is the case in Winnipeg and Brandon, or contract out policing to the RCMP or other municipalities.

In addition to this requirement, since 2009, the Police Services Act also requires the establishment of Police Boards (PBs). The province introduced PBs to provide greater civilian oversight over police action. However, in practice they restrict municipalities' ability to shape and direct police spending and policy. Prior to the introduction of police boards, municipalities with their own police force had direct control over the police budget and police services. Today, police services boards act as an intermediary between municipal councils and police services. While municipal councils appoint members to the boards and have final say on the size of budgets, they cannot direct service or require changes to how police allocate their resources. For many larger municipalities, particularly those with their own police service, policing is the single largest tax-supported operating expense. In Brandon, police services account for roughly 37 percent of the tax-supported operating budget, and in Winnipeg for 28 percent. In both cities, the cost of policing, along with fire services, has been growing faster than other services, due largely to increased labour costs. As with the cost of health care at the provincial level, these cost increases have squeezed other municipal services and capital expenditures. As a result, many municipal councillors have been challenging proposed budget increases for policing, placing them in direct confrontation with members of the police boards, which often include other members of council, and the police service itself.[15]

For those municipalities relying on RCMP services, the collective agreement negotiated between the federal government and the union representing RCMP officers in summer 2021 has further exacerbated this issue. This new collective agreement increases the wages of average RCMP officers by $20,000, and awards officers retroactive pay going back to 2017.[16] While the federal and provincial governments offset some of the cost of policing for smaller municipalities, this new agreement, which did not include any input from municipal government in Canada, will significantly increase the cost of policing in most medium and smaller municipalities in Manitoba, at a time when they are already struggling with their budgets. As with larger municipalities that have their own police forces, many municipalities that contract with the RCMP may have to raise taxes or make cuts to other services or infrastructure maintenance to cover the increasing cost of policing.

Such constraints to municipal revenue play an important role in shaping not only the provision and delivery of municipal services but also municipal politics. Many municipalities in Manitoba have expressed concerns over the rising costs of policing[17] and their inability to control costs due to the absence of direct communication between municipal council and police services. In Winnipeg, these concerns have resulted in open conflict between Winnipeg city councillors, the city's PBs, police chiefs, and police union.[18] The problem is bigger than policing, though. At the core of the debate over police budgets in Manitoba is the broader politics surrounding the public's conflicting demands for low property taxes and better services. Municipalities must either constrain their spending or raise taxes. They do not have the luxury of borrowing money indefinitely to pay for their largesse. This means they are constantly dealing with the tension between maintaining or improving the services they provide, while avoiding the ire of the public should they raise property taxes.

Municipal Councils and Municipal Elections

Along with the fiscal restrictions that municipalities face, the nature of their elected government in Manitoba is also very different from that at the provincial and federal levels. At the provincial and federal levels, political parties dominate. Most political discussion and debate occur along clear partisan lines, and the number of seats a party holds determines who forms the government and executive (premier or prime minister and cabinet). At the municipal level in Manitoba, party politics is absent, and voters directly elect an executive—a mayor in urban municipalities or a reeve in rural ones. In Winnipeg, the mayor also appoints the chairs of five standing committees (subcommittees of council).[19] The mayor and these five committee chairs form the Executive Policy Committee (EPC), which functions somewhat like a cabinet at the federal and provincial levels. For good or bad, the absence of political parties and the separation of the legislative and executive functions of municipal government significantly alter the nature of government and politics at the municipal level. These differences also alter the relationship between elected officials, the public, and city staff.

Municipal Elections

Once every four years, municipalities in Manitoba hold municipal elections. Voters in all municipalities elect a mayor or reeve at-large, while election for council member vary by municipality. Roughly half of Manitoba's 137 municipalities also elect their council members at-large, while the other half elect their councillor via single-member, two-member, or three-member ward (a geographic division of the municipality akin to a federal or provincial riding).[20] The absence of political parties changes the dynamics of municipal elections, as do the size and nature of the municipality. Candidates for mayor, reeve, and councillor have their own political leanings—some may even be card-carrying members of federal or provincial parties—but they do not run under a party banner. This means that candidates must rely on their own name recognition among the voting public to attract votes. Given the limited attention the news media devotes to municipal campaigns outside of Winnipeg, reaching potential voters with one's message can be difficult.[21]

In very small municipalities, where most residents know each other, the absence of partisan labels may have only a limited impact on the success of a given candidate. However, as municipalities grow larger in population, communal ties are usually insufficient to get oneself elected. The larger the municipality, the more funding candidates need to raise in order to compete for election. Without a well-funded party to provide support, candidates must raise their own funds. This self-reliance for funding favours well-connected individuals. In the past, this often meant members of the business community or organized labour, though this is changing.[22]

Provincial and municipal laws in Manitoba limit who can donate to a campaign (only individual residents) and how much they can donate (see Manitoba, the Municipal Act, s. 93, note 6, and individual municipal financing bylaws). However, even with such restrictions in place, having many "friends" with deep pockets is often necessary to run a successful campaign. Thus, while the barrier to *run* for council, mayor, or reeve is quite low, the barrier to *winning* can be quite high. Such barriers continue to undermine attempts to diversify councils.[23]

Where there is no incumbent (current elected official) running for re-election, the winner of most municipal races, barring races for mayor in some of the largest cities, is often a winner of a popularity contest heavily dependent on a candidate's capacity to raise funds. When an incumbent is running, the capacity of a challenger to defeat them is very low, particularly in races for council positions.

At the federal and provincial levels, we tend to vote for a candidate based on their partisan ties rather than their individual merit. With significant media coverage of party politics, the voting public can assess the performance of the existing government, and vote for or against their candidates in the elections based on this assessment. This can lead to significant turnover among incumbents. At the municipal level in Manitoba, such mechanisms for holding incumbent councillors accountable is absent, however.

Even in a large city like Winnipeg, with significant media coverage of municipal and local affairs, the news media provides few accounts of the actions and voting behaviour of individual councillors. Without such knowledge, voters have little information with which to assess an incumbent councillor's performance. The absence of any media oversight enables incumbent councillors to avoid accountability for their past decisions. With their existing name recognition, they can successfully seek re-election repeatedly. This cycle leads to a perverse situation where residents in municipalities with wards tend to view council negatively but their own councillor positively.

Voters view council negatively because of its perceived inertia or incompetence when it comes to pursuing city-wide objectives or overseeing the administration of the city.[24] However, the nature of council races encourages incumbent councillors to adopt parochial stances on most city-wide issues. To curry favour with their constituents, incumbent councillors with wards focus on obtaining funds for projects in their ward while opposing development or policies that their residents find objectionable. Residents will notice and reward councillors for this, even though adopting such an approach to politics and governance undermines the capacity of council to achieve any broader objectives.[25]

In contrast, voters equate the state of their municipality with the mayor and reeve and will punish them when they feel the city, town, or RM is going in the wrong direction (even though, outside of Winnipeg, reeves and mayors have little authority to direct the course of the municipality on their own). The higher profile of the head of council draws more media coverage, even in the smallest of municipalities, which allows for races that are more competitive, which, in turn, allows for some element of accountability. However, in comparison with the federal and provincial levels, unseating an incumbent mayor or reeve can still be very difficult, as they often already command support among donors and enjoy a high public profile.[26]

The consequence of the municipal electoral systems in Manitoba is often inertia, as voters are unable or unwilling to punish and remove elected officials who hinder necessary change. This lack of electoral accountability can result in significant failures in government oversight, a fact exacerbated by the part-time status of municipal councillors and of many mayors and reeves outside of Winnipeg. With low remuneration and part-time status, the role of councillor, reeve, or mayor is more akin to community volunteering than the full-time positions of MLAs (Members of the Legislative Assembly) and MPs (Members of Parliament). These facts can undermine oversight and accountability in two ways: lack of adequate specific knowledge of municipal government, and failure to follow prescribed codes of conduct and legislation.

Oversight and Accountability

Part-time elected officials—councillors, mayors, and reeves—often lack enough specific knowledge of the operations and function of municipal government to provide adequate oversight. Even in Winnipeg, where all members of council are full time, elected officials rely on the information and guidance that municipal staff provide, with limited means to assess or challenge the veracity of this information.[27]

The ongoing police headquarters (HQ) saga in Winnipeg is illustrative of this. The story of Winnipeg's new police HQ is very complex—it includes a construction company with alleged ties to organized crime and allegations of kickbacks to members of city staff, among other things. One of the central elements of the scandal is the purported reliance of councillors on the word of city staff as the cost of the project continued to escalate. News media reports suggest that senior city administrators convinced council that the purchase of a former Canada Post headquarters and sorting facility was the only option for a new police HQ. Councillors did not appear to question the wisdom of such a purchase or the estimated value of the office building that came with the purchase. In addition, for years council had accepted inaccurate budgets for the construction and renovation of the building, while staff managed to authorize cost increases that legally required council authorization.[28]

Eventually, following the news that the RCMP was investigating the firm involved in the construction of the police HQ, the city's new mayor began questioning the behaviour and decision making of the municipal administration.[29] The local news media has also vigorously pursued the issue. Nevertheless, for years the system failed in providing oversight, and the city may never achieve full accountability. Despite two RCMP investigations relating to the HQ scandal, Crown prosecutors have yet to charge anyone with criminal wrongdoing, and the provincial government repeatedly refused former Winnipeg mayor Brian Bowman's request for a formal public inquiry to investigate the scandal.[30]

If full-time city councillors in a city the size of Winnipeg struggle to maintain oversight of municipal operations, how can we expect part-time elected officials with far fewer resources to do better? There has been a growing process of professionalization among municipal staff across Manitoba, as in the rest of Canada. This process of professionalization often includes the introduction of new and more transparent practices and internal oversight measures to government administration. However, there remain important questions about how part-time elected officials can provide adequate oversight of municipal operations when they are so highly dependent on city staff for information.

Along with concerns regarding their capacity for oversight, elected officials at the municipal level often fail in following their own codes of conduct or provincial legislation governing the nature and function of council and council meetings, further undermining the capacity of municipal government to deliver transparent and accountable government. The consequences of such absences in oversight usually materialize only when someone successfully engages the interests of the news media. In recent years there have been several notable issues surrounding the malfunctioning of municipal councils in this province that illustrate the problematic nature of the current municipal government system in Manitoba.

For instance, beginning in 2017, several small-town and rural Manitoba councillors, many newly elected women, raised concerns regarding bullying and harassment on council. These accounts suggest that longer-serving incumbent councillors would bully or try to silence new councillors and mayors when they would challenge or question decisions and decision-making processes.[31] While the provincial government responded to these allegations by passing new, stringent codes of conduct for councillors, so far these new codes are largely untested.

More recently, the *Brandon Sun* uncovered a practice among the city's council of holding informal meetings, in chambers, with no record of the content or nature of the meeting.[32] This practice is in clear violation of section 152(1) of the province's Municipal Act, which requires that all council meetings occur in public and for minutes to be recorded. The only exception to this rule is meeting on certain sensitive issues, in which case council can close the meeting to the public, though they must still notify the public and record the meeting. The absence of any recording or minutes is highly problematic, as it substantially erodes transparency. The mayor of Brandon at the time argued that the council made no decisions in such meetings.[33] However, if the meetings informed the decisions of council in any way, then this information should be available to public. Otherwise, how can the public evaluate the decisions of council? How can voters hold council accountable for their decisions?

The Provincial Role in Municipal Politics

Provincial legislation and regulation play a very important role in shaping the internal politics of Manitoba municipalities, as they establish the responsibilities and constraints of municipal government and govern municipal electoral systems and elected officials. The role of the province and its impact on local politics do not end with legislation and regulation, however. Although the province often chooses to remain aloof when it comes to local politics and governance, it can and does intervene when it believes doing so is to its own benefit.

The capacity of the provincial government to control all aspects of municipal government, and to choose when or when not to intercede at the local level, often results in significant tension between municipal governments and the province. Provincial control over municipalities also regularly leads to conflicts between the political interest of the governing provincial party and the political and policy interest of individual communities and their residents. For instance, in 2019 the provincial government decided to unliterally cap its contribution to the cost of transit in the City of Winnipeg, effectively shifting the entire burden of future cost increases to the city.[34] The provincial government in past years has also held up promised provincial and federal funding for various municipal infrastructure projects by placing conditions on how these funds can be used.[35] The provincial government also imposed the establishment of the Police Boards that are now the bane of many municipalities across the province. These often arbitrary and usually politically motivated decisions can make life very difficult for municipalities that are already struggling to balance the demands of their own residents with the limits of the property tax.

While many academic scholars like to insist that municipal governments are no longer the "creatures of the provinces" in Canada,[36] the continued intervention of provincial government into municipal affairs suggests that this is not the case. The most striking examples of such interventions in Manitoba are the province's repeated applications of forced amalgamation on unwilling municipalities.

Forced Amalgamation

Amalgamation is the process of taking two or more existing municipalities and combining them into one larger municipality. The Province of Manitoba used this authority most famously when it amalgamated the former City of Winnipeg with twelve surrounding municipalities in 1972 to form the new City of Winnipeg, known colloquially as "Unicity." At the time of this amalgamation, the New Democratic Party (NDP) government argued the amalgamation was necessary to address inequality between the different municipalities that comprised the city region of Winnipeg. Prior to amalgamation, many of the wealthier suburban municipalities surrounding the old city enjoyed much lower property taxes, growing population, and industrial development, while the central city declined and poverty grew.[37] At the time, the decision to amalgamate the entire city region faced significant opposition from many of the existing municipalities and their residents. However, in the end, local opposition did not sway the province.

Today, there is little evidence that amalgamation addressed inequality in the region. Suburban councillors dominated the new city council following amalgamation, as they do today. And while property taxes levelled out across the new city, the council directed much of the funding for services and infrastructure to growing areas at the city's fringe, rather than older, inner-city neighbourhoods,[38] a practice that continues today.

While Unicity remains the most famous example of amalgamation in Manitoba and was the first of many amalgamations of large city regions across Canada, in the past decades the province of Manitoba, particularly under the premiership of Greg Selinger, imposed several amalgamations on smaller urban and rural municipalities throughout the province. The government's justification for this wave of amalgamations differs substantially from those used for the creation of Unicity. The province largely promoted these new amalgamations as a means to save money by reducing duplication and achieving economies of scale—where services can be delivered at a cheaper cost per capita the larger the user base.[39] In reality, the political rationale for the amalgamation of urban municipalities with surrounding rural municipalities is to use the tax base of the urban municipalities to offset the cost of maintaining infrastructure and services in the rural areas. While the provincial government provides subsidies via grants to all municipalities in Manitoba, the subsidies tend to be greater to rural areas, as rural municipalities in the province are responsible for providing services over larger areas with a limited tax base. Thus, the province, not the municipalities or their residents, benefits the most from such amalgamations.

The main reason for the original separation of urban and rural areas into distinct municipalities arose due to the conflicting interests of urban and rural property owners and the different needs of urban and rural residents. Urban areas tend to require more services, including municipal water and basic welfare services, and greater investments in infrastructure, from roads to sewer systems. Rural areas need fewer services and municipally provided infrastructure, such as water, as many rural residents rely on their own sources for these needs. What rural residents do need is properly maintained rural roads, basic services such as fire and policing, and properly maintained electrical grids, services that the province either provides directly or subsidizes. By forcing the amalgamation of these disparate communities, the province has created tension between urban and rural residents.[40]

In addition to the conflicting interests of rural and urban residents, in several of the newly amalgamated municipalities, rural residents, particularly farmers, have experienced significant increases in their property tax rates, as the municipalities align the rates for both urban and rural property. While in other provinces municipalities can adjust the property tax rates for different types of property, in Manitoba, the province dictates how rates vary by land use. Municipal property rates, known as the "mill rate" in Manitoba, must be consistent across all usage types. As the value of farm property has increased much faster than the value of urban properties in many areas, the tax burden of these amalgamated municipalities has shifted toward the rural farmers and away from urban residents.[41]

Provincial capriciousness adds another layer to the already complex nature of municipal politics and governance. Municipalities have little control over what the province does, while provincial decisions can significantly shift municipal politics and governance. In the short run, municipal elected officials can and will blame the provincial government for any unwanted interventions or decisions, but in the long run, municipalities must deal with the consequences of provincial decisions.

Conclusion

Municipal politics in Manitoba is far more complex than can be conveyed in one chapter. However, the nature of municipal government as outlined above captures many of the fundamental aspects of Manitoba municipalities that determine and shape municipal politics and governance. Notably, municipal politics is typified by parochialism and the conflicting desire to expand services while limiting tax increases. These characteristics of municipal politics serve to undermine any attempts to implement progressive, municipal-wide policies and municipal governments' capacity to maintain transparency, oversight, and accountability. The threat of provincial intervention and capriciousness adds an additional layer of complexity to all of this.

While it is easy to blame elected officials and municipal staff for the failings of municipal politics and governance in the province, the voting public plays a substantial role in perpetuating the many issues that plague municipalities. Voter inattentiveness is significant in shaping opaque governance. Moreover, while the municipal electoral system plays a role in perpetuating parochialism in the absence of political parties, that parochialism mirrors the parochialism of the electorate. After all, municipal councillors focus largely on interests of their own constituents, and if those interests are parochial, then so, too, will be the policy decisions of the councillor.

The fundamental issue with municipal politics in Manitoba is the broader public's lack of interest in municipal politics. This is not specific to Manitobans. Low voter turnout and attentiveness are common at the municipal level through Canada and the U.S. When residents engage at the local level, it is usually because of a policy or proposal that they feel will negatively affect them in their personal life. This makes municipal politics primarily reactive. If change is to occur for the better at the municipal level, then the average voter must become more engaged and proactive in their engagement, otherwise breakdowns in governance and failures in oversight and accountability will continue.

There are some reasons to be optimistic about the future of municipal government and politics in Manitoba, however. While allegations of bullying and otherwise bad behaviour among municipal elected officials may cast a pall on these institutions of government, they also suggest an important change is occurring among municipalities in Manitoba. A growing number of elected officials, often reflecting under-represented demographics at the municipal level, as well as journalists and members of the public, are challenging old norms of behaviour and upending traditional council consensus. These changes may result in greater public debate over municipal policy and greater oversight and scrutiny of council and municipal staff decision making, even in the smallest municipalities.

As the editors of this volume note in the introduction, there are traditions of accommodation and consensus building in Manitoba politics. In an era where conflict seems to dominate political discourse, particularly at the federal level, there is great appeal to these twin traditions. However, in some instances consensus can lead to stagnation or lack of innovation, and failure to protect the interest of the public. While sustained periods of conflict could erode municipal capacity to govern, and the public trust, shorter periods of unrest followed by real change could lead to better governance and policy making at the local level in Manitoba.

Notes

1   *14957 Canada Ltée (Spraytech, Société d'arrosage) v Hudson (Town)*, [2001] 2 S.C.R. 241, 2001 SCC 40.
2   Gordon Goldsborough, *With One Voice: A History of Municipal Governance in Manitoba* (Portage la Prairie: Association of Manitoba Municipalities, 2008).
3   Ibid.
4   Gerald Friesen and Barry Potyondi, *A Guide to the Study of Manitoba Local History* (Winnipeg: University of Manitoba Press, 1981).
5   The two remaining local government districts are Mystery Lake and Pinawa.
6   Manitoba, The Municipal Act, C.C.S.M. c. M225, https://web2.gov.mb.ca/laws/statutes/ccsm/m225.php.
7   Ibid.
8   Manitoba, The City of Winnipeg Charter, S.M. 2002, c. 39, https://web2.gov.mb.ca/laws/statutes/2002/c03902e.php.
9   Manitoba, The Planning Act, C.C.S.M. c. P80, https://web2.gov.mb.ca/laws/statutes/ccsm/p080.php.
10 For instance, the Manitoba Municipal Act's omnibus provision (section 3 of the Act) states: "the purposes of a municipality are (a) to provide good government; (b) to provide services, facilities or other things that, in the opinion of the council of the municipality, are necessary or desirable for all or a part of the municipality; and (c) to develop and maintain safe and viable communities."
11 *114957 Canada Ltée (Spraytech, Société d'arrosage) v Hudson (Town)*, [2001].
12 Winnipeg is the exception to this rule. The Winnipeg Charter enables the municipality to collect water charges as part of the municipality's general revenue. This means the city can increase water fees beyond the basic cost of operation and use the revenue to offset property tax increases.
13 In Manitoba, the provincial government (or the City of Winnipeg) assesses the value of each property in the province every two years. The province also establishes what they call "a portioned percentage" by property type. For instance, the current portioned percentage for residential property in the province is .45 (i.e., 45 percent) while for commercial property it is .65 (65 percent). The portioned percentage is the percentage of a property's value that municipalities apply property tax to. For example, if the province values a residential property at $200,000, the respective municipality will apply the property tax to 45 percent of that value, or $90,000. Municipalities then set the mill rate. The mill rate is the number of dollars a municipality will collect in property taxes for every 1,000 dollars of a property's portioned valuation. So, for instance, if the mill rate is 5, the municipality will collect five dollars for every 1,000 dollars of a property's value (or .05 percent).

The property tax is a valuable source of revenue for municipalities, as, unlike the provincial and federal sales and income tax, it does not fluctuate with the economy. However, this means that the property tax does not grow with inflation. Many residents believe, erroneously, that the amount of property tax they pay, and thus property tax revenue, goes up as the value of property increases. This is not the case. While a municipality could leave their property tax rate fixed, and, in theory at least, recoup significant dividends from the recent surge in housing prices, in practice, municipalities will adjust the actual property tax rate down as prices rise. They do this because few residents could afford tax increases at the rate of housing price increases today, and because they are legislatively required to balance their budget (they cannot budget for massive surpluses).

Because property tax does not increase with inflation, if a municipality needs to increase its revenue, it needs to adjust property tax rates. This can result in municipalities announcing an increase in property taxes each year. In practice, when a municipal government says it is increasing property taxes by, say, 2 percent, they are communicating the average increase that property owners will have to pay. The property tax rate may go down in some cases if property prices have increased significantly. Unfortunately, for municipalities, property tax increases are necessary if they wish to keep their revenue in line with inflation.

14 Manitoba, The Police Services Act, S.M. 2009, c. 32, https://www.canlii.org/en/mb/laws/stat/ccsm-c-p94.5/latest/ccsm-c-p94.5.html#:~:text=The%20Police%20Services%20Act%20of,accountability%20in%20policing%20(preamble).

15 Cameron MacLean, "Fractious Finance Committee Meeting Reveals Doubts over Winnipeg Police Oversight," *CBC News*, 12 November 2021, https://www.cbc.ca/news/canada/manitoba/winnipeg-police-board-finance-committee-police-oversight-1.6247963.

16 Catharine Tunney, "Mounties to See Their Salaries Soar as First Collective Agreement Is Ratified," *CBC News*, 17 August 2021, https://www.cbc.ca/news/politics/rcmp-union-deal-1.6142305.

17 Association of Manitoba Municipalities, "Municipalities Seek to Prevent Impacts to Emergency Services, Ensure Public Safety Remains Top Priority," News Release, 23 November 2021, http://www.amm.mb.ca/download/news_releases/2021.11.23-AMM-News-Release-Municipalities-seek-to-prevent-impacts-to-emergency-services-ensure-public-safety-remains-top-priority.pdf.

18 MacLean, "Fractious Finance Committee Meeting."

19 Scott Gillingham reduced the number of standing committees from six to five once he took office in winter 2022. This reduction resulted from his pledge to reduce the city's Executive Policy Committee.

20 Under at-large systems, voters can vote for as many candidates as there are council seats. For instance, if a municipality has a five-member council, voters will vote for up to five candidates from a list of all council candidates. Under single-member, two-member and three-member ward systems, voters can vote for one, two, or three candidates within their ward, respectively.

21 Aaron A. Moore, "The Potential and Consequences of Municipal Electoral Reform," IMFG Perspectives No. 20 (Toronto: Institute on Municipal Finance and Governance, Munk School of Global Affairs, University of Toronto, 2017); Aaron A. Moore, R. Michael McGregor, and Laura B. Stephenson, "Paying Attention and the Incumbency Effect: Voting Behaviour in the 2014 Toronto Municipal Election," *International Political Science Review* 38, no. 1 (2017): 85–98.

22 Moore, "Potential and Consequences."

23 Ibid.

24 Ibid. See also Probe Research's post, "The City Election in Three Parts," from 19 August 2022, https://probe-research.com/news/civic-election-three-charts. Drawing on their earlier poll, Probe found that 60 percent of Winnipeggers felt the city was going in the wrong direction, and 44 percent felt that the majority of councillors should be defeated in the next election, versus 14 percent who believed most deserved to be re-elected. Despite many voters' negative assessment of city

councillors, in the subsequent fall election in 2022, voters returned all but one incumbent councillor who ran for re-election. The incumbent for Transcona, Shawn Nason, lost to the ward's previous councillor, Russ Wyatt, who chose not to run in the 2018 election. In addition, in one of the two open races, voters returned a councillor who lost his seat in 2018, after his ward, St. Charles, merged with St. James. As a result, voters elected only one new councillor to council in 2022.

25 Moore, "Potential and Consequences."
26 Joseph Kushner, David Siegel, and Hannah Stanwick, "Ontario Municipal Elections: Voting Trends and Determinants of Electoral Success in a Canadian Province," *Canadian Journal of Political Science* 30, no. 2 (1997): 539–53; Moore, "Potential and Consequences."
27 Andrew Sancton, *Canadian Local Government: An Urban Perspective*, 3rd ed. (Toronto: Oxford University Press, 2021).
28 CTV Winnipeg, "Audit of Over-Budget Police Headquarters Finds Lack of Oversight," *CTV News*, 15 July 2014, https://winnipeg.ctvnews.ca/audit-of-over-budget-police-headquarters-finds-lack-of-oversight-survey-states-building-provides-value-1.1914189.
29 *CBC News*, "Brian Bowman Says 'Heads Should Roll' if Police HQ Probe Uncovers Wrongdoing," *CBC News*, 11 December 2014, https://www.cbc.ca/news/canada/manitoba/brian-bowman-says-heads-should-roll-if-police-hq-probe-uncovers-wrongdoing-1.2870089; KPMG, n.d., *Winnipeg Police Service Headquarters Construction Project Audit*, report, https://legacy.winnipeg.ca/audit/pdfs/reports/2014/WinnipegPoliceServiceHeadquartersConstructionProjectAudit.pdf.
30 Caroline Barghout and Joanne Levasseur, "Crown Downplays Value of Inquiry in Winnipeg Police HQ Scandal, Doubles Down on Decision Not to Lay Charges," *CBC News*, 3 October 2022, https://www.cbc.ca/news/canada/manitoba/winnipeg-police-hq-charges-crown-1.6601320.
31 Jeff Cottrill, "Manitoba Mayor, Councillors Resign After Alleged Bullying," *OHS Canada*, 9 May 2017, https://www.ohscanada.com/manitoba-mayor-councillors-resign-alleged-bullying/; Ian Froese, "Province Moves to Clamp Down on Misbehaving Manitoba Municipal Officials with Standardized Code of Conduct," *CBC News*, 22 November 2018, https://www.cbc.ca/news/canada/manitoba/manitoba-government-harassment-abuse-municipal-1.4917227.
32 Colin Slark, "Behind Closed Doors: Council's Informal Meetings May Violate the Municipal Act, Expert Says," *Brandon Sun*, 28 May 2022, https://www.brandonsun.com/local/2022/05/27/councils-informal-meetings-called-into-question.
33 Colin Slark, "Informal Council Meetings Common Under Chrest: Data," *Brandon Sun*, 3 August 2022, https://www.brandonsun.com/local/2022/08/03/informal-meetings-common-under-chrest-data.
34 Maggie Macintosh, "Most in City Support 50-50 Transit Split: Poll," *Winnipeg Free Press*, 27 September 2019, https://www.winnipegfreepress.com/breakingnews/2019/09/27/most-in-city-support-50-50-transit-split-poll.
35 Sam Samson, "Province's Removal of Conditions on Federal Cash for Winnipeg Sewage Upgrades 'Helps Move Things Along': CFO," *CBC News*, 10 May 2022, https://www.cbc.ca/news/canada/manitoba/winnipeg-funding-sewage-transit-manitoba-1.6448173.

36 Kristen Good, "The Fallacy of the Creatures of the Province Doctrine," *IMFG Papers* 46 (Toronto: Institute on Municipal Finance and Governance, Munk School of Global Affairs, University of Toronto, 2019).

37 James Lightbody, "The Reform of a Metropolitan Government: The Case of Winnipeg, 1971," *Canadian Public Policy* 4, no. 4 (1978): 489–504.

38 Ibid.

39 William Ashton, Wayne Kelly, and Ray Bollman, "Municipalities Amalgamate in Manitoba: Moving towards Rural Regions," *Manitoba Law Journal* 38, no. 2 (2015): 123–54.

40 Bud Robertson, "Pair of Rural Councillors in Westman Quit," *Winnipeg Free Press*, 15 April 2022, https://www.winnipegfreepress.com/local/2019/04/15/pair-of-rural-councillors-in-westman-quit.

41 Allan Dawson, "Farmers Fail to Rally to Tax Revolt Talk," *Manitoba Co-operator*, 20 October 2016, https://www.manitobacooperator.ca/news-opinion/news/local/manitoba-farmers-fail-to-rally-to-farmland-tax-revolt-talk/.

PART 4
Parties and Elections

CHAPTER 11

The Manitoba Progressive Conservatives

ROYCE KOOP

This chapter explores the Progressive Conservative (PC) Party of Manitoba from several perspectives. First, it provides a historical overview of the party's electoral and ideological record. Second, the chapter examines the leaders of the party in detail. As with most other parties in Canada, the party leader has always occupied an important and special place in the PC Party, and understanding the party requires understanding the personalities who have led it variously to both victory and defeat over the decades. This pattern of victory and defeat is then explored in an assessment of the party's organizational performance. This then leads into an assessment of the future of the party following the 2023 election loss.

The Progressive Conservative Party of Manitoba is an old party, having emerged and contested public office as an integrated organization with the federal Conservative Party in the 1800s. John Norquay, premier from 1878 to 1887, is considered the province's first Conservative premier, given his support for Conservative Prime Minister John A. Macdonald, but he did not lead a coherent party at the provincial level, and, indeed, many Conservatives opposed his premiership.[1] Norquay's defeat led to the party's first lengthy period on the Opposition benches. The party returned to power in 1899, led by Hugh John Macdonald, but Rodmond Roblin became leader and premier shortly thereafter and was re-elected in the 1903 election. As premier, Roblin oversaw an activist government that increased spending and government activity, including the creation of North America's first publicly owned telephone system. The growth of the provincial state under Roblin hit a snag when questions were raised about possible fraud in the construction of the new legislative building. Roblin resigned as leader and the party was defeated in the subsequent 1915 election. The party then entered its second lengthy period in the Opposition—what Christopher Adams refers to as the "Winter Years."[2] While Conservative members joined John Bracken's coalition government in this period, it is likely this only heightened the loss of identity and organizational decay faced by the party.[3]

Leaders of the party through its long winter were oriented towards the PCs' rural base and largely failed to break through in Winnipeg. Members at the 1946 annual conference formally adopted the federal party's new name—the Progressive Conservative Party—and updated the party's policies to emphasize greater government activity, including a boost to old-age pensions. But these changes did not help the party return to power until after the selection of a new leader: Duff Roblin, who was selected as leader in 1954. The grandson of Rodmond Roblin, the new leader rode the PC wave created by federal PC leader John Diefenbaker, and Roblin finally brought the party back to power in the 1958 provincial election. The party's new youthful and comparably urbane leader led it to winning several Winnipeg seats.

In office, Roblin oversaw an activist government and an expansion of the provincial state in Manitoba. Spending increased significantly and the provincial government shepherded massively expanded investments in health, education, and social services. The government also spent on infrastructure and capital projects. Under Roblin, the party went on to win three more times, in the 1959, 1962, and 1966 elections. Following Roblin's departure as premier in 1967, he was replaced by Walter Weir, who, Adams argues, "signaled a shift back to the more rurally based 'small government, low tax' orientation of the party."[4] Despite some promising polls, Weir went down to defeat and the Progressive Conservatives' time in government came to an end.

The party's time out of office saw conflict between the conservative, rural faction of the party and the more pragmatic urban faction. Weir was replaced by the Winnipeg MLA (Member of the Legislative Assembly) and former minister Sidney Spivak. The new leader was an uncomfortable fit in a party that was still dominated by rural perspectives, and he lost in the 1973 election. Spivak's hold on the party was challenged in a bitter leadership battle with Sterling Lyon, with Lyon emerging as the new leader in 1975. An urban MLA, Lyon was nevertheless on the right-wing side of the party, and was an adherent to the Thatcherite consensus that, contra Duff Roblin, government spending and interventions in the economy should be minimized. With this new coalition of perspectives, Lyon went on to win a resounding majority government in 1977 based on promises of austerity, lower taxes, and pro-business policies. Lyon's government lasted only one term with the New Democratic Party (NDP) winning a majority victory in the 1981 election.

The PCs would return to power in 1988 under the leadership of Gary Filmon, another leader who hailed from Winnipeg. Filmon, upon becoming leader, hoped to put a moderate stamp on the party, claiming that "the vast majority of Manitobans are at the centre of the political spectrum."[5] Both prior to winning and once in office, Filmon struggled to maintain the Tory coalition between rural and urban MLAs and activists, and between ideological conservatives and those who wanted Filmon to govern in the centrist manner he had promised in the prior leadership contest. In a minority government, Filmon succeeded in balancing competing pressures: his first budget, for example, featured increased spending on health and community services but also the abolition of the payroll tax. The PC campaign played up their leader's profile, and Filmon won a majority government in 1990 based on both his policies and his enhanced profile on the national stage during constitutional negotiations surrounding the Meech Lake Accord.

The provincial PCs were aware that their party's "brand" was tarnished by Brian Mulroney and his federal PCs. A new force across the western provinces was Preston Manning and his Reform Party, which succeeded to win seats in many parts of Manitoba in the 1993 federal election. Furthermore, despite Mulroney's departure from federal politics, the 1993 federal election decimated the PC government by reducing it to two seats in the House of Commons. An added problem for the PCs in Manitoba was a downturn in the province's economic conditions and changes in the mid-1990s to the amount transferred from the federal to the Manitoba government. This forced Filmon into introducing cutbacks across several government sectors, including health and education. Filmon won re-election in 1995 despite this, once again by emphasizing the "Team Filmon" label and distancing the provincial party from their unpopular federal counterparts.

The party's defeat in the 1999 election was both a regular alteration in power and a result of short-term factors. The party suffered because of a scandal related to electoral skullduggery and because of economic conditions. The defeat was not substantial, but the PCs lost several Winnipeg seats that had been key to their previous victories. The party would remain out of power—with different leaders employing different unsuccessful strategies—until Brian Pallister finally led it back into public office in the 2016 election.

What this brief overview of the historical development of the Manitoba PC Party illustrates is a multi-dimensionality that has shifted but remained remarkably resilient over several decades. From an ideological perspective: the party contains a range of opinions from the Red Toryism of Duff Roblin to the conservatism of several leaders. Even the nature of the dominant conservatism within the party has shifted from the old-fashioned establishment conservatism of Walter Weir to the ideological, austerity-minded neo-liberalism of Sterling Lyon and, to a lesser extent, Gary Filmon. This tension has remained in the party over time and across its various leaders, and tracing which of its ideological factions is ascendent is a useful way to understand the electoral appeals and behaviour of the party.

From a geographic perspective: ideological traditions have been associated with different regions, with the right-wingers tending to hail from the countryside and more pragmatic centrists emerging from Winnipeg. Sometimes those divisions in the party have clearly aligned, with, for example, the countryside as the home of the harder-edged conservatism that has seemed to put the party at a disadvantage. But at other times, region and ideology have come at least partially unglued. And the importance of suburban Winnipeg has become clearer over time, with the interests of these communities sometimes aligning with those of rural Manitoba and at other times with the more NDP-friendly areas of inner-city Winnipeg.

Multi-dimensionality in the Manitoba PC Party also manifests itself in terms of its organization. Like all parties, the Manitoba PC Party has multiple sites of power that complement and conflict with one another: the leader, the caucus, the constituency organizations, the membership, and activists. Of these, the most important in the Manitoba PC Party is the leader. Also, recent events demonstrate the importance of the caucus as a site of power within the party. The comparably sleek and adaptable organization evolved by the PCs has likely given it an electoral advantage over the more organizationally dense and complex NDP.

Federalism also adds some complexity to the party. While long since organizationally distinct from the federal Conservative Party, the PC Party shares common members, activists, and elites. In some cases, such as with former Conservative Member of Parliament (MP) Candice Bergen, movement between the federal and provincial parties can be seamless.

What is remarkable is how understanding the Manitoba PC Party as a multi-dimensional party—one with predictable factions of belief spread across both geographic and organizational locations—helps us to better understand the party over such a long period of time, despite widespread changes in the sociological and technological environments within which the party competes for power. The following sections use this as a framework to understand the party from the mid-2000s to the present.

Leaders and Premiers

Leaders are of great importance in Canadian political parties. To differing degrees between parties, leaders are given substantial leeway to make their priorities and concerns also those of their parties. Parties can often become synonymous with their leaders, and an important strength or liability. Once in power, premiers exercise even more substantial power over their parties through discipline of the party caucus and cabinet, and the perks of office can be used to keep the party in line. While candidate nomination is traditionally a right given to local party members, leaders and the party bureaucracy can and do sometimes interfere in these local processes. All these things are true in the Manitoba PC Party, and so the roles of leaders and premiers in any consideration of the party is important.

Hugh McFadyen was selected as leader of the PC Party in 2006 and was the last leader of the party's time on the Opposition benches before Pallister took the party back to power in 2016. McFadyen was a consummate political insider in Manitoba: he served as Filmon's principal secretary; was the Manitoba chair of Belinda Stronach's campaign to become leader of the Conservative Party of Canada in 2004; was the campaign manager for Sam Katz's mayoral campaign in the City of Winnipeg in 2004; and subsequently became a senior political advisor to Katz. McFadyen secured the nomination for the safe Tory seat of Fort Whyte and was soon mentioned as a potential successor to leader Stuart Murray, who resigned in 2005.

McFadyen was one of three candidates in the 2006 leadership race, the others being MLA Ron Schuler and former Neepawa mayor Ken Waddell. The race was conducted under a new one-member-one-vote (OMOV) selection system that would allow party members and activists to have a say in who the next leader would be. McFadyen was quickly seen as the favourite in the race and amassed endorsements and support from throughout the party establishment. As Kelly Saunders notes, McFadyen was seen as a "golden boy" who could potentially rescue the party from its long period in opposition.[6] McFadyen steered clear of ideological pitfalls and focused on unifying Tory issues, with special emphasis on his perceived ability to beat the NDP. "New day, winning day, join the winning way today," was his awkward campaign slogan. When the votes were finally counted, McFadyen had scored an overwhelming victory with 67 percent of the votes cast.

McFadyen was seen to have a shot at winning the next provincial election against an NDP government that was getting quite "long in the tooth," but the PCs flubbed the opportunity. McFadyen ran a middle-of-the-road, optimistic campaign, adopting "Together We Can" as a campaign slogan. But McFadyen and the party's thin policy platform meant the party was vulnerable to attacks from the NDP and indeed seemed to not be particularly committed to its own ideas. Premier Gary Doer was able to effectively capture the momentum of the campaign. The result was an historic win in 2007 for the NDP. Despite successfully holding on to the leadership of the party and introducing organizational reforms to modernize the PCs, McFadyen once again went down to defeat in the subsequent 2011 election. McFadyen once again had run a middle-of-the-road, optimistic campaign. But he was unable to effectively hold the NDP and its leader accountable for a series of scandals and missteps, and the PCs were assailed by the NDP and its allies for the PCs' allegedly far-right hidden agenda that McFadyen hoped to impose on Manitobans if elected. McFadyen, despite a relatively innocuous campaign platform, was unable to counter this attack, and resigned after the election result.

McFadyen was well travelled in Manitoba politics, was young, modern, professional, and impeccably moderate in his presentation to Manitoba voters. Despite this, he lost in two elections against a long-time NDP government. Further, the party suffered losses in places like the suburban Winnipeg seats it needed if it ever hoped to form a government. McFadyen's losses threw many in the party into a state of sorrow. These losses also called into question the wisdom that, to win, the party simply needed to present a more moderate, urban face to challenge the NDP on its centrist, Winnipeg turf. McFadyen seemed to have done so but had still not prevailed. What was the way forward for the PCs?

Ultimately, the party's next leader, Brian Pallister, provided that way forward. Like McFadyen, Pallister was a well-travelled and -connected politician. But there were important ideological and stylistic differences between these two men. Unlike McFadyen, Pallister already had substantial experience as an elected official before becoming leader. Pallister previously served as an MLA and minister in Filmon's government as well as an MP. Pallister had experience both winning and losing while running for public office. Indeed, he had staged a run for the leadership of the federal Progressive Conservative Party in 1998 but was defeated by former prime minister Joe Clark.

But whereas McFadyen was a polished and disciplined politician firmly rooted in the urban politics of Winnipeg—an image consultant's dream come true—Pallister maintained a degree of folksiness from his origins as a rural politician hailing from Portage la Prairie. His plain-spoken manner sometimes landed Pallister in hot water, and this would be accentuated upon his return to Manitoba politics; in 2013, for example, Pallister flubbed when he jokingly wished atheist "infidels" a merry Christmas.[7] In other situations, Pallister wore his heart on his sleeve, especially when talking about his family and his childhood struggles, over which he often teared up.

In selecting Pallister as leader, the party seemed to be diverging sharply from the path set out by McFadyen. But the race was hardly competitive: Pallister was acclaimed in July 2012 when no other candidates entered the leadership race. In part, this reflected despondency in the party after yet another unexpected defeat at the hands of the NDP. But Pallister's supporters had also worked behind the scenes to discourage potential challengers and short-circuit their campaigns. The result was that Pallister secured the leadership, but the party was deprived of a potentially exciting leadership race that could have drawn attention and driven new memberships and contributions to the party.

As leader, Pallister took up his new role in the Legislative Assembly by assailing Greg Selinger's faltering government. More importantly, he pursued an aggressive program of intra-party reform within the party, pushing for organizational change, growth, and renewal at the constituency level to better prepare the party for an upcoming provincial election. In particular, the party developed a modern and effective fundraising strategy and machine in this period. Pallister and those around him also focused on individual constituencies, encouraging the development of constituency associations across the province that could engage local Tories, organize competitive nomination races, and support the election of PC candidates. Pallister directly involved himself in these efforts, often travelling to constituencies to support local PC activists. Eventually, Pallister's organizational spadework in the constituencies would pay off.

By 2016, Selinger had endured a caucus rebellion and led a badly fractured NDP into the provincial election campaign. Ahead in the polls, Pallister and his candidates ran a disciplined front-runner campaign, keeping the focus squarely on NDP incompetence in office and on Selinger's broken promise to not raise the PST. Indeed, the party's straightforward campaign theme was focused on the NDP: "broken trust, broken government." The PC themes in the campaign were somewhat bland; the centrepiece promise to reduce the PST by 1 percent was designed to keep attention focused on Selinger's broken promise.[8] The party made concerted efforts to recruit women and members of visible minority communities to run in competitive seats.[9] Pallister's campaign was disciplined and Pallister himself withstood personal attacks from NDP candidates, refusing to be baited over his past socially conservative statements. The PC leader, who was known to shoot from the hip, was listening to his advisors and so was remarkably, surprisingly disciplined throughout the campaign, sticking to the campaign's pre-selected themes. The party had benefited from organizational improvements under the new leader.

On election day, Pallister won the largest majority in Manitoba history: forty out of fifty-seven seats. Most importantly, Pallister's big win saw the party clinch a swath of suburban seats across Winnipeg, especially south Winnipeg, that would prove crucial to the party's future success. This was in addition to the expected solid performance for the party outside Winnipeg.

Pallister ran a fiscally conservative government that cut taxes, reduced spending across the board, reduced the deficit, and began to pay down the debt. The government cut costs in part by reducing the overall size of the public service, and soon came into conflict with public sector unions. This conflict would grow in magnitude over Pallister's time in office. The government also pursued major reforms of the province's health sector, including a recommended plan to shut down several emergency rooms in Winnipeg and replace them with "urgent care" centres.

Pallister prided himself on not shying away from difficult problems and on getting results no matter the circumstances, and his own popularity and that of his party were dented as a result. Nevertheless, in the 2019 election (which was called one year prior to the set date election of 3 October 2020), Pallister cruised to re-election with another impressive majority, dropping only two seats from his previous result in 2016. While the party moderated its fiscally conservative reputation with promises to boost health care spending and child-care spaces, the PCs also effectively cast doubts on NDP leader Wabanakwut "Wab" Kinew's personal character and abilities.[10] In any case, the NDP was still rebuilding from its disastrous conclusion in government.[11] Pallister was not particularly well liked by Manitobans, but he had nevertheless scored a significant victory. And, while there were some warning signs, the PCs had once again performed well across suburban Winnipeg.[12]

In his second term, Pallister faced a rejuvenated NDP and a more restive provincial society that provided stronger opposition to Tory cuts and reform programs. The government, for example, confronted a significant and sustained campaign opposed to legislation designed to reform the administration of public-school districts through the abolition of elected boards (the legislation was ultimately never passed). The Pallister government also struggled with its response to the COVID-19 pandemic, with the leader making matters worse by insisting on making himself the public face of the government's pandemic response, holding frequent press conferences where his performances were sometimes praised but oftentimes panned.

Pallister was particularly poorly prepared to grapple with an increase in protests and activism in support of Indigenous reconciliation and resurgence. Following protests in front of the legislative building that saw a statue of Queen Victoria vandalized, the premier delivered a tone-deaf lecture to reporters in which he seemed to defend European colonizers. Pallister's comments were widely criticized, including indirectly by members of his own caucus. Events came to a crisis point when Minister of Indigenous and Northern Relations Eileen Clarke left the cabinet over the premier's behaviour regarding Indigenous issues. The debacle, together with Pallister's low approval ratings, convinced many members of the caucus that the leader had become a millstone around the neck of the party and following a caucus meeting in Brandon, in which the premier was told he no longer had the confidence of his caucus, Pallister announced he would not seek re-election. In the fall of 2021, he resigned as premier and leader.[13]

Pallister had led the PC Party to two impressive majority governments after the party had spent a long period in the political wilderness. Nevertheless, figures in the PC Party had become spooked, in the final days of Pallister's time as leader, by both the increasing NDP fortunes and low polling numbers for their party. There was a sense in the party that it was headed for defeat and a course correction was needed.

A leadership race following Pallister's resignation could provide that opportunity. However, those same figures in the party were skittish about the possibility of an outsider candidate who could rally enough support and new members to crash the party and take the leadership. As a result, early on in the race, there was significant elite coalescing around one establishment candidate: Tuxedo MLA and long-serving cabinet minister Heather Stefanson. A quick campaign was scheduled by party brass in such a way that was seen to benefit Stefanson, especially since the timing made it very difficult for any MPs (particularly for the federal party's deputy leader, Candice Bergen, who was seen as a viable candidate) to effectively contest the leadership while running in their own seat during the 2021 federal election. On the day of her announcement, Stefanson had recruited almost two dozen MLAs who showed up to support her leadership bid. The message was clearly that Stefanson had very substantial support in the party, and that the party appeared to be coalescing around her candidacy for leader. In this way, Stefanson's rise to power closely resembled McFadyen's, who also enjoyed substantial institutional support in the party but who struggled to connect with voters.

Like Pallister, Stefanson brought long-standing political experience and strong support to the role of leader. She first entered the legislature in 2000, replacing Filmon as the MLA for Tuxedo. Unlike many other MLAs, Stefanson played an active role in party building while the PCs were in opposition, for example by visiting constituency association meetings and building her own profile in the party along the way. Under Pallister, Stefanson served in high-profile cabinet portfolios and as deputy premier. Stefanson was not irascible in the same way as Pallister, and was well liked in the party caucus, where Pallister could sometimes be seen as a distant, stern authority figure.

Stefanson was a disciplined urban politician with deep connections within the party. She did not suffer from Pallister's proclivity to shoot from the hip but was also not particularly charismatic. Any rural, folksy populism that was a part of Pallister's style was not present in the new leader. To her benefit, Stefanson promised to change the government's tone from that of the easily irritated Pallister.

While Stefanson's elite support in the PC Party proved invaluable, she faced a formidable opponent for the party leadership in previous Conservative MP Shelly Glover. The former Winnipeg police officer was incensed at rules imposed by party brass on the leadership race that seemed to favour Stefanson's campaign. In contrast to Stefanson, Glover was an earthy, right-wing populist, decrying the PC Party for drifting too far from the party grassroots and promising to reconnect if she was elected as leader. Glover drew on support from new members, particularly people in rural Manitoba concerned with vaccine mandates and opposed to the government as a result. In contrast, Stefanson's advantage was organizational: she drew on deep experience and connections with the party to sign up new members and bring existing members on-board. Stefanson's very broad support in the caucus meant she could count on a network of people in constituencies across the province to recruit new members and turn out the vote.

The result was a quick but eventful and highly competitive leadership race. Despite her institutional advantages, Stefanson won with only a small margin of victory over Glover: 51.1 percent to Glover's 48.9

percent. The former MP and her supporters were convinced there had been fraud in the counting of ballots and so went to court to challenge the result. Stefanson and the party eventually successfully defended themselves from this challenge, but the close margin and Glover's reaction tainted Stefanson's victory. Glover's accusation that the party establishment had closed ranks around Stefanson and subsequently put its thumb on the scale for her leadership campaign stung the new leader.

Once in office, Stefanson confronted the challenge of distinguishing herself from her unpopular predecessor. This task was made more difficult by her reputation as an establishment insider who had served as Pallister's deputy premier. Ultimately, Stefanson was quick to make personnel and policy changes that would help to close the book on Pallister's time in government. For example: Stefanson dismissed David McLaughlin, the Clerk of the Executive Council and former PC campaign manager who was seen to be close to Pallister.

But Stefanson did not successfully chart a policy course that was significantly different from Pallister's. Early on, she drew attention for loosening COVID-19 restrictions and justifying doing so by noting that "it's up to Manitobans to look after themselves."[14] And she held the line on spending on such portfolios as health care up until the months leading to the 2023 provincial election, in which Stefanson approved significant new spending. Despite the hope that Stefanson could rebrand the PC Party after Pallister's final days in power, both she and her party remained low in the polls.

Party and Performance

This discussion of leaders and policy has focused on the Manitoba PC Party since Hugh McFadyen assumed the leadership of the party. But what can be said of the long-term performance of the PC Party? Does Manitoba have a naturally governing party and, if so, is it the Tories?

The Conservatives are an old party in Manitoba, and in fact governed under the title from 1879 to 1888 and again from 1899 to 1915. But the modern pattern of electoral competition in Manitoba commenced following a period of realignment in 1958, the election when Duff Roblin became premier. When the party eventually lost power in the 1969 election, it would lose to the NDP, not the Liberals, ushering in a new system characterized by alteration of power between the PCs and the NDP.

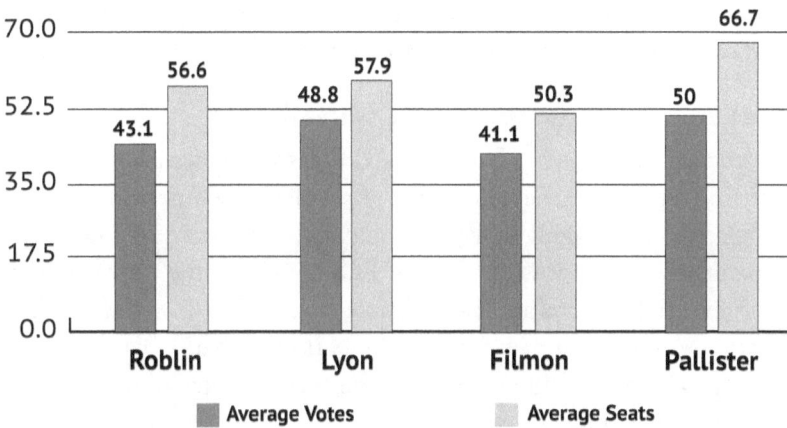

Figure 11.1. Average Vote and Seat Shares by Premier (figures compiled by author from data maintained by Elections Manitoba).

The PC Party has won ten of the nineteen elections held since (and including) the 1958 election, which makes it a somewhat electorally more successful party than the NDP/CCF (Co-operative Commonwealth Federation). Has support for the party changed over time? The story for most old parties in developed democracies is one of long-term secular decline in popular support; this is not so for the PC Party of Manitoba. Figure 11.1 illustrates the average vote and seat shares for the PC leaders in their winning elections.

The vote shares that PC leaders receive have not shifted significantly over the past half-century: Roblin's vote share averaged 43.1 percent across his four winning elections, whereas Filmon's were slightly lower and Pallister's were higher. The difference in seat shares is starker: whereas Roblin and Lyon led relatively safe governments, Filmon's average was on the edge. In contrast, Pallister's majority governments were very safe. The figure also illustrates how Manitoba's electoral system has provided a bonus to the PC Party: Pallister received a whopping average seat bonus of 17 percent. In part, this reflected his ability to score seats in suburban Winnipeg in both elections in which he led the party.

Manitoba party politics has been stable for some time featuring regular shifts in power between the PCs and the NDP, with the Liberal Party winning small and varying numbers of seats in each election.

While the PCs under Heather Stefanson lost the 2023 provincial election, even this was not a stunning loss, as the party won 41.9 percent of the popular vote, less than four points below the winning NDP.

The Future of the Progressive Conservatives

When the Manitoba PC Party showed Pallister the door, it was ostensibly in response to the view that the premier's own personal lack of popularity was dragging down the popularity of the party, and he would make it next to impossible for the PCs to win in the next election. The new leader therefore had a simple task: to break with Pallister's legacy and provide a new face for the party that had a better chance of keeping the party in power, or at the very least avoiding a disaster in the next election.

Stefanson was seen as a candidate who could potentially provide a break with the Pallister legacy, though not someone who would upend the policy agenda of the previous premier. But Stefanson also benefited from strong if not unanimous support from the party establishment. In retrospect, it seems risible that Stefanson—Pallister's deputy premier and a high-profile cabinet minister in both his governments—would be able to provide much of a break from the past. But Stefanson was also reliable and, perhaps most importantly, a known quantity who worked well with others in the party and enjoyed substantial support where it mattered: in the party caucus. While Glover may have provided a clearer break from Pallister's time in government, she was seen to be unpredictable, and it was not clear whether she would work well with others in the party. Indeed, Stefanson played this up in the leadership campaign, at one point claiming Glover would force incumbent MLAs to compete in contested nomination contests.[15] Glover's subsequent legal challenge of the results seemed to confirm that she was not a team player.

There were initial signs that Stefanson would successfully break from Pallister's time in office. The day she announced her candidacy, with most of the PC caucus standing behind her, for example, Stefanson announced that the government's controversial education bill, Bill 64, would be withdrawn. More importantly, Stefanson worked to change the tone of governing in Manitoba, moving from Pallister's seemingly irascible approach to one characterized by greater consensus and conciliation. That approach bore fruit, as the premier improved relationships with the federal government, the government of Winnipeg, and Indigenous organizations. Stefanson has overseen new agreements on child care, transit, infrastructure, and the Hudson Bay Railway.[16]

But, contrary to the party's hopes, Stefanson did not successfully provide a boost to the PC Party's standing in the polls. Indeed, she remained the country's least-popular premier through the first half of 2022 and remained in this position a year after winning the leadership of the party.[17] In part, this reflected some early fumbles as Stefanson adjusted to the new role of leader. In early 2022, for example, Stefanson awkwardly responded to an NDP question about the death of a COVID-19 patient by taking the opportunity to congratulate her son's hockey team before getting to addressing the tragedy, which was widely viewed as insensitive and for which the premier subsequently apologized.[18] Problems in the health care sector continued to dog the premier even after the COVID-19 pandemic waned, and wait times in the province's emergency and urgent care wards remained stubbornly high.

Nevertheless, Stefanson tried in this period to position herself for the coming provincial elections. She signalled that she was open to a pivot to the centre by announcing that the provincial minimum wage would increase[19] and that the government would invest substantial new funding in school lunch programs.[20] Indeed, Stefanson increased program spending substantially in the lead-up to the 2023 election campaign. At the same time, the new premier indicated she would take a tough-on-crime approach in the next campaign, following a wave of violent assaults in Winnipeg.[21]

This manoeuvring aside, the 2023 PC election campaign ultimately seemed to represent the triumph of the right-wing faction of the party. Indeed, the party seemed to take a turn to the populist right that was also characterizing other right-wing parties in Canada and North America.[22] The PCs focused on tax cuts and unveiled a new set of promises to protect "parental rights" in public education.[23] The campaign took a notable turn when the party began trumpeting Stefanson's decision to not fund a search of the Prairie Green landfill for the remains of four murdered Indigenous women.[24] The PC campaign released advertisements touting Stefanson's decision to "stand firm" on her decision despite public pressure to change her mind.

The campaign was designed to consolidate support for the party to avoid a crushing defeat. In part, the campaign succeeded: the party scored 41.9 percent of the vote and held onto twenty-two seats. But, in losing to Wab Kinew's NDP, the PCs lost all but three seats in the city of Winnipeg. Even formerly rock-solid suburban Winnipeg seats like Lagimodiere and Waverley in the South swung to the NDP, though with narrow margins.

The result is that the PC caucus is now dominated by rural MLAs, and this will have consequences for how the party positions itself for the next election. If the PC Party must now win as a rural-suburban coalition, then attention must now focus on how to rebuild support in the suburbs. The party will also have to grapple with the fallout of its divisive 2023 campaign, which immediately drew heated criticism from within the party itself following the loss.[25]

The history of the PC Party of Manitoba is one of varying factions—urban versus rural, right wing versus Red Tory—rising and falling inversely to one another. Both Pallister and Stefanson were ideological conservatives who seemed to have more in common with Walter Weir than with Duff Roblin, and the 2023 campaign called into question the overall moderation of the party. The biggest question facing the party is which faction the next leader will hail from, and what consequences this will have for the future of the PC Party.

Notes

1. Christopher Adams, *Politics in Manitoba: Parties, Leaders, and Voters* (Winnipeg: University of Manitoba Press, 2008), 24–25.
2. Ibid., 29.
3. Murray Donnelly, *The Government of Manitoba* (Toronto: University of Toronto Press, 1963), 48.
4. Adams, *Politics in Manitoba*, 40.
5. Ibid., 47.
6. Kelly Saunders, "Manitoba's Progressive Conservative Party: A 'Great Renewal' or Continued Disarray?" in *Manitoba Politics and Government*, ed. Paul G. Thomas and Curtis Brown (Winnipeg: University of Manitoba Press, 2010), 114.
7. Lara Schroeder, "Manitoba Conservative Leader Offers Holiday Greetings to 'Infidel Atheists,'" *Global News*, 3 December 2013, https://globalnews.ca/news/1003282/watch-pallister-video-sparks-ire-ridicule/.

8   Kelly Saunders, "Riding the Blue Wave: Brian Pallister and the Progressive Conservative Victory," in *Understanding the Manitoba Election 2016: Campaigns, Participation, Issues, Place*, ed. Karine Levasseur, Andrea Rounce, Barry Ferguson, and Royce Koop (Winnipeg: University of Manitoba Press, 2016), 11.

9   Royce Koop, "Nominations and Candidates in the 2016 Manitoba Election," in *Understanding the Manitoba Election 2016: Campaigns, Participation, Issues, Place*, ed. Karine Levasseur, Andrea Rounce, Barry Ferguson, and Royce Koop (Winnipeg: University of Manitoba Press, 2016), 21.

10 See Christopher Adams, "The Manitoba New Democratic Party," in this volume.

11 Kelly Saunders, "The Progressive Conservatives," in *Understanding the Manitoba Election 2019: Campaigns, Participation, and Issues*, ed. Royce Koop, Barry Ferguson, Karine Levasseur, Andrea Rounce, and Kiera Ladner (Winnipeg: University of Manitoba Press, 2019), 8.

12 Barry Ferguson and Royce Koop, "Snap Election, Flat Campaign, Clear Results," in *Understanding the Manitoba Election 2019: Campaigns, Participation, and Issues*, ed. Royce Koop, Barry Ferguson, Karine Levasseur, Andrea Rounce, and Kiera Ladner (Winnipeg: University of Manitoba Press, 2019), 40.

13 Deveryn Ross, "Mis-timed Mutiny Created PC Predicament," *Winnipeg Free Press*, 9 August 2022, https://www.winnipegfreepress.com/opinion/analysis/2022/08/09/mis-timed-mutiny-created-pc-predicament.

14 Dylan Robertson and Carol Sanders, "'It's Up to Manitobans to Look after Themselves': Premier," *Winnipeg Free Press*, 12 January 2022, https://www.winnipegfreepress.com/breakingnews/2022/01/12/everyone-will-likely-be-exposed-to-the-virus-manitobans-warned.

15 Bartley Kives, "PC Leadership Candidate Heather Stefanson Accuses Rival of Threatening to Defeat or Fire Sitting MLAs," *CBC News*, 28 September 2021, https://www.cbc.ca/news/canada/manitoba/stefanson-glover-forum-leader-pcs-manitoba-wfpcbc-cbc-1.6193005.

16 Colin Slark, "Tories Work to Regain Ground After Pallister," *Brandon Sun*, 11 August 2022, https://www.brandonsun.com/local/2022/08/11/tories-work-to-regain-ground-after-pallister.

17 Kevin Rollason, "Stefanson Dogged by Low Popularity," *Winnipeg Free Press*, 14 June 2022, https://www.winnipegfreepress.com/breakingnews/2022/06/14/stefanson-dogged-by-low-popularity.

18 Ian Froese, "Premier Apologizes for Boasting of Son's Hockey Success When Asked about Patient's Death," *CBC News*, 17 March 2022, https://www.cbc.ca/news/canada/manitoba/manitoba-premier-hockey-accomplishment-patient-transfer-death-1.6389008.

19 Tom Brodbeck, "Tories Find Middle Ground with Minimum-Wage Compromise," *Winnipeg Free Press*, 18 August 2022, https://www.winnipegfreepress.com/local/2022/08/18/tories-find-middle-ground-with-minimum-wage-compromise.

20 Judy Peters, "Province Injects $1.3 Million into School Meal Programs," *Steinbach Online*, 22 September 2022, https://steinbachonline.com/articles/province-injects-13-million-into-school-meal-programs.

21 Government of Manitoba, "Statement from Premier Stefanson on Unwavering Support for Winnipeg Police Officers," 12 July 2022, https://news.gov.mb.ca/news/?archive=&item=55460.

22 Brian Budd, "Maple-Glazed Populism: Political Opportunity Structures and Right-Wing Populist Ideology in Canada," *Journal of Canadian Studies* 55, no. 1 (Winter 2021): 152–76.

23 Cameron MacLean, "Manitoba PCs Promise Expanded Parental Rights in Schools If Re-elected," *CBC Manitoba*, 17 August 2023, https://www.cbc.ca/news/canada/manitoba/manitoba-pcs-promise-expanded-parental-rights-in-schools-if-re-elected-1.6939489.

24 Brittany Hobson and Steve Lambert, "Manitoba Progressive Conservatives 'Pulling Out Stops' with Attack Ads: Analyst," *CTV News*, 27 September 2023, https://winnipeg.ctvnews.ca/manitoba-progressive-conservatives-pulling-out-stops-with-attack-ads-analyst-1.6580449.

25 Steve Lambert, "Ads Opposing Landfill Search 'Deeply Regrettable,' Says Manitoba PC Cabinet Minister Who Lost Seat," *CBC News*, 4 October 2023, https://www.cbc.ca/news/canada/manitoba/tory-strategy-criticize-by-former-members-1.6986864.

CHAPTER 12

The Manitoba New Democratic Party

CHRISTOPHER ADAMS

Introduction

In its "Statement of Principle," the Manitoba New Democratic Party (NDP) reveals its commitment to social issues over economic issues: "Our society must change from one based on competition to one based on co-operation. We wish to create a society where individuals give according to their abilities and receive according to their needs."[1] Since the late 1960s, the NDP's core support has been in Manitoba's "two norths." The first north is Winnipeg's blue-collar North End, the urban core of the city historically populated by immigrants of non-British extraction and, in more recent decades, by Indigenous peoples. The North End has also served as an historical hotbed for Canadian labour politics. The second north is northern Manitoba, with its many Indigenous communities, public servants in health and education, and resource-sector workers. These two norths have served as a counterweight to the Progressive Conservatives (PCs) and their "two souths," which consist of 1) the fertile farmlands and small towns of southern Manitoba, and 2) middle- and upper-middle-class voters in the southern neighbourhoods of Winnipeg. Historically the two souths were populated by those more sympathetic to the interests of commerce and business, and of British extraction.[2]

Party History

The NDP's origins are located in Winnipeg's labour movement and date back to the early years of the last century. In 1900, Manitoba Labour Party candidate Arthur Puttee was elected in Winnipeg and sent to sit in the House of Commons.[3] He was the first MP (Member of Parliament) to be elected under a "labour" banner in Canada. It was a time in which Winnipeg's industry began expanding, with many left-wing political organizations emerging out of Winnipeg's North End. These ranged from those promoting evolutionary labour-oriented activities based on a British model rooted in Fabianism, to revolutionary parties inspired by eastern European and Russian Marxism. In 1919, many of these left-wing political forces, including organized labour, converged to trigger the Winnipeg General Strike.[4] In 1920, out of the strike's ashes arose the Independent Labour Party (ILP). It was modelled on the British Labour Party, which would soon form its first national government in the United Kingdom in 1924.

The ILP elected ten MLAs (Members of the Legislative Assembly) in the 1920 provincial election, sending them to what was then a fifty-five-seat assembly. Unfortunately for the party, this was its highwater mark, and it elected fewer members in subsequent elections.[5] In the meantime, one of Canada's most influential labour politicians was James Shaver Woodsworth, who had studied at the universities of Toronto and Oxford and, as a Methodist minister, served the needs of immigrants and poverty-stricken families through his All Peoples' Mission.[6] He left the ministry in 1918 due to the Methodist Church's support for the war, and became deeply involved in the 1919 General Strike. In the 1921 federal election, he successfully ran for the ILP in Winnipeg Centre.

A decade later, neither the Conservatives nor the Liberals appeared capable of handling the economic crisis of the Great Depression. While factories shut down and farmers lost their farms, many Canadians were looking for a radical solution. One response was the formation of the Co-operative Commonwealth Federation (CCF), which was founded in 1932 with the ILP's Woodsworth as its first national leader. The CCF was an amalgam of the ILP, radical farmers, Social Gospel proponents, and a group of academics known as the League for Social Reconstruction. Within Manitoba and at the provincial level, ILP candidates ran under the ILP-CCF banner in the 1936 provincial election, and as the CCF thereafter.[7]

Seymour James Farmer, an ardent ILP organizer who served briefly as mayor of Winnipeg from 1922 to 1923, became the provincial CCF's first leader. In 1940, while Canada was at war with Germany, Farmer joined Premier John Bracken's Liberal-Progressive wartime government coalition. As the province's minister of Labour, he was the first Canadian CCF politician to serve in a cabinet.[8] In 1942, Farmer withdrew from the coalition and resigned from cabinet. His party was asserting its independence at a time the CCF was making gains in public opinion across Canada. In the Ontario provincial election of 1943, the CCF won thirty-four of ninety seats. In the same year a national Gallup poll surprised many people by showing the party with a slight lead over both the Liberals and PCs. Might Canada be heading to a postwar labour-oriented government? Meanwhile in Manitoba, the CCF won three by-elections in 1943. These were in the provincial ridings of The Pas and Brandon and the federal riding of Selkirk. More significantly, Tommy Douglas's CCF won the 1944 Saskatchewan election, shocking many people across Canada.[9] The CCF supporters and activists were therefore looking forward to a postwar era in which the national party would seize power and initiate new social and economic programs. However, it would be Mackenzie King's Liberal Party that would initiate many of the programs advocated by the CCF and take the credit for expanding social programs and pensions in the postwar era.[10]

The CCF never regained momentum, either federally or provincially. Two factors worked against the party, with the first being Cold War politics. Anti-Soviet hysteria led voters to suspect any party associated with socialism. Both the Liberals and the PCs took advantage of this, and effectively painted the CCF as being a pro-Soviet communist party. With many Manitobans being of East European descent, and with families having fled their Soviet-dominated homelands, the CCF was particularly vulnerable to these attacks. The CCF was forced to distance itself from the Marxist left, so much so, that in 1949 the provincial CCF expelled two of its sitting MLAs for harbouring anti-NATO opinions.[11]

The second factor working against the CCF, with its reliance on urban labour, was an electoral system in Manitoba that overrepresented the rural voter by more than two to one. In 1952, for example, forty rural MLAs represented 224,083 voters, compared with Winnipeg's urban region, which elected only seventeen MLAs representing 228,280 voters.[12] This rural-urban imbalance was only slightly corrected in 1957 to a rural-urban ratio of 7:4 by legislation arising from recommendations of the newly established Electoral Divisions Boundary Commission.[13] The impact was slightly positive for the CCF. The party had won only five seats in the 1953 provincial election but then, following the redistricting, eleven seats in the 1958 election and ten in 1959. Meanwhile, the federal CCF was facing severe problems, losing official party status by winning a mere eight seats in the face of John Diefenbaker's PCs and their 1958 landslide election victory. As the 1960s approached, it was clear that both provincially and federally the CCF was going nowhere.

The "New" Party

Out of the national CCF's ashes in 1961 there emerged the New Democratic Party. More than a simple rebranding, the new party now had formal ties to the Canadian Labour Congress.[14] At the same time, as was its predecessor, the national party continued to be a federation of its provincial parties, with a reliance on their support for financing its national office and federal campaign.[15] (Fortunately for the national party, this changed with the Election Expenses Act in 1974, which provided public funding to federal parties.)[16] The provincial CCF under its leader Andrew Russell ("Russ") Paulley fell into step in adopting the party's new identity, becoming the Manitoba NDP, with formal ties to the Manitoba Federation of Labour and the Winnipeg District Labour Council.[17] To this day the provincial party continues to maintain formal links to organized labour, and, as discussed later in this chapter, the affiliated unions continue to play a major but not exclusive role in how the party chooses its leaders.

The newly launched Manitoba NDP had a disappointing campaign for the 1962 provincial election, fielding only thirty-nine candidates among the province's fifty-seven constituencies. It obtained only 15 percent of the vote and seven seats.[18] A continuing problem was the electoral system's overrepresentation of rural voters. However, this was largely corrected in 1968 when the province's electoral boundaries were further adjusted to better reflect the distribution of the population. With these changes, almost half of the fifty-seven seats were now located in Winnipeg and its suburban neighbourhoods.[19] This laid the groundwork for the party's 1969 breakthrough.

The 1969 Election

In 1967, Duff Roblin, the popular Progressive Conservative premier, left the provincial scene to seek the leadership of the federal PCs. (He was unsuccessful, losing to Robert Stanfield.) Walter Weir, a funeral director by trade, representing the rural riding of Minnedosa, was chosen by party delegates to serve in his place. (Roblin's and Weir's leadership are discussed by Royce Koop elsewhere in this volume.) In 1969, the Liberals chose Bobby Bend, a self-declared right-of-centre candidate representing the rural wing of that party.[20] With the selection of these two leaders, both the Liberals and the PCs had veered to the right, leaving space in the centre for the NDP. Another development was that with positive polling numbers and a budget surplus, Weir expressed confidence in his party's fortunes by calling an early election. In the meantime, following on a promise made to his party members at the 1968 NDP convention, Paulley stepped down as leader in 1969. This triggered a leadership race that overlapped with the early part of the provincial election. The leadership race, which was widely covered by the media, included televised debates featuring Edward Schreyer, the federal NDP MP for Selkirk, and Sidney Green, the MLA for the North End riding of Inkster. Schreyer won the leadership and proceeded immediately into the provincial campaign. Styled as a "Man for All Seasons,"[21] the youthful leader, aged thirty-three, appeared better suited to the times than the leaders of the two older parties. On election day, 25 June 1969, the Manitoba NDP scored a minority victory based on support from both urban and northern communities, including many First Nations.[22] It was fifty years to the day that the Winnipeg General Strike had ended,[23] and it was the first time that an NDP government was elected anywhere in Canada.

The 1969 election was more than just a breakthrough for labour and the political left; it signalled a long-term realignment of Manitoba's party system. Up until then the provincial party system resembled that of Ontario, with the PCs, Liberals, and NDP all contending for power. As Kelly Saunders writes in this volume, since 1969, and except for the period of 1988 to 1995, the Liberals have largely been sidelined by the ongoing battles between the PCs and the NDP, both of which, to varying degrees, have sought out swing voters and the middle class. Since then, the NDP has achieved many electoral victories, all of which were majorities: in 1973 under Schreyer; in 1981 and 1986 under Howard Pawley; and, after a long hiatus, electoral victories under Gary Doer in 1999, 2003, and 2007, followed by Greg Selinger in 2011. And, of course, most recently in 2023 with Wabanakwut "Wab" Kinew's NDP's majority victory.

Doer's Third Way Politics

The PCs like to paint the NDP as the "tax and spend" party. Leading up to the 1999 provincial election, Gary Doer, however, positioned the NDP as prudently pragmatic, startling many observers by supporting the governing PCs' balanced budget legislation. The NDP's 1999 platform rested on five pillars that were meant to appeal to the middle class: improving the health care system, making post-secondary studies affordable, promoting safer communities, balancing the budget, and collaborating with the business sector.[24] Polling data from the time reveal that support for the NDP came mainly from middle-class and middle-aged voters and women.[25] Despite attempts in the party to avoid using the term "Third Way" politics, in many particulars, Doer's approach was similar to that of the British Labour Party's leader Tony Blair, who campaigned on a platform that combined the "innovative energy" of private capital with community development.[26] From 1999 onward, Doer's NDP expanded its urban core of support into the southern parts of Winnipeg—ridings once thought to "belong" to the PCs—winning three consecutive majority victories in 1999, 2003, and 2007. The PCs in the meantime felt they could go nowhere in what they termed "Fortress Winnipeg" until Doer retired.[27] With some people suspecting backroom plotting between the PCs and their national Conservative counterparts, in 2009 Doer was appointed by Prime Minister Stephen Harper to serve as Canada's ambassador to the United States. He held this post until 2016.

After Doer's departure, in 2009 Greg Selinger was chosen by the party members as their new leader, thereby immediately becoming premier. An MLA since 1999 and a social worker educated at the London School of Economics, Selinger had served as Doer's long-time finance minister. It had been a good time to be a finance minister, with the economies of both Manitoba and North America on the upswing (at least until 2008) and at a time in which transfer payments from the federal government for social and health programs were increased. In

2011, Selinger led the NDP to yet another majority victory. However, the political waters soon turned stormy. Facing growing deficits, in 2013, Selinger's government increased the provincial sales tax from 7 to 8 percent. It was seen as a mishandled decision with poor communications both internally and externally.[28] In 2014, five cabinet ministers—termed by the media as the "gang of five"—left cabinet, citing their unhappiness with the premier's performance and leadership style. In an unusual move to shore up his leadership, the premier asked the NDP party executive to schedule a leadership vote for the 2015 party convention. In the ensuing leadership race, Manitobans witnessed the strange sight of a sitting premier running for his own job against two contenders (Steve Ashton and Theresa Oswald). It took two ballots for the party's delegates to decide that the premier could remain as leader. This did nothing to increase the premier's popularity among the general public, with a December provincial poll showing support for the NDP having declined to third place behind the Liberals.[29] Fortunately for the NDP, as discussed by Kelly Saunders elsewhere in this volume, the Liberals were unable to translate this support into seats during the 2016 provincial election. Regardless, on election day, 19 April 2016, the long-governing NDP was smashed by Brian Pallister's PCs, leaving it with only fourteen seats in the fifty-seven-seat assembly.[30] On that same evening, Selinger stepped down as party leader.

Party Structure and Leadership Selection

The Manitoba NDP is governed by its Provincial Council.[31] This consists of the Provincial Executive, which is a large group consisting of the party leader, party president, six regional vice-presidents, the treasurer, the provincial secretary (who serves as the chief administrative officer), ten members at large, two caucus members, and the chair of the Status of Women, Gender Equity, and Gender Diversity Committee. In addition to the provincial executive, the provincial council includes two individuals from each constituency association (the president and another member), three representatives of the Manitoba Youth New Democrats (MYND), five affiliated union members, Manitoba's Federal Council party members, and the chairs of the standing committees.

Party conventions are centrally important to the party's business and in selecting its leaders. Each year the NDP holds a Provincial Convention, which, according to the party's constitution, is deemed to be "the supreme governing body of the Provincial Party." In addition to the annual convention, a "special" provincial convention is held by a decision of the provincial council or on request by a majority of constituency associations. The party's constitution outlines the rules for electing a leader at a party convention. Unlike the federal NDP,[32] as well as most other parties, including the provincial PCs and Liberals, which currently choose their leaders by using a one-member-one-vote (OMOV) system, the Manitoba NDP continues to use the more traditional system of having convention delegates choose their leader.[33] There are four types of delegates at a Manitoba NDP leadership convention, with each representing a major component of the party. First, there are those representing constituency associations. Second, there are those from the affiliated labour groups. Third and fourth are the youth delegates from the MYND, and those who are termed "automatic delegates," consisting of members of the provincial council, MLAs, and MPs. Overall, the number of constituency delegates far outweighs those of the other three groups. For example, at the 2015 leadership convention at which Selinger was re-elected to remain as party leader (and premier), the breakdown of delegates was as follows: 1,212 from the constituencies, 296 labour group delegates, 77 MYND, and 157 automatic delegates.[34]

Wab Kinew

Wab Kinew is only the second Indigenous person to lead one of the Manitoba's major parties. One has to go back to the nineteenth century when John Norquay, a leader of mixed First Nations and European heritage, served as premier from 1878 to 1887.[35] Kinew is a member of the Onigaming First Nation community, which is located in northwestern Ontario, and the son of Chief Tobasonakwut Kinew. Unlike other party leaders, who often come to their positions as lawyers, business owners, or educators, or, in the case of the NDP, through the labour movement, Kinew's background is in the creative arts, which includes writing, hip hop music, and broadcasting. In addition to this eclectic professional background, Kinew also got into trouble in his early adulthood. It was during his first campaign to enter the legislature in 2016 for the riding of Fort Rouge as one of the bright lights in a troubled NDP campaign that the media reported on Kinew's anti-gay and misogynist tweets dating back to 2009 and 2010.[36] Other issues from his past have included two criminal charges stemming from impaired driving and assaulting a taxi driver. Prior to running for office, Kinew applied for and received a formal pardon.[37] A former partner also made an allegation of domestic assault dating back to 2003, which Kinew has always denied. The Crown stayed the charges.[38] Despite these controversies, Kinew won his riding against Liberal leader Rana Bokhari and PC candidate Audrey Gordon.

At the NDP leadership convention, which was held on 16 September 2017, one candidate challenged Kinew for the leadership. This was Steve Ashton, a veteran campaigner who had served in the cabinets of both Doer and Selinger. First elected to the assembly in 1981, he had twice run previously for the party leadership—in 2009 and 2015. He subsequently lost his Thompson seat—as did many others in his caucus—in the 2016 election. The loss to Kinew signalled what is likely the end to his long political career when he garnered 253 votes to Kinew's 728.[39]

Under Kinew's leadership, the NDP gained four seats in the 2019 campaign, which translated into a stronger Official Opposition of eighteen seats in the assembly. The NDP subsequently watched the PCs lurch from one crisis to the next. As discussed by Royce Koop in this volume, Premier Brian Pallister picked fights with the Indigenous community,[40] organized labour, and health care workers, including doctors and nurses. The PCs also reorganized the province's hospitals, which included shutting down some of the city's emergency departments. Added to this, and more disastrously, the government was largely seen as inept in handling the COVID-19 pandemic.[41] When Pallister stepped down in 2021, with the PCs low in the polls, his replacement, Heather Stefanson, proceeded to have her own problems with the media and in dealing with the ongoing pandemic, a nurses' shortage, and overcrowded hospital emergency departments, which was reflected in publicly released polls.[42] To counter this, Stefanson moved the party to the centre by putting forward major increases in social spending, including health care, with the spring budget prior to the fall 2023 provincial election. Kinew and his party's task was to appear competent in the assembly, make few gaffs, and prepare itself for the coming election. This approach proved successful. With Brian Topp as the party's campaign manager, the NDP ran a flawless campaign, promising to cut the provincial gasoline sales tax so long as inflation remained high, reopen hospital emergency rooms, address issues pertaining to Indigenous reconciliation, and correct other matters ailing the province. On 3 October 2023, the NDP elected thirty-four MLAs, sweeping almost all of Winnipeg, producing a majority victory with the PCs winning twenty-two seats and the Liberals reduced to one seat.[43]

Similar to the party's successes in 1999, 2003, 2007, and 2011, Kinew's NDP victory rested on a combination of support from its traditional bastions in the North and working-class Winnipeg, as well as successfully campaigning for middle-class votes across Winnipeg, most particularly among women. Polling data from Probe Research revealed in the spring of 2023 that only one out of every four women in seat-rich Winnipeg, compared with two out of five men, was willing to support the PCs.[44] In the end, the NDP was able to defeat a long-governing but unpopular PC government by appealing to mainstream voters.

Kinew's first cabinet reveals a party priority to elevate those who have been under-represented in the past, and includes individuals from Indigenous communities such as Kinew, Nahanni Fontaine, Bernadette Smith, and Ian Bushie. Kinew has assigned himself two portfolios: Intergovernmental Relations and International Affairs as well as Indigenous Reconciliation. Fontaine has the following three portfolios: Families, Accessibility, and Women and Gender Equity. Smith was tasked to handle Housing, Addictions and Homelessness, and Mental Health. Bushie was given Municipal and Northern Relations, and Indigenous Economic Development. The cabinet includes visible minorities as well, such as Uzoma Asagwara, the province's first non-binary MLA, who was appointed minister of Health, Seniors and Long-Term Care.[45]

While Kinew has gained national attention as Canada's first First Nations premier, he has garnered positive press locally due to his ease at such public events as a Chinese New Year's dinner or Winnipeg Jets playoff hockey games. Six months into his election, a photograph went viral featuring the premier by the highway—en route from a funeral and kneeling in his formal suit—changing someone else's tire.[46] At the time of writing, Kinew and his party's polling numbers are very high. Time will tell whether Kinew and his party will be able to translate the party's success into successive victories.

NDP Leaders and Premiers

Russell Paulley, Party Leader, 1961–1969

Edward Schreyer, Party Leader, 1969–1978; Premier, 1969–1977

Howard Pawley, Party Leader, 1979–1988; Premier, 1981–1988

Gary Doer, Party Leader, 1988–2009; Premier, 1999–2009

Greg Selinger, Party Leader, 2009–2016; Premier, 2009–2016

Wab Kinew, Party Leader, 2016; Premier, 2023–?

Notes

1. Manitoba NDP, "Manitoba New Democratic Party. Constitution, As amended by Convention 2022, As amended by Provincial Council 2024," https://assets.nationbuilder.com/mbndp/pages/15/attachments/original/1734306878/MBNDP_Constitution_2024_-_Updated_December_14__2024.pdf.
2. Christopher Adams, *Politics in Manitoba: Parties, Leaders, and Voters* (Winnipeg: University of Manitoba Press, 2008), 133–37.
3. A. Ross McCormack, *Reformers, Rebels, and Revolutionaries: The Western Canadian Radical Movement, 1899–1919* (Toronto: University of Toronto Press, 1977), 79.
4. It is beyond the scope of this chapter to discuss the Winnipeg Strike in any detail. Among the many works on this subject are the following two: David Bercuson, *Confrontation at Winnipeg: Labour, Industrial Relations, and the General Strike* (Montreal: McGill-Queen's University Press, 1974); and Reinhold Kramer and Tom Mitchell, *When the State Trembled: How A.J. Andrews and the Citizens' Committee Broke the Winnipeg General Strike* (Toronto: University of Toronto Press, 2010).
5. Results reported in this chapter for all elections up to 2007 are sourced from Appendix B in the present volume.
6. Adams, *Politics in Manitoba*, 102–3.
7. Nelson Wiseman, *Social Democracy in Manitoba: A History of the CCF/NDP* (Winnipeg: University of Manitoba Press, 1983), 21.
8. Adams, *Politics in Manitoba*, 106.
9. Ibid., 106–7.
10. John Duffy, *Fights of our Lives: Elections, Leadership, and the Making of Canada* (Toronto: HarperCollins, 2002), 167–68.
11. Wiseman, *Social Democracy*, 57–60. Of course, the purging of communists, or suspected communists, was happening across the continent, including such large American unions as the United Auto Workers. Amity Shlaes, *Great Society: A New History* (New York: HarperCollins, 2019), 64.

12 While Winnipeg had yet to amalgamate its suburbs, these numbers include Winnipeg and its surrounding areas.
13 Christopher Adams, "Electoral System," in *Encyclopedia of Manitoba*, ed. Ingeborg Boyens (Winnipeg: Great Plains Publications, 2007), 198.
14 Desmond Morton, *The New Democrats, 1961–1986: The Politics of Change* (Toronto: Copp Clark Pitman, 1986), 23–30; Walter D. Young, *The Anatomy of a Party: The National CCF, 1932–61* (Toronto: University of Toronto Press, 1969), 132–34.
15 Nelson Wiseman, "The Success of the New Democratic Party," in *Manitoba Politics and Government: Issues, Institutions, Transitions*, ed. Paul G. Thomas and Curtis Brown (Winnipeg: University of Manitoba, 2010), 74. See also David McGrane, *The New NDP: Moderation, Modernization, and Political Marketing* (Vancouver: UBC Press, 2019), 41–43.
16 F. Leslie Seidle and Khayyam Zev Paltiel, "Party Finance, the Election Expenses Act, and Campaign Spending in 1979 and 1980," in *Canada at the Polls, 1979 and 1980: A Study of the General Elections*, ed. Howard R. Penniman (Washington DC: American Enterprise Institute, 1981), 250–52.
17 Wiseman, *Social Democracy*, 100–102.
18 Adams, *Politics in Manitoba*, 112–13. The federal NDP fared equally poorly in the 1962 and 1963 federal elections, winning only nineteen and seventeen seats, respectively. These early campaigns were deemed by *Maclean's* political writer Blair Fraser as a "twice-proven failure." Blair Fraser, "Will the NDP Turn Parliament Upside Down?" *Maclean's* (24 July 1965): 38.
19 Adams, "Electoral System," 198; James McAllister, *The Government of Edward Schreyer: Democratic Socialism in Manitoba* (Montreal: McGill-Queen's University Press, 1984), 116.
20 Paul Barber, "Manitoba Liberals: Sliding into Third," in *Manitoba Politics and Government: Issues, Institutions, Transitions*, ed. Paul G. Thomas and Curtis Brown (Winnipeg: University of Manitoba, 2010), 140–41.
21 The contrast in styles is stark when one looks at two newspaper advertisements that appeared just prior to election day, with one featuring Weir and the other featuring Schreyer. Christopher Adams, "Realigning Elections in Manitoba," in *Manitoba Politics and Government: Issues, Institutions, Transitions*, ed. Paul G. Thomas and Curtis Brown (Winnipeg: University of Manitoba, 2010), 165.
22 Adams, "Realigning Elections," 166.
23 Wiseman, "The Success," 73.
24 Adams, "Realigning Elections," 168–69.
25 Adams, *Politics in Manitoba*, 127–28.
26 On Third Way politics, see Anthony Giddens, *The Third Way: A Renewal of Social Democracy* (London: Polity Press, 1998); and Tony Blair, *The Third Way: New Politics for the New Century* (London: Fabian Society, 1998). Regarding the backlash in the NDP for those promoting "Blairism" or Third Way politics, see also McGrane, *New NDP*, 26–27.
27 Adams, *Politics in Manitoba*, 62.
28 This account is largely based on first-hand experience, as this author was the political analyst for the CBC at the time the budget was announced.
29 Probe Research, Media Release, 26 December 2015, https://tinyurl.com/3nthycrs.
30 *CBC News*, "Brian Pallister's PCs Win Majority Government in Manitoba,"

20 April 2016, https://www.cbc.ca/news/canada/manitoba/manitoba-election-results-1.3543735.
31   This section is largely based on the NDP's constitution. Manitoba NDP, "Manitoba New Democratic Party, Constitution."
32   In 2003, Jack Layton was the first federal leader of the party to be elected using "one-member-one-vote" (OMOV) rules. McGrane, *New NDP,* 34.
33   The Manitoba NDP has mulled the option of moving to the OMOV system. See Sean Kavanagh, "Status Quo Result after Hours of Debate on 1 Member, 1 Vote at NDP Convention," *CBC News,* 18 March 2017, https://www.cbc.ca/news/canada/manitoba/status-quo-result-after-hours-of-debate-on-1-member-1-vote-at-ndp-convention-1.4031576.
34   Manitoba NDP, "Manitoba New Democratic Party, Constitution," Article 9.
35   See Royce Koop, "The Manitoba Progressive Conservatives," in this volume. See also Gerald Friesen, *The Honourable John Norquay: Indigenous Premier, Canadian Statesman* (Winnipeg: University of Manitoba Press, 2024).
36   Canadian Press, "Drop Candidate Wab Kinew over Offensive Comments, Manitoba Liberals Urge NDP," *Toronto Star,* 11 March 2016, https://www.thestar.com/news/canada/2016/03/11/drop-candidate-wab-kinew-over-offensive-comments-manitoba-liberals-urge-ndp.html; Steve Lambert, "Selinger Stands by Wab Kinew, Despite Social-Media Slurs," *Winnipeg Sun,* 12 March 2016, https://winnipegsun.com/2016/03/11/liberals-demand-wab-kinew-step-down.
37   Nick Martin, "Kinew Sought Pardon for Crimes before Running for Office," *Winnipeg Free Press,* 20 September 2017, https://www.winnipegfreepress.com/breakingnews/2017/09/20/kinew-sought-pardon-for-crimes-before-running-for-office.
38   Steve Lambert, "Woman at Centre of Wab Kinew Domestic Assault Allegations Says She Was Thrown," *CBC News,* Canadian Press, 14 September 2017, https://www.cbc.ca/news/canada/manitoba/wab-kinew-domestic-assault-allegations-1.4290885.
39   *CBC News,* "Manitoba's NDP Chooses Wab Kinew as New Leader," 16 September 2017, https://www.cbc.ca/news/canada/manitoba/ndp-manitoba-vote-2017-1.4291711.
40   At one point, his attitude towards First Nations peoples caused his minister to resign from cabinet in protest. Caitlyn Gowriluk, "Manitoba Indigenous Relations Minister Resigns from Cabinet After Premier's Comments on Colonial History," *CBC News,* 14 July 2021, https://www.cbc.ca/news/canada/manitoba/eileen-clarke-resigns-cabinet-pallister-indigenous-1.6102299.
41   See Andrea Rounce, Karine Levasseur, and Shannon Furness, "Manitoba's Mixed Bag of Policy Responses to the COVID-19 Pandemic," in *COVID-19 in Manitoba: Public Policy Responses to the First Wave,* ed. A. Rounce and K. Levasseur (Winnipeg: University of Manitoba Press, 2020), 1–6.
42   See the discussion by Royce Koop in this volume.
43   The official results can be found at: https://www.electionsmanitoba.ca/en/Results/Elections/2023.
44   Probe Research June 2023 survey results, based on the Winnipeg-specific tables released at https://probe-research.com/polls/ndp-pcs-head-pre-election-period-dead-heat-june-2023-provincial-voting-intentions.

45 Province of Manitoba, "Cabinet Ministers," accessed 6 January 2025, https://www.gov.mb.ca/minister/index.html. Worth noting is that Brian Pallister made efforts to promote diversity in the PC Party. See Christopher Adams, "Looking Back at the 2016 Manitoba Election: The Engagement of Métis People," *Prairie History* 3 (Fall 2020): 18–30, http://www.mhs.mb.ca/docs/prairie history/03/index.shtml.

46 See APTN's news coverage of this incident and the positive press that followed: https://www.aptnnews.ca/videos/manitobas-premier-changing-a-tire-sparks-viral-memes/.

CHAPTER 13

The Manitoba Liberal Party

KELLY SAUNDERS

On the face of it, the Manitoba Liberal Party (MLP) appears to represent a conundrum of sorts. On the one hand is the party's perpetual third-place position behind the Progressive Conservatives (PCs) and the New Democratic Party (NDP) in provincial elections. Over the past three decades, the MLP has not been able to capture more than 15 percent of the popular vote, and, with the exception of a fourteen-month period in 2018–19, has failed to gain the required four seats necessary for official party status in Manitoba. Reduced in the 2023 provincial election to a single seat in the Manitoba legislature, the Liberals continue to struggle to have their voice heard within the corridors of Manitoba provincial politics.

On the other hand are several factors suggesting that the Manitoba Liberal Party should be more successful than it is. To begin with are the party's deep roots in Manitoba's political history. For the first seven-plus decades of its existence in the province, the Liberal Party was a dominant player in Manitoba politics, holding power either on its own or in union with others in half of the elections held between 1883 and 1958. A second factor is the province's political culture. Situated in the "Heart of the Continent" and colloquially referred to as Canada's "Keystone Province," Manitoba reflects a modest and moderate political culture, grounded in the principles of progressive centrism, pragmatism, and flexible partisanship.[1] In many ways Manitoba represents a microcosm of the larger country within which it is located: it is both rural and urban, progressive and conservative, and diverse in its economy, population, and culture—essentially, the prairies' political middle ground.[2] This middle-of-the-road political culture suggests an appetite for brokerage politics in Manitoba, and for those parties and leaders best able to bridge the ethnic, geographic, and class cleavages that exist within the province. Indeed, Manitoba's most successful provincial party leaders over the past fifty years have forged their electoral coalitions around the progressive centre, eschewing extremist positions on both the right and the left on the road to electoral victory.[3]

A further factor in the conundrum that is the Manitoba Liberal Party is the nature of the province's party system. Despite the moderation of its political culture, contemporary provincial politics in Manitoba remains deadlocked between the Progressive Conservatives and the NDP in a classical two-party system. Indeed, no other party has formed government in the province outside of these two parties since the 1950s, although the Liberals came close in 1988 by winning five seats shy of the Progressive Conservatives to form the Official Opposition in Manitoba. With no other parties constituting a serious contender for power, voters are left with only two choices.[4] As a result, power in Manitoba has tended to swing from the Manitoba PCs to the provincial NDP every eight to ten years or so; as voters become frustrated with one party, they have little choice but to vote for the other.

Together, these factors—the once-formidable power of the Manitoba Liberal Party in the province's early years; Manitoba's centrist, progressive, and moderate political culture; and the lack of viable alternatives for Manitoba voters other than the Progressive Conservative and NDP parties—would suggest a more dominant role for the Manitoba Liberals in provincial politics. Yet the MLP continues to languish in provincial polls and elections, much to the dismay of its supporters and the succession of leaders who have attempted to break through this logjam.

This chapter will explore some of these questions and challenges facing the Manitoba Liberal Party as it seeks to reposition itself as a serious contender for political office in the province. It begins with a brief overview of the historical and geopolitical context that continues to shape Manitoba politics. This will be followed by an examination of the leaders, performance, and organization of the Manitoba Liberal

Party, notably over the past three decades. As I argue, despite the factors that would suggest a more robust Liberal Party in Manitoba, the ability of the NDP and the PCs to broker geographic, class, and ethnic cleavages and claim the ideologically moderate centre has left little room for the MLP. This lack of ideological space has been compounded by the party's perennial struggles on the organizational, financial, and leadership fronts.

The Geographical and Historical Context of Manitoba Politics

Manitoba politics has long been described by scholars as shaped by a diagonal line traversing the province from the Swan River Valley in the northwest corner to the Lake of the Woods in the southeast region, providing a geographic expression to the province's political outcomes.[5] As Christopher Adams explains, this spatial lens is helpful in understanding the province's class cleavages and the historical link between territorial politics, social class, and electoral party support in Manitoba.[6] The line from the northwest to the southeast regions of Manitoba effectively separates the province into three, distinct, physical and political divisions. The first division consists of the southern region of the province, home to abundant farming areas and settled by Ontarian farmers of British ancestry who, Adams says, exemplified "farmer-oriented liberal individualism."[7] Constituents in these communities, historically and to this day, tend to vote Progressive Conservative. The second geographic area is in the northern region of Manitoba and is populated by Indigenous and natural resource–based communities (primarily nickel and copper mining and hydroelectricity) as well as marginal farming activity; this confluence of voters and interests tends to vote NDP.

The third, and most important, region of the province from a political and economic standpoint, consists of the City of Winnipeg. With a population of 750,000 people, Winnipeg represents the sixth-largest city in Canada.[8] Like the province itself, Winnipeg can be divided into distinct geographic areas, representing another layer of territorial expression in Manitoba politics. The North End of Winnipeg, consisting of a rich diversity of Indigenous and East European labourers who were followed by subsequent waves of newcomers from all over the globe, tends to vote NDP. In contrast is the southern part of Winnipeg, settled by Ontarians of English and Scottish descent and dominant in the city's business and professional sector, which has historically favoured the Progressive Conservatives.

While this geographic schema appears to leave the Manitoba Liberal Party without a natural constituency, this was not always the case. Indeed, prior to the electoral shakeup that culminated in the 1969 election and the realignment of the Progressive Conservatives and the NDP, the Manitoba Liberals were, depending on the leader, able to draw significant support from a variety of groups including farmers, labour, the business sector, and ethnocultural communities.[9] Making its first formal appearance in the 1883 provincial election, the Manitoba Liberal Party has its roots in the prosperous British settlers who arrived in the province from Ontario.[10] With the ascension of Thomas Greenway to the premiership in 1888, the Manitoba Liberals would go on to become a dominant political force in Manitoba over the next seventy years, competing for power with their main rivals in the Conservative Party. Greenway was a key figure in the country's growing provincial rights movement, and, as premier, James Mochoruk describes, "presided over the final transition of Manitoba from a communally-based entity ... into a 'modern' political culture where partisanship, majoritarianism, and liberal capitalism determined political power."[11] Manitoba's second Liberal premier, Tobias Crawford Norris, rode to power in 1915 on a progressive platform that drew together farmers, workers, and suffragettes along with various social reform groups. While in office, he led a government described as one of the most active and important in the history of the province, passing progressive legislation in the areas of women's and worker's rights, education, health, and prison reform.[12]

The fortunes of the Manitoba Liberal Party over the following five decades would be marked by the emergence of the United Farmers of Manitoba, later renamed the Progressive Party. Merging with the Progressive government of John Bracken in 1932, the Liberal Party was reconfigured into the Liberal-Progressive Party, which governed the province until its eventual defeat in 1958. Reflecting the views of its leader, the Liberal-Progressive Party, despite its name, represented a rural, small c-conservative ideology.[13] Aligning itself with a farmers' movement that emphasized fiscal frugality, the Manitoba Liberals abandoned their earlier progressivism and embarked on a course that, according to Paul Barber, would "leave them vulnerable in a modern urban world that wanted a more activist state than their inherited beliefs would permit."[14]

The collapse of the Liberal-Progressives came in the 1958 election at the hands of Duff Roblin and his renamed Progressive Conservative Party, denoting what one scholar labelled the beginning of a "quiet revolution" in Manitoba politics.[15] While the Liberals managed to hold on to second place in both popular vote and seats during the PCs' grip on power from 1958 to 1969, this period would also mark the start of the long descent of the Manitoba Liberal Party.[16] Its future would be cemented over the next decade in the face of its inability to modernize and seize upon the social, economic, and political changes sweeping across Manitoba at the time and transform itself into a more progressive and urban party. Outflanked by the centrist and change-oriented governance of Duff Roblin's Progressive Conservatives on one side and Ed Schreyer's recasting of the Manitoba NDP as a moderately left-of-centre party on the other, the Liberals found themselves left behind. Squeezed out of the ideological centre with no electoral base to count on for support, the Manitoba Liberal Party would languish over the next two decades.

The election of Sharon Carstairs as leader in 1984—the first woman to lead a major provincial party in Canada—would regalvanize the Manitoba Liberals and bring them their greatest electoral success of the modern era. In 1986, Carstairs was elected to a seat in the Manitoba legislature and doubled her party's vote share; two years later in a snap election, the Liberals would win a whopping twenty seats and 35 percent of the popular vote to form the Official Opposition in Manitoba. Despite hopes that they would replace the NDP as the main challenger to the Progressive Conservatives, the Liberals' success would not hold. Rather than a Liberal resurgence, the 1988 election reflected Manitobans' considerable discontent with both the NDP and the PCs. Victim to the geographical and electoral divide that defines Manitoba politics, by the time the next election was called in 1990, the Liberals would find themselves once again frozen out of the southern and northern regions of the province (firmly entrenched in PC and NDP hands, respectively), and, within the City of Winnipeg, unable to sufficiently differentiate themselves from their rivals on the centre left and the centre right. Five years later in the 1995 election, the Liberal Party would be back down to three seats, one seat shy of official party status.

From the Lady in Red to the Loneliest Man in Politics

Sharon Carstairs—dubbed the "Lady in Red" by the local media—repositioned the Manitoba Liberal Party into an urban, reformist, and centrist option for voters looking for a viable alternative to the status quo in provincial politics. A dynamic leader, Carstairs was lauded for her ability to seize control of emerging issues to the Liberals' advantage: most notably, her sharp and immediate criticism of the much-reviled Meech Lake Accord that dominated provincial and national politics from 1988 to 1990. By staking her ground on this issue and taking advantage of voter frustrations with the NDP and the PCs, Carstairs was able to force open an ideological space for the Manitoba Liberals and come up the middle in the 1988 election. Describing this election as the "happiest moment" of her political career, Carstairs made history by taking a perennially third-place party and turning it into the Official Opposition in the space of four short years, and, in so doing, becoming the first woman in Canadian history to become a leader of the Official Opposition.[17] Holding the balance of power in a minority PC government, the Liberals were able to capture nineteen of twenty-nine seats in Winnipeg, drawing together a cross-section of upper- and lower-middle-class voters, multicultural communities, and even working-class districts.[18] By 1990, however, as the PCs and NDP regrouped and reclaimed the ideological centre, it was clear that the Manitoba Liberals would not be able to sustain this success. Watching the MLP slip back to seven seats in the Manitoba legislature in the 1990 provincial election, and tired, as she said, from "carrying so much of the burden of the party on my back," Sharon Carstairs—the most successful Liberal leader in Manitoba in the past sixty years—stepped down from provincial politics.[19]

Carstairs was followed as leader by Winnipeg lawyer Paul Edwards and former party president Ginny Hasselfield, but it would be the leadership of Jon Gerrard that would come to define the MLP over the next fifteen years. A medical doctor by training, Gerrard served as the secretary of state for Science, Research and Development in the federal Liberal government of Jean Chrétien, and, following the loss of his riding to the Reform Party in the 1997 general election, took over the helm of the Manitoba Liberals in 1998. Considered to be a decent, thoughtful, and dedicated leader, Gerrard received high marks for his policy ideas and election platforms. He was, however, an awkward campaigner uncomfortable with retail politics and the cut and thrust of political debate; as one former Liberal Party candidate noted, "for Jon, politics is about policy."[20] While Gerrard would successfully bring the Winnipeg riding of River Heights into the Liberal fold, the party languished under his leadership. During his time as leader, from 1998 until 2013, the Liberal Party's share of popular support decreased in every subsequent provincial election, from a high of 13.4 percent in 1999 to the party's worst showing ever of 7.52 percent in the 2011 election. Over this period the MLP would win only six seats, four of which were Gerrard's own constituency of River Heights.

Gerrard's inability to inspire Manitobans and make inroads into the soft party bases of the PCs and the NDP made it difficult for him to solidify control within his own party. He survived a leadership challenge in 2008 only to face further dissension within party ranks following the Liberals' devastating showing in the 2011 election. In the aftermath of this disappointing campaign, Liberals began openly criticizing Gerrard and calling for his resignation, describing a party that was both dysfunctional and divided.[21] Faced with little choice but to resign, Gerrard agreed to do so—but insisted on staying on for an additional eighteen months on an interim basis until a leadership contest could be held. He was labelled the "loneliest man in Canadian politics" by *Maclean's* magazine, and Gerrard's long goodbye would further tarnish the Manitoba Liberal brand in the province.[22]

The Liberals' performance in the 2011 election is illustrative of the myriad challenges they faced throughout much of this period, most of which continue to this day. The party's small membership base makes fundraising difficult, and its inability to secure official party status in the Manitoba legislature (which requires a minimum of four seats) means that it is perennially struggling to finance its operations and election campaigns. The Liberals' financial problems were exacerbated by changes to the Manitoba Elections Finances Act (EFA) in 1999, which banned corporate and union donations and limited individual donations to $3,000. While these changes applied to all the provincial parties, the Liberal Party was notably damaged by the EFA's new reporting requirements.[23] Prior to 1999, the Manitoba Liberal Party and the provincial wing of the Liberal Party of Canada had operated under a joint Provincial Territorial Association model, in which both parties shared a single executive, staff, membership, and accounting system.

The amendments to the EFA necessitated the creation of two separate entities for the provincial and federal parties, leaving the Manitoba Liberals without the benefit of membership sales from the 2003, 2006, and 2008 federal Liberal leadership contests.

The loss of a significant amount of financial and organizational support throughout this period put the Manitoba Liberals in an ever-more weakened position heading into the 2011 election. Standing at only 10 percent in the polls and close to $100,000 in debt, the party did away with its previous free membership system, and Gerrard was forced to use his own car as a campaign bus. Some Liberal candidates even mused that their party was in danger of being "wiped off the political map."[24] The dissension within the party became abundantly clear when two former Liberal MPs signed a letter in support of the NDP candidate in the Winnipeg riding of Seine River. When the ballots were counted, Gerrard managed to hang on to his seat, but for the first time in decades the Liberals failed to capture 10 percent of the popular vote, a necessary threshold to qualify for reimbursement of campaign expenses. Winning less than 8 percent of the ballots cast—almost half of what it received in the 2007 election—the 2011 election was seen as "an unqualified disaster" for the Manitoba Liberal Party.[25]

Missed Opportunities: The Bokhari Years

Despite having only one seat in the Manitoba legislature, a declining membership base, and mounting financial problems, the Liberals were nonetheless able to launch a legitimate leadership race in 2013. Three candidates threw their hats into the ring—Rana Bokhari, a Winnipeg lawyer and political neophyte; Dougald Lamont, a small-business owner and long-time party member; and Bob Axworthy, brother to both long-time federal Liberal powerhouses Lloyd and Tom Axworthy. Seen as an outsider compared with her rivals, Bokhari managed to bring in over 600 new members in only two months. She would go on to win the leadership on the first ballot with 431 votes to Lamont's 285 votes and Axworthy's 131 votes.[26] At only thirty-six years of age, Bokhari would be the youngest ever leader of the Manitoba Liberal Party and the first ever leader in the province of South Asian descent.

With a new leader, triple the number of party members from a year previously, and the financial boost that a well-contested leadership campaign brings, the Manitoba Liberal Party appeared ready to embark on a new chapter in its political history. These hopes would soon be dashed as long-standing fractures within the party deepened in the face of what had been a particularly acrimonious leadership campaign. No sooner were the ballots counted in Bokhari's favour when some party members expressed their disappointment, lamenting that "Manitoba Liberals lost their souls today."[27]

Bokhari's rocky start as leader would only worsen with time. Rather than seeking a seat in the legislature at the first opportunity, as Sharon Carstairs had done, Bokhari decided to focus on building the party's organization and membership base. This proved to be a tactical error for the new leader. She was chastised for her failure to publicly raise the profile of the MLP and for alleged attempts to shut down dissent within the organization, and a growing number of party members openly dismissed their new leader as being, a *Winnipeg Free Press* article reported, "more interested in the title (of leader) than the task (of leading)."[28] Some disenchanted Liberals even launched a new organization encouraging voters to support the PCs in order to defeat the NDP. Dissent within the party reached such a breaking point that former leader Jon Gerrard had to step in and call for party unity.[29]

In the months leading up to the 2016 general election, Bokhari would be given the opportunity to prove her critics wrong. The combination of several factors—the stellar success of the Trudeau Liberals in the 2015 federal election that saw seven Liberal MPs elected from Winnipeg; the open revolt within the governing NDP caucus and cabinet against incumbent premier Greg Selinger; and voter dislike of the newly elected (and uncontested) leader of the PC Party Brian Pallister—positioned the Manitoba Liberals in a situation not unlike that of 1988. Not only was a woman once again at the helm of the Manitoba Liberal Party, the image of Bokhari as a young, progressive woman of colour stood in sharp contrast to her opponents, both of whom were middle-aged white men. The polls also showed a surge in support for the Liberals, placing them second to the PCs and growing in popularity amongst women voters. For the first time in close to three decades, the MLP appeared poised to replace the NDP as the main alternative to the Progressive Conservatives.

Unfortunately for Bokhari and the Manitoba Liberals, however, the 2016 election proved to be yet another example of missed opportunity.

While the party tripled its seat count from one to three and doubled its popular vote from 2011, the election did not lead to the kind of systemic realignment it had hoped for. The problem did not appear to be the party's campaign promises, which were seen as clever, well-conceived, and imaginative, and included a guaranteed annual income, proportional representation, and the allocation of 10 percent of seats in the Manitoba legislature for Indigenous peoples.[30] Rather, it had more to do with the inexperience of the leader, the party's perpetual financial struggles, and a shortage of practiced advisers and volunteers. Uncontested nominations, incomplete vetting processes, and the direct appointment of candidates in some ridings by the party leader led to the removal of six Liberal candidates over the course of a few days. This not only sparked a wildfire of media criticism for Bokhari and the Liberal brand, and chaos and uncertainty in the campaign, but it also meant that the Liberals were unable to run a full slate of candidates in the 2016 election—the first time since 1999.

Then there were the tactical errors by Bokhari herself. Revealing her lack of experience and political savvy, Bokhari often appeared ill-prepared in debates and media scrums, failing to clearly articulate what set the Manitoba Liberals apart from the PCs and the NDP and accusing the media of unfairness.[31] Thus, rather than a campaign built on meaningful change and a new generation of leadership, the 2016 election saw the Liberals once again squander the opportunity to take advantage of a weakened NDP and a popular federal Liberal brand and, in so doing, break the PCs' and NDP's stranglehold on power.[32]

Despite losing her own election in the Winnipeg riding of Fort Rouge, Bokhari at first declared that she would stay on as Liberal leader. One month later, following a meeting with her provincial executive, Bokhari announced that she would be stepping down, declaring to the press that "I just want to go back to normal life and have fun."[33] While the party denied that she had been pushed out, statements by former candidates cast much of the blame for the MLP's dismal showing in the 2016 election on Bokhari's shoulders, and highlighted the challenges her ongoing leadership would present for the party moving forward. "Every day that she is here we are less valid in the eyes of Manitobans," declared one unsuccessful Liberal candidate.[34] Once again, the Manitoba Liberals found themselves in search of a new leader.

Failure to Launch

Saddled with yet more campaign debt and the ever-present infighting amongst its ranks, the MLP set a date for fall 2017 to choose their next leader. Four candidates entered the race: former leader Jon Gerrard, incumbent MLAs Cindy Lamoureux and Judy Klassen (who had also served as interim leader following Bokhari's departure), and former leadership candidate Dougald Lamont. With Klassen subsequently withdrawing from the race, Lamont went on to win the leadership on the second ballot, securing 296 votes to Lamoureux's 288. Heeding the lesson from Bokhari's failed leadership, Lamont ran for, and handily won, a by-election in the Winnipeg riding of St. Boniface nine months after becoming leader. With this win, the Liberals now had four elected MLAs in the Manitoba legislature, and more importantly, official party status. This afforded the Liberals increased public funds to finance their activities and hire researchers, while also being able to formally participate in Question Period and on legislative committees. It also meant more media attention—and hence more public attention—for Lamont and the Liberal Party.

It was in this spirit of optimism that the Manitoba Liberals kicked off their 2019 provincial election campaign. Despite lagging in third place in the polls leading up to the writ drop, the Liberals were nonetheless able to mount a full slate of candidates and present an ambitious electoral platform. Under the theme of a "New Way Forward," the MLP ran a strategically left-of-centre campaign with the aim of outflanking the NDP. Campaign promises included a fifteen-dollar minimum wage, mental health initiatives, and a commitment to make Manitoba carbon-neutral by 2030. Lamont proved to be a skilled leader, performing well in the debates and speaking effectively to the MLP's policy initiatives. As a more seasoned and savvier campaigner, Lamont also avoided the kinds of obvious missteps and controversies that had plagued Bokhari. Despite these advantages, the party found itself unable to replace the NDP as the main opposition voice to the Progressive Conservatives, or to grow its vote in the northern and rural areas of the province. In the end, despite having run a solid campaign, the party lost the northern riding of Keewatinook to the NDP and found itself relegated once again to three seats in the Manitoba legislature.[35]

In his assessment of the Liberals' performance in the 2019 election, Allen Mills highlights the financial pressures placed upon the party by further amendments to the Election Financing Act (EFA) passed by the Pallister government in 2016. As in 1999, these changes had a significant bearing on the party, cutting in half the public subsidy of eligible election expenses, which, for the Liberals, accounted for a quarter of their annual budget. These ongoing financial woes and the lack of organizational strength at the centre denied the Manitoba Liberals the kind of foundation necessary for political success, including a steady stream of financial contributions; extensive and expanding membership lists; and civil society supporters, media attention, attractive candidates, and competent advisors.[36]

Under the slogan of "Real Choice for Real Change," the Manitoba Liberals launched their 2023 election campaign in a direct attempt to appeal to fiscally responsible, yet progressive, voters frustrated with the incumbent PC government but wary of returning the NDP to power.[37] Yet, despite the positive optics of this scenario, the party was not able to attract a full slate of candidates (again), or defeat the NDP's tactical courtship of Liberal voters. With endorsements by former federal Liberal MP Lloyd Axworthy and entreaties to Liberal supporters to vote strategically for the NDP, along with a strong ground-game in Liberal-held ridings, NDP leader Wabanakwut "Wab" Kinew made it clear that he had Liberal voters in his sights. In the end, the NDP's unabashed attempts to target Liberal voters and ridings worked. With just over 10 percent of the popular vote, the MLP managed to win only one seat in the election, that of popular incumbent Cindy Lamoureux (and daughter of long-time Liberal MP Kevin Lamoureux) in the Winnipeg riding of Tyndall Park. The Manitoba Liberal Party, yet again, proved itself unable to rise to the challenge and launch itself as a credible contender in Manitoba electoral politics.

The Challenges of Being a Third Party

In a piece written for the *Canadian Parliamentary Review* after her departure from provincial politics, Sharon Carstairs discussed the challenges she faced going from a caucus of one (herself) when she first became leader of the Manitoba Liberal Party in 1984 to managing a caucus of twenty following the 1988 election. Referring to this scenario as an "adult day care centre," which undoubtedly did not enamour her to her former caucus colleagues, Carstairs's observations reiterate the problems involved in trying to meld individual and inexperienced members into a cohesive group, particularly in an organization not used to the rigours of governing. As she recounted, "the reality was that most members had never been in the Manitoba legislative building or even attended a sitting. In fact, many had been elected without believing that they ever would be."[38] These observations underscore a common, and perennial, theme within the Manitoba Liberal Party: the structural and logistical inadequacies that persist because of limited finances, a small membership base, and the difficulties in attracting qualified and experienced candidates, organizers, and volunteers. It is this absence of organizational depth, compounded by a constant struggle for funds, that remains a defining albatross around the neck of the MLP. Indeed, past Liberal candidates have spoken about winning nomination contests only to discover the non-existence of riding organizations and the challenges of having to build a viable and legitimate electoral machine from scratch.[39] Without any kind of structure in place, it is nearly impossible for the Liberals to recruit candidates, sell memberships, or raise funds, a situation only made worse by the lack of official party status.

The lack of organizational and financial strength has also made internal conflict, factionalism, and dysfunctionalism ingrained features within the Manitoba Liberal Party. Going back decades, a succession of Liberal leaders have been dogged by infighting and discord from within their ranks, hampering their ability to unify their base and put their own stamp on the party. Despite an apparent willingness on the part of Manitobans for a viable third-party option, the MLP remains unable to take advantage of opportunities to establish itself as a legitimate contender for government. These kinds of internal disagreements are part and parcel of being a third party; as Royce Koop explains, power is good in terms of being able to exert discipline within a party and keep members in line. However, when a party hasn't had power for some time, that leads to "more of these internal disagreements and internal battles."[40]

Then there is the question of ideology and leadership. In his book on the history of the Manitoba Liberal Party, former leader Jon Gerrard describes the party's ideology as one based on the traditions of Canadian and international liberalism, which he defines as a combination of fiscal responsibility and social justice, respect for diversity, and the building of successful rural and urban economies and communities.[41] He sees the Manitoba Liberals as occupying the centre of the political spectrum in Manitoba, and a constant reminder to the other two parties that there is an "innovative, forward-thinking middle way."[42] This fluid and rather nondescript ideology benefits the MLP by affording it flexibility in its policies and platforms, allowing it to shift to the centre left or the centre right depending on time and circumstance. At the same time, however, it also makes a consistent policy approach difficult, thus potentially causing confusion among voters as to what the party actually stands for. Paul Thomas points to this ideological inconsistency as a problem for the MLP; he maintains that while the party's ideology over the past fifty years has become decidedly centrist, the Manitoba Liberals "have presented a blurred image as they shifted in successive elections from centre-right to centre-left in their policy messages to voters."[43]

These ideological inconsistencies have been exacerbated by the frequent leadership changes within the MLP. Since 1969, there have been no fewer than eighteen full or interim leaders of the Manitoba Liberal Party, compared with eleven for the PCs and just six for the NDP. In this era of leader-dominated parties, the image of the leader and that of the party they lead become fused in the minds of voters. Reflecting this logic, it is not difficult to surmise that the turnover in leaders has made it harder for the Manitoba Liberals to carve out an identifiable base of support and maintain these voters from election to election.[44] The lack of a core constituency, in turn, is compounded by the single member plurality (SMP) electoral system in Manitoba. It is not surprising that the Manitoba Liberals have long called for an end to SMP, given its tendency to reward parties like the NDP and the PCs whose voters are more territorially concentrated, and disadvantage parties like the Liberals with more dispersed support across the province.

Together, these factors have resulted in what one pundit has called the Manitoba Liberals' demonstrated habit of "snatching defeat from the jaws of victory."[45] Polling well between elections, notably when voters are disillusioned with the NDP, the Liberals tend to fizzle out once the race is on. This is the perennial challenge of the Manitoba Liberals: despite changes in leadership, innovative policy ideas, and increasing frustrations on the part of many Manitobans with status quo politics in the province, they cannot seem to break out of their third-party status. This appears to be part of a larger trend in provincial party systems across western Canada, which are increasingly characterized by two-party competition involving the NDP and a centre-right alternative under a variety of different party labels.[46] Given this scenario, the ability of the Manitoba Liberal Party to find its way out of the conundrum that is Manitoba liberalism appears bleaker than ever.

Notes

1. Jared Wesley, "Political Culture in Manitoba," in *Manitoba Politics and Government: Issues, Institutions, Traditions*, ed. Paul Thomas and Curtis Brown (Winnipeg: University of Manitoba Press, 2010), 60.
2. Jared Wesley, *Code Politics: Campaigns and Cultures on the Canadian Prairies* (Vancouver: UBC Press, 2011), 175. While Manitoba shares much with Alberta and Saskatchewan, it also has close ties with Ontario demographically, socially, and culturally, given that the first waves of immigrants after Manitoba's entry into Confederation in 1870 came from Ontario. The Ontario Liberal Party has also had considerable electoral success throughout that province's history, most recently its fifteen-year stint in office prior to its defeat in the 2018 provincial election.
3. Jared Wesley, "Staking the Progressive Centre: An Ideational Analysis of Manitoba Party Politics," *Journal of Canadian Studies* 45, no. 1 (2011): 143–77. Manitoba's centrist political culture is also reflected in its federal voting patterns. Federal elections in Manitoba have tended to be a three-way race between the federal Conservatives, NDP, and Liberal parties. Since 2000, Manitoba voters have elected a total of twenty-eight Liberal MPs; in the 2015 election, Manitoba elected seven of fourteen Liberal MPs. While this number would decline to four in the 2019 and 2021 elections, Liberal candidates placed a strong second to Conservative and NDP candidates in federal ridings across the province. It is clear that, unlike its prairie neighbours to the west, Manitobans are not averse to voting Liberal at the federal level.
4. There is a provincial Green Party in the province, which has never won a seat in the Manitoba legislature. The Manitoba Greens typically win only about 5 percent of the vote in provincial elections. Manitoba has been, and continues to be, home to a plethora of minor parties at the provincial level. None of these parties, however, has ever managed to secure a notable percentage of the popular vote.
5. See Paul Barber, "Manitoba's Liberals: Sliding into Third," in *Manitoba Politics and Government: Issues, Institutions, Traditions*, ed. Paul Thomas and Curtis Brown (Winnipeg: University of Manitoba Press, 2010), 131; Christopher Adams, *Politics in Manitoba: Parties, Leaders, and Voters* (Winnipeg: University of Manitoba Press, 2008); Tom Peterson, "Ethnic and Class Politics in Manitoba," in *Canadian Provincial Politics: The Party Systems in Ten Provinces*, ed. Martin Robin (Scarborough: Prentice-Hall, 1972), 61–70; and Meir Serfaty, "Electoral Behavior in Manitoba: The Convergence of Geography and Politics," in *The Geography of Manitoba: Its Land and Its People*, ed. John Welsted (Winnipeg: University of Manitoba Press, 1996), 177–94.
6. Adams, *Politics in Manitoba*, 5–8.

7   Ibid., 6.
8   Statistics Canada, 2022, *Census Profile*, 2021 Census of Population, https://www12.statcan.gc.ca/census-recensement/2021/dp-pd/prof/details/page.cfm?Lang=E&SearchText=Winnipeg&DGUIDlist=2021A00054611040&GENDERlist=1,2,3&STATISTIClist=1,4&HEADERlist=0.
9   Peterson, "Ethnic and Class Politics."
10 Barber, "Manitoba's Liberals."
11 James Mochoruk, "Thomas Greenway," in *Manitoba Premiers of the 19th and 20th Centuries*, ed. Barry Ferguson and Robert Wardhaugh (Regina: Canadian Plains Research Center, 2010), 80.
12 Morris Mott, "Tobias C. Norris," in *Manitoba Premiers of the 19th and 20th Centuries*, ed. Barry Ferguson and Robert Wardhaugh (Regina: Canadian Plains Research Center, 2010), 140; Adams, *Politics in Manitoba*, 71. Under Norris, Manitoba would become the first province in Canada in 1916 to grant women the right to vote.
13 Robert Ermel, "The Manitoba Liberals: Gerrard's Dilemma," in *Disengaged? Fixed Date, Democracy, and Understanding the 2011 Manitoba Election*, ed. Andrea Rounce and Jared Wesley (Regina: University of Regina Press, 2015), 83.
14 Barber, "Manitoba's Liberals," 134.
15 Alex Netherton, "Paradigm and Shift: A Sketch of Manitoba Politics," in *The Provincial State in Canada: Politics in the Provinces and Territories*, ed. Keith Brownsey and Michael Howlett (Toronto: University of Toronto Press, 2001), 215.
16 Allen Mills, "The Manitoba Liberal Party," in *Understanding the Manitoba Election 2016: Campaigns, Participation, Issues, Place*, ed. Karine Levasseur, Andrea Rounce, Barry Ferguson, and Royce Koop (Winnipeg: University of Manitoba Press, 2016), 9.
17 Kevin Rollason, "Carstairs Announces Retirement from Politics," *Winnipeg Free Press*, 26 March 2011, https://www.winnipegfreepress.com/local/2011/03/26/carstairs-announces-retirement-from-politics.
18 Serfaty, "Electoral Behavior in Manitoba," 185.
19 Sharon Carstairs, *Not One of the Boys* (Toronto: Macmillan Canada, 1993), 216.
20 Quoted in Ermel, "Manitoba Liberals," 93.
21 Steve Lambert, "Manitoba Liberal Dissent Grows; Party Called 'Dysfunctional': Director Says Manitoba Liberals 'Dysfunctional,'" *Canadian Press*, 6 March 2012.
22 Jonathon Gatehouse, "The Last Liberal Standing in Manitoba" *Maclean's* (26 October 2011), https://macleans.ca/news/canada/the-loneliest-number/.
23 Ermel, "Manitoba Liberals," 85–86.
24 Steve Lambert, "Manitoba Liberals Get Help from Sheila Copps as Election Campaign Winds Down," *Canadian Press*, 29 September 2011, https://globalnews.ca/news/160635/manitoba-liberals-get-help-from-sheila-copps-as-election-campaign-winds-down/.
25 Dan Lett, "Lowly Liberals Lacking Leadership Candidates," *Winnipeg Free Press*, 25 October 2011, https://www.winnipegfreepress.com/local/2011/10/25/lowly-liberals-lacking-leadership-candidates.
26 Larry Kusch, "An Emotional 'Roller-Coaster' for New Liberal Leader," *Winnipeg Free Press*, 27 October 2013, https://www.winnipegfreepress.com/breakingnews/2013/10/27/liberals-have-a-new-leader.

27 Steve Lambert, "Manitoba Liberal Leadership Race Ends with Some Bitterness," *CBC News*, 28 October 2013, https://www.cbc.ca/news/canada/manitoba/manitoba-liberal-leadership-race-ends-with-some-bitterness-1.2255065.
28 Deveryn Ross, "Can Bokhari Rise to the Challenge?" *Winnipeg Free Press*, 25 April 2014, https://www.winnipegfreepress.com/opinion/analysis/2014/04/25/can-bokhari-rise-to-the-challenge.
29 Steve Lambert, "Former Manitoba Liberal Leader Calls for Party Unity in Support of His Successor," *Canadian Press*, 25 April 2014, https://www.ctvnews.ca/winnipeg/article/former-manitoba-liberal-leader-calls-for-party-unity-in-support-of-his-successor/.
30 Mills, "Manitoba Liberal Party," 9–10.
31 Mary Agnes Welch, "Party Leaders and the Media: A Tale of Two (or Three?) Campaigns," in *Understanding the Manitoba Election 2016: Campaigns, Participation, Issues, Place*, ed. Karine Levasseur, Andrea Rounce, Barry Ferguson, and Royce Koop (Winnipeg: University of Manitoba Press, 2016), 16.
32 Andrea Rounce and Karine Levasseur, "Introduction: Blue Manitoba 2016," in *Understanding the Manitoba Election 2016: Campaigns, Participation, Issues, Place*, ed. Karine Levasseur, Andrea Rounce, Barry Ferguson and Royce Koop (Winnipeg: University of Manitoba Press, 2016), 5.
33 Kristen Annable, Larry Kusch, and Nick Martin, "'I Just Want to Go Back to a Normal Life,'" *Winnipeg Free Press*, 10 May 2016, https://www.winnipegfreepress.com/breakingnews/2016/05/09/liberal-caucus-thanks-bokhari-for-hard-work-commitment.
34 Kristen Annable and Carol Sanders, "Grits Tight-Lipped on Bokhari Resignation: Losing Candidates Blame Leader," *Winnipeg Free Press*, 9 May 2016.
35 Judy Klassen, the incumbent MLA and interim leader of the Liberal Party following the resignation of Rana Bokhari, stepped down to run for the federal Liberals in the 2019 general election.
36 Mills, "Manitoba Liberal Party," 13.
37 Manitoba Liberal Party, "Manitoba Liberals Launch 2023 Election Campaign," Press Release, 6 September 2023, https://www.manitobaliberals.ca/post/manitoba-liberals-launch-2023-election-campaign-real-choice-for-real-change.
38 Sharon Carstairs, "Some Reflections on the Role of Caucus," *Canadian Parliamentary Review* 21, no. 1 (1998): 2–3.
39 Dan Lett, "Liberal Machine Missing Parts," *Winnipeg Free Press*, 9 January 2016, https://www.winnipegfreepress.com/breakingnews/2016/01/09/liberal-machine-missing-parts.
40 Quoted in Steve Lambert, "Several Resignations Hit Manitoba Liberal Party Ahead of Key Byelection," *CBC News*, 1 May 2018, https://www.cbc.ca/news/canada/manitoba/manitoba-liberal-party-resignations-1.4643343.
41 Jon Gerrard, *Battling for a Better Manitoba: A History of the Provincial Liberal Party* (Winnipeg: Heartland Associates, Inc., 2006), 12.
42 Ibid., 13.
43 Paul Thomas, "Can Manitoba's Liberal Party Become a Real Contender Again?" *CBC News, Opinion*, 17 October 2017, https://www.cbc.ca/news/canada/manitoba/manitoba-liberal-party-leader-1.4343861.

44 This trend continues, as the lone Liberal MLA in the Manitoba legislature—Cindy Lamoureux—is also the interim leader of the Manitoba Liberal Party following the defeat of former leader Dougald Lamont in the 2023 election. At the time of writing, the party has not set a date for its next leadership convention.

45 Dan Lett, "Lamont Victory Brings Grits in from the Cold," *Winnipeg Free Press*, 18 July 2018, https://www.winnipegfreepress.com/local/2018/07/17/lamont-victory-brings-grits-in-from-the-cold.

46 Royce Koop, "Liberals' Fate Seems Sealed in the West," *Winnipeg Free Press*, 27 October 2023, https://www.winnipegfreepress.com/opinion/analysis/2023/10/27/liberals-fate-seems-sealed-in-the-west.

Conclusion

KELLY SAUNDERS AND CHRISTOPHER ADAMS

On 3 October 2023, Manitobans went to the polls to cast their ballots in the province's forty-third general election. As the polls closed and the results began to pour in, it was evident that the evening would not turn out well for either the Progressive Conservatives (PCs) or the Manitoba Liberal Party (MLP). The New Democratic Party (NDP) would prove to be the big winner on election night, securing 45.6 percent of the popular vote and a comfortable majority of thirty-four seats in the provincial legislature.[1] For the incumbent PCs, who had been in power since winning one of the province's largest ever majority governments in 2016, the results would be a crushing disappointment. Despite winning 41.9 percent of the vote (a difference of less than 4 percent compared with the NDP), the PCs were reduced to twenty seats, all but three of which were located outside Winnipeg.[2] The results would prove to be even more devastating for the Liberals. Dropping down to 10.6 percent of the popular vote, the Liberals would lose three of their four seats, including that of party leader Dougald Lamont.

Not surprisingly, the PCs and their supporters downplayed the election results, pointing to the fact that the party came within 19,000 votes of defeating the NDP and holding onto power. Others maintained that it was simply time for a new government, that the election reflected nothing more than the straightforward alternation of power between Manitoba's two dominant parties, the NDP and the PCs. Indeed, as the election results contained in Appendix B reveal, since the 1960s, political power in Manitoba has typically swung from the NDP to the PCs and back again, roughly every eight to ten years. Seen through this lens, it was clear that the clock was running out on the Stefanson government. Already in power for seven years, the Tories were due for a defeat, as they ran out of steam and voters grew restless for change. Added to the natural aging of their administration was the fact that the PCs had also struggled through other challenges, as Royce Koop outlines in Chapter 11, including a leadership change while they were in power and problems in managing the COVID-19 pandemic. The impact of these challenges were reflected in the polls; throughout 2021 and 2022, the PCs lagged behind the NDP, particularly in Winnipeg, where they trailed by double digits. A poll prior to the election showed the NDP leading by eleven points over the PCs (49 percent versus 38 percent), and by a whopping twenty-nine points in seat-rich Winnipeg (57 percent versus 28 percent).[3]

While mindful of these factors, and what appears at first glance to be the natural ebb and flow of Manitoba provincial politics, it would be a mistake to see the 2023 election as merely a status quo electoral event. Instead, we argue, this election is indicative of a central theme of this book. Manitoba, while sharing much of the same legislative, constitutional, and structural framework as its provincial cousins (for example, the Westminster parliamentary system, the single member plurality electoral system, the constitutional division of powers), is also a "world among other worlds" in Canadian politics. The 2023 election reveals evidence of Manitoba's uniqueness on several fronts. To begin with, Manitoba's two largest parties, the NDP and the PC Party, were led respectively by an Indigenous person and a woman, meaning that no matter what the results would be, history would be made on election night. And, while the results of the election brought to an end the careers of two of Manitoba's three party leaders,[4] it also, more importantly, brought to power the country's first ever First Nations premier, Wabanakwut "Wab" Kinew. Kinew is in fact the third Indigenous person to lead the province, following John Norquay (1878 to 1887) and Louis Riel, who negotiated Manitoba's entry into Confederation (and was subsequently bestowed the honorary title of "the first premier of Manitoba" by the Kinew government shortly after taking office).[5] In addition to Kinew, ten other Indigenous candidates were elected to the provincial legislature in 2023, accounting for just under 20 percent of all MLAs.

While the number of Indigenous people elected in 2023 is historic, as Joan Grace points out in Chapter 8, this election also brought with it the most gender-diverse Legislative Assembly in the province's history. A record number of women and gender-diverse candidates were elected to office in 2023: twenty out of fifty-seven MLAs, representing 35 percent of the provincial legislature, and higher than the national average of 31 percent in the House of Commons.[6] This includes Logan Oxenham, the newly elected MLA for Kirkfield Park in Winnipeg's west end, who became not only the first openly transgender person elected in Manitoba but in all of Canada, as well as Uzoma Asagwara, appointed minister of Health and deputy premier, and Manitoba's first non-binary political representative.[7] Commenting on the record number of women and gender-diverse people elected in the province, Chi Nguyen, executive director of Equal Voice Canada, stated, "This is more than just a win for Manitoba; it's a resounding victory for gender representation in political establishments across Canada."[8]

The diversity in the Legislative Assembly extends to Manitoba's executive branch. Upon taking office, Premier Kinew created not only the province's first (nearly) gender-balanced cabinet but also the most racialized in its history. Seven out of fifteen MLAs picked to sit in cabinet are women or non-binary, five are Indigenous (including two First Nations women, also a first for Manitoba), two are members of the LGBTQIA+ community, and eight are racialized.[9]

While the diversity of MLAs, cabinet ministers, and the premier himself who were elected and appointed in 2023 sets Manitoba apart in many ways from its provincial counterparts, the provincial election also revealed other aspects of what we have termed the "Big World" of Manitoba provincial politics. The election proved to be one of the most divisive and polarized events in the province's history. While many of the issues that became points of contestation were not surprising, including such topics as affordability, crime, and health care, the extent to which they were "weaponized," notably by the PCs as the NDP began to pull out even further ahead in the polls, was a first for the province. A controversial issue that emerged during the final stages of the campaign was the proposed search of a Winnipeg landfill for the remains of four Indigenous women who were believed to have been murdered at the hands of a serial killer. While the PCs opposed the search on safety and financial grounds, they took the extra step of making it a campaign issue, taking out billboards and newspaper ads publicizing their commitment to "standing firm" and pushing back against those calling for a search. Many saw this move on the part of the Stefanson team as heartless and traumatizing to the families of the victims, and Indigenous people in general, and it was later criticized by former cabinet ministers and senior officials within the PC party itself.[10]

The landfill search was not the only contentious issue on which the PCs staked their fortunes and lost. They also came under fire for their public stance on "parental rights," which some people argued was a thinly veiled attack on vulnerable trans and gender non-conforming youth in public schools, as well as for their campaign ads that appeared to play into negative stereotypes of Indigenous and racialized peoples. Speaking to these PC tactics, Liberal Leader Dougald Lamont declared the 2023 election campaign to be "one of the most disgusting" he had ever seen. "It's going to be bad for the [Progressive Conservatives] because it says that they don't care about anything. They'll stoop to anything to try to get elected, and that's disgraceful," he added.[11] Political scientist Paul Thomas agreed, calling the PC attack ads "nastier" and "more vicious and mean" than usually seen in provincial election campaigns. These efforts, he concluded, "seemed to reek of desperation" on the part of the Progressive Conservatives.[12]

In contrast to the PCs, the NDP's approach was far less reactive. Early in the campaign Kinew announced that his party would be fiscally prudent and tough on crime, while at the same time focusing on the problems within the province's ailing health care system, a hot-button issue that had plagued the PCs throughout their second term. With health care the number-one issue for most Manitobans, the NDP promised a range of new measures, including a commitment to hire close to 1,000 new health professionals (doctors, nurses, paramedics) and reopen the emergency departments at several Winnipeg hospitals closed by the previous administration. In an attempt to neutralize the Opposition's efforts to paint them as financially irresponsible, the New Democrats also put forth what they called a "responsible" and "balanced" fiscal platform, including promises to balance the budget in their first term in office, to not raise the provincial sales tax, and to continue with the property tax cuts that had begun under the Stefanson government. As Christopher Adams observed in an interview with Global TV, the NDP campaign represented a clear attempt to strike a centrist approach, appealing to both middle-class voters as well as the undecided. "There's that sweet spot of middle-class voters that go back and forth," he noted, and these sorts of announcements are designed "to get those swing voters to feel comfortable with voting for the NDP again."[13]

The NDP's centrist approach was also a clear attempt to target supporters of the Manitoba Liberal Party. While Liberal leader Dougald Lamont criticized the NDP for selling out on its progressive roots and for adopting the same right-wing fiscal policies as the PCs, the Liberals were soon forced onto the sidelines of what was clearly a two-way race between the two front-runner parties. As Kelly Saunders notes in Chapter 13, as in past campaigns, the Manitoba Liberals boasted some of the more creative campaign policies in the election, including a minimum income for seniors and people with disabilities, electoral reform, and medical coverage for mental health services. Yet, once again the 2023 election proved to be another crushing blow for the Manitoba Liberal Party.

In the end, Manitobans rejected the PCs and chose the more positive and aspirational messaging of the NDP. In this we can see evidence of a second theme of this book—that despite the conflicts and challenges that the province has faced since its inception in 1870, Manitobans have shown a marked tendency to find common ground with those they disagree with. This desire for consensus, the accommodation of difference, and social harmony are rooted in the principle of *wahkohtowin*, described by Robert Coutts in the opening chapter of this book. It is also reflective of the electorate's disdain for extremism and polarization, preferring instead a more centrist, pragmatic, approach to political affairs in the province.[14] While our moderate political culture may be seen as boring and banal by some, it has also brought communities and individuals from all sectors and walks of life together in unique and fascinating ways, establishing Manitoba as truly a Big World in Canadian politics.

Notes

1   Elections Manitoba, "Results of the 43rd General election, October 3, 2023," https://www.electionsmanitoba.ca/en/Results/Elections/2023.
2   The NDP would subsequently win the Tuxedo seat vacated by former PC leader and premier Heather Stefanson in a by-election in June 2024, thereby reducing the number of Conservative ridings in Winnipeg to a mere two.

3   Probe Research, "Manitoba Provincial Politics: 2023 Election Survey," https://probe-research.com/sites/default/files/2023-09/202309%20Omnibus%20-%20Party%20Support%20UPDATED.pdf.
4   Both Dougald Lamont, leader of the Manitoba Liberal Party, and PC leader and premier Heather Stefanson announced their resignations on election night. While Lamont lost his Winnipeg seat to the NDP, Stefanson would remain as MLA for an additional six months, stepping down from her seat in May 2024.
5   The Legislative Assembly of Manitoba, The Louis Riel Act (bill 206), https://web2.gov.mb.ca/bills/42-2/b206e.php. The Louis Riel Act was the first piece of legislation introduced by the Kinew government, following a long-standing promise to the Métis people of Manitoba to recognize Riel as the founder of Manitoba and the province's Father of Confederation.
6   Statistics Canada, *Gender Representation among Canadian Members of Parliament and Cabinet*, 8 March 2024, https://www150.statcan.gc.ca/n1/en/pub/11-627-m/11-627-m2024001-eng.pdf?st=rcVB872V.
7   Asagwara also made history in 2019, becoming the province's first Black queer person elected to provincial office.
8   Glen Dawkins, "Record Number of Women, Gender-diverse Candidates Elected Tuesday," *Winnipeg Sun*, 9 October 2023, https://winnipegsun.com/news/provincial/record-number-of-women-gender-diverse-candidates-elected-tuesday.
9   Bartley Kives, "Gender, Ethnocultural Representation Strong in Manitoba Premier Wab Kinew's 1st Cabinet, *CBC News*, 18 October 2023, https://www.cbc.ca/news/canada/manitoba/cabinet-wab-kinew-representation-1.7000444.
10 Steve Lambert, "Ads Opposing Landfill Search 'Deeply Regrettable,' Says Manitoba PC Cabinet Minister Who Lost Seat," *CBC News*, 4 October 2023, https://www.cbc.ca/news/canada/manitoba/tory-strategy-criticize-by-former-members-1.6986864. Nearly eighteen months after the election, Interim PC leader Wayne Ewasko apologized to the families of the four murdered Indigenous women for the party's refusal to search for their remains, noting that "we (the PCs) lost our way in regards to empathy." Tessa Adamski, "Manitoba PCs Apologize to Families of Murdered Women Believed to Be in Winnipeg-area Landfill," *CBC News*, 5 March 2025, https://www.cbc.ca/news/canada/manitoba/pc-party-landfill-search-apology-1.7475657.
11 Brittany Hobson and Steve Lambert, "Manitoba Progressive Conservatives 'Pulling Out Stops' with Attack Ads: Analyst," *CTV News*, 27 September 2023, https://winnipeg.ctvnews.ca/manitoba-progressive-conservatives-pulling-out-stops-with-attack-ads-analyst-1.6580449.
12 Quoted in Bartley Kives, "PCs Step Up Attack Ads Against NDP in Waning Days of Manitoba Campaign," *CBC News*, 27 September 2023, https://www.cbc.ca/news/canada/manitoba/pc-attack-ad-2023-election-1.6979875; Caitlyn Gowriluk, "Manitoba NDP Bet Big on Health Care, Rode Wave of Discontent with Tories on Way to Victory," *CBC News*, 4 October 2024, https://www.cbc.ca/news/canada/manitoba/2023-election-analysis-kinew-stefanson-1.6986075.
13 Nicole Buffie, "Manitoba Election: NDP Fiscal Plan Includes Balanced Budget, No Tax Increase," *Global News*, 9 August 2023, https://globalnews.ca/news/9886526/manitoba-ndp-promises-balanced-budget-no-tax-increase-if-elected/.
14 This doesn't mean that Manitoba hasn't experienced extremist events in the past or even in the present. It just doesn't typically show itself at the polls.

APPENDIX A

Evolution of Voting and Elections in Manitoba[1]

1870
- Voting occurs at public constituency meetings where each voter publicly declares his preference. The electoral officer records the votes, and the simple plurality (or "first-past-the-post") system is used to elect members for the 24 seats in the Legislative Assembly.
- Only males who are established members of the community, in good financial standing, can vote.

1888
- Requirement to be in good financial standing eliminated.
- Residency requirement for voting increased to six months in Manitoba and one month in the electoral division.
- The secret ballot becomes a permanent feature of Manitoba elections.

1892
- Manitoba Assembly increased from 24 to 40 seats.

1914
- Manitoba Assembly increased to 49 seats.
- A new system of representation is introduced: Winnipeg is divided into three constituencies, each represented by two members. Voters in each constituency are issued two ballots, one for each seat. No candidate can be listed on both ballots. So, although Winnipeg voters, in effect, vote twice, the ballots are counted and the candidates declared elected as if there were two separate constituencies. The rural constituencies, meanwhile, retain the simple first-past-the-post system.

1916
- Manitoba is the first Canadian province to extend the franchise to women.

1920
- A "proportional representation" system of voting is introduced in Winnipeg. The city is consolidated into a single constituency electing 10 members. Voters indicate their preferences by numbering the candidates' names on the ballot paper 1, 2, 3, etc. A complex method of counting these ballot papers is provided by amendments to The Elections Act.
- Manitoba Assembly increased to 55 seats.

1927
- The rural constituencies abandon the simple plurality system in favour of an "alternative" or "referential" balloting system, which is used until 1958. In constituencies where more than two candidates are nominated, voters indicate their preferences by marking the ballot 1, 2, 3, etc.
- The practice of members of the Assembly who had been chosen to enter the Cabinet (Executive Council) resigning their seats to face a by-election is abolished.
- The practice of "deferring" elections is becoming increasingly common, especially in northern constituencies where transportation and communication are difficult. Elections in these constituencies are held after the General Election, when results from the remainder of the province were already known. Deferred elections are last held in 1966.

1932
- First Nations persons in Armed Forces enfranchised.
- Advance voting first introduced during the 1932 General Election.

1946
- Three members are elected to represent the three branches of the Armed Forces (Army, Navy, and Air Force). These representatives are elected by Manitobans in the Armed Forces, many of whom are overseas. The addition of these seats increases the size of the Assembly to 58.

1949
- The three Armed Forces seats in the Assembly are eliminated, while the number of constituencies within Manitoba is increased to 57, as it is today.
- First mention of Chief Electoral Officer. Appointed by Lieutenant Governor in council to be Clerk of Executive Council and administer elections.

- The single, 10-member constituency of Winnipeg is replaced by three constituencies, each represented by four members. In addition, the constituency of St. Boniface is given two members. The preferential balloting system is retained for these multi-member seats.

1952
- Manitoba's Treaty Indian population enfranchised.

1957
- Electoral Divisions Boundaries Commission formed to independently review boundaries. Manitoba is the first province with an independent boundaries commission.

1958
- Winnipeg is divided into 20 single-member constituencies. The system of referential or alternative voting is abandoned in favour of the first-past-the-post plurality system in all constituencies, rural and urban.

1962
- Provisions for hospital patients to vote (special blank ballot) first used.

1969
- The voting age is lowered from 21 to 18 on 10 October.

1970
- $200 fee for nomination abolished and replaced with the requirement of signatures of 50 eligible voters in the electoral division in which the potential candidate wishes to become nominated.

1980
- The Office of the Chief Electoral Officer is established to serve as an independent office of the Legislative Assembly in order to administer fair elections.
- The Elections Finances Act (EFA) is proclaimed. It introduces advertising spending limits for candidates and parties, a tax credit system for contributions to registered political parties and candidates, and provisions for financial disclosure.
- Paid advertising of elections is allowed.
- Nomination papers now require 100 signatures.

1983
- Election day is always to be a Tuesday.

1986
- Effective 1 July, only Canadian citizens can vote (British subjects and landed immigrants are not eligible).

1988
- Patients in mental health care facilities are eligible to vote for the first time (result of a Court of Queen's Bench decision).
- Inmates in correctional institutions eligible to vote for the first time (result of a Court of Queen's Bench decision in March 1986). Subsequent decisions in November 1988, August 1990 and August 1999 uphold this eligibility.

1990
- Persons with a mental disability residing in an institution are eligible to vote for the first time (result of a Court of Queen's Bench decision in August 1990).

1997
- Eligible voters can have their names omitted or obscured from the voters list under rules of personal security protection.
- Voters list no longer posted for public viewing or available for public use.

1998
- Voters given the option of placing ballot in ballot box themselves.
- Judicial recounts deemed to be solely for the purpose of declaring as elected the candidate with the highest number of votes.

2001
- Tie votes resolved through a by-election rather than having the returning officer cast the deciding ballot.
- The minimum election period is shortened from 36 to 33 days.

2006
- Advance voting extended to seven days. Eligible voters can vote at any advance voting station in Manitoba. Identification required.
- Homebound voting extended to persons with any disability and to caregivers, if applicable.

2008
- Set election date established, with the first election set to take place on 4 October 2011, and subsequent elections to take place on the first Tuesday of October every four years.
- Political parties are now entitled to public funding (referred to as an "annual allowance").
- Ban on government advertising and publications extended to 90 days before a set date election.

2012 • Provision for a different date for a provincial election if overlapping with a federal election.

2016 • Annual allowance (public funding) for parties is repealed.
- Updated government advertising provisions shorten the pre-election period to 60 days from 90.
- Number of signatures required for nomination reduced from 100 to 50.

2017 • Mandatory ID instituted for voting.

2019 • Candidates required to disclose offences under the Criminal Code of Canada, the Controlled Drugs and Substances Act and under provincial and federal income tax laws. Excludes youth offences and offences for which a pardon has been granted.

2022 • The use of vote counting machines (tabulators) introduced. Non-resident votes are counted in the electoral district in which they are cast.

Notes

1 Elections Manitoba, "History of Electoral Process from 1870 to 2011," with modifications, https://www.electionsmanitoba.ca/en/Resources/History. Used with permission.

APPENDIX B

Manitoba Election Results, 1870 to 2023

Table A: Provincial Elections in Manitoba, 1870 to 1915.[1]

Election Year	Political Party	# Seats	% Total Votes	Party and Premier
1870	Government	18	56%	Alfred Boyd (1870–71) – n.a.
	Opposition	4	23%	Marc Girard (1871–72, 1874) – Cons.
	Other*	2	21%	
				Henry Clarke (1872–74) – n.a.
1874	Government	9	19%	Robert Davis – n.a.
	Opposition	6	18%	
	Other*	9	63%	
1878	Government	7	9%	John Norquay – Cons.
	Other*	17	91%	
1879	Conservative	14	34%	John Norquay – Cons.
	Liberal	2	7%	
	Other*	8	59%	
1883	Conservative	20	55%	John Norquay – Cons.
	Liberal	10	45%	
1886	Liberal	14	48%	John Norquay – Cons.
	Conservative	21**	51%	David Harrison (1887) – Cons.
	Other*	0	1%	
1888	Liberal	32	57%	Thomas Greenway – Lib.
	Conservative	5	34%	
	Other*	1	10%	
1892	Liberal	24	50%	Thomas Greenway – Lib.
	Conservative	9	41%	
	Other*	7	9%	

Appendix B

1896	Liberal	32	50%	Thomas Greenway – Lib.
	Conservative	5	40%	
	Patrons of Industry	2	8%	
	Independent	1	2%	
1899	Liberal	17	50%	Hugh Macdonald – Cons.
	Conservative	18	44%	Rodmond Roblin – Cons.
	Other/ Independent	5	7%	
1903	Liberal	9	45%	Rodmond Roblin – Cons.
	Conservative	29	48%	
	Other/ Independent	2	8%	
1907	Liberal	13	48%	Rodmond Roblin – Cons.
	Conservative	28	51%	
	Labour	0	2%	
1910	Liberal	13	44%	Rodmond Roblin – Cons.
	Conservative	28	51%	
	Socialist/ Labour	0	4%	
	Independent	0	1%	
1914***	Liberal	20	43%	Rodmond Roblin – Cons.
	Conservative	28	47%	
	Labour	0	5%	
	Independent	1	6%	
1915***	Liberal	40	55%	T.C. (Tobias) Norris – Lib.
	Conservative	5	33%	
	Labour²	0	3%	
	Independent	2	9%	

* Candidate was undeclared or affiliation is unknown. For 1879 results, this includes such designations as Independent-Conservative, National Party, and Independent Liberal.

** This includes David Glass who ran as an independent but then became Speaker in the Norquay Government (Joseph Alfred Hilts, "The Political Career of Thomas Greenway," PhD dissertation, University of Manitoba, 1974, 98).

*** The 1914 provincial election gave Winnipeg voters two ballots each in order to vote for candidates for an "A" riding and a "B" riding. Percentage figures provided here are based on Elections Manitoba figures that have been adjusted to equalize the Winnipeg number of votes cast within the provincial voting population.

Table B: Provincial Elections in Manitoba, 1920 to 1949.

Election Year	Political Party	# Seats	% Total Votes	Party and Premier
1920	Liberal	21	35%	T.C. Norris – Lib.
	Conservative	9	19%	
	Farmers	9	14%	
	Labour	10	18%	
	Independent	4	12%	
	Socialist	2	3%	
1922	Liberal	8	23%	
	Conservative	7	16%	
	UFM	28	33%	John Bracken – UFM
	Labour	6	16%	
	Independent	6	13%	
1927	Liberal	7	21%	John Bracken – Lib.-Progressive
	Conservative	15	27%	
	Progressive	29	32%	
	Farmer-Labour	3	11%	
	Independent	1	9%	
1932	Liberal-Progressive	38	40%	John Bracken – Lib.-Progressive
	Conservative	10	35%	
	Farmer-Labour	6	17%	
	Independent	1	7%	
	Liberal (non-fusion candidates)	0	2%	
1936	Liberal-Progressive	23	35%	John Bracken – Lib-Progressive
	Conservative	16	28%	
	Ind. Labour/CCF	7	12%	
	Social Credit	5	9%	
	Independent	3	12%	
	Communist	1	2%	

1941	Govt. Coalition:			John Bracken – Lib.-Progressive S.S. Garson (1943–) – Lib.-Progressive
	Liberal-Progressive	27	35%	
	Conservative	12	16%	
	CCF	3	17%	
	Social Credit	3	2%	
	Independent	5	11%	
	Anti-Coalition:			
	Conservative	3	4%	
	Social Credit	0	6%	
	Independent	1	5%	
	Communist	1	3	
1945***	Govt. Coalition:			S.S. Garson – Lib.-Progressive D.L. Campbell (1948–) – Lib.-Progressive
	Liberal-Progressive	25	32%	
	Progressive Conservative	13	16%	
	Social Credit	2	1%	
	Independent	3	5%	
	Anti-Coalition:			
	CCF	9	34%	
	Social Credit	0	1%	
	Labour-Progressive	1	5%	
	Independent/Ind. CCF	2	6%	
1949	Govt. Coalition:			D.L. Campbell – Lib.-Progressive
	Liberal-Progressive	30³	38%	
	Progressive Conservative	9	12%	
	Ind. Lib/Lib. Prog.	1	4%	
	Independent	4	4%	
	Anti-Coalition:			
	CCF	7	26%	
	Cons & Ind. PC	4	7%	
	Ind. Lib/Lib. Prog.	1	3%	
	Others	1	6%	

Table C: Provincial Elections in Manitoba, 1953 to 1966.

Election Year	Political Party	# Seats	% Total Votes	Party and Premier
1953	Liberal-Progressive	33	39%	D.L. Campbell – Lib.-Progressive
	Progressive Conservative	12	21%	
	CCF	5	16%	
	Independent Lib.-Progressive	3	5%	
	Social Credit	1	13%	
	Independent	2	4%	
	Communist	1	1%	
	Labour-Progressive	0	1%	
1958	Liberal-Progressive	19	35%	Duff Roblin – PC
	Progressive Conservative	26	40%	
	CCF	11	20%	
	Independent	1	2%	
	Other	0	2%	
1959	Liberal	11	30%	Duff Roblin – PC
	Progressive Conservative	36	46%	
	CCF	10	22%	
	Independent and Other	0	1%	
1962	Liberal	13	36%	Duff Roblin – PC
	Progressive Conservative	36	45%	
	NDP	7	15%	
	Social Credit	1	3%	
1966	Progressive Conservative	31	40%	Duff Roblin – PC Walter Weir (1967–) – PC
	Liberal	14	33%	
	NDP	11	23%	
	Social Credit	1	4%	

Table D: Provincial Elections in Manitoba, 1969 to 2023.

Election Year	Political Party	# Seats	% Total Votes	Party and Premier
1969	Progressive Conservative	22	35%	Edward Schreyer – NDP
	NDP	28	38%	
	Liberal	5	24%	
	Social Credit	1	1%	
	Independent	1	1%	
1973	Progressive Conservative	21	37%	Edward Schreyer – NDP
	NDP	31	42%	
	Liberal	5	19%	
1977	Progressive Conservative	33	49%	Sterling Lyon – PC
	NDP	23	38%	
	Liberal	1	12%	
1981	Progressive Conservative	23	44%	Howard Pawley –NDP
	NDP	34	47%	
	Liberal	0	7%	
1986	Progressive Conservative	26	40%	Howard Pawley – NDP
	NDP	30	41%	
	Liberal	1	14%	
1988	Progressive Conservative	25	38%	Gary Filmon – PC
	NDP	12	24%	
	Liberal	20	35%	
1990	Progressive Conservative	30	42%	Gary Filmon – PC
	NDP	20	29%	
	Liberal	7	28%	
1995	Progressive Conservative	31	43%	Gary Filmon – PC
	NDP	23	33%	
	Liberal	3	24%	
1999	Progressive Conservative	24	41%	Gary Doer – NDP
	NDP	32	44%	
	Liberal	1	13%	
2003	Progressive Conservative	20	36%	Gary Doer – NDP
	NDP	35	49%	
	Liberal	2	13%	
	Green Party	0	1%	

Year	Party	Seats	%	Leader
2007	Progressive Conservative	19	38%	Gary Doer – NDP
	NDP	36	48%	
	Liberal	2	12%	
	Green Party	0	1%	
2011	Progressive Conservative	19	44%	Greg Selinger – NDP
	NDP	37	46%	
	Liberal	1	8%	
	Green Party	0	3%	
2016	Progressive Conservative	40	53%	Brian Pallister – PC
	NDP	14	26%	
	Liberal	3	14%	
	Green Party	0	5%	
2019	Progressive Conservative	36	47%	Brian Pallister – PC
	NDP	18	32%	
	Liberal	3	15%	
	Green Party	0	6%	
2023	Progressive Conservative	22	42%	Wab Kinew – NDP
	NDP	34	45%	
	Liberal	1	11%	
	Green Party	0	<1%	
	Keystone Party	0	<1%	

Notes

1. This and subsequent tables are based chiefly on results in Elections Manitoba, "Historical Summaries," as printed in Christopher Adams, *Politics in Manitoba: Parties, Leaders, and Voters* (Winnipeg: University of Manitoba Press, 2008), Appendix B. The author reviewed each election and summed up the results for each party for all elections up to 2007. Percentage figures are rounded to the nearest percentage; totals may therefore exceed 100 percent for each election period. For this volume, the updated results for elections from 2011 to 2023 are also drawn from Elections Manitoba data.

2. There is some discrepancy among different accounts of both the 1914 and 1915 provincial elections (as discussed in Adams, *Politics in Manitoba*, Chapter 4) and seats that were won for a "Labor Party." This table reflects the results as reported by Elections Manitoba with adjustments based on newspaper coverage of the elections.

3. This figure (as well as percent of popular support) is adjusted from Elections Manitoba, "Historical Summaries," which incorrectly has Robert Bend identified as a Liberal-Progressive. As discussed in Adams, *Politics in Manitoba*, Chapter 3, Bend ran in 1949 as an "Independent Progressive Conservative." He is placed here as an Independent Government Coalition candidate.

CONTRIBUTORS

Christopher Adams is the rector of St. Paul's College and an adjunct professor in both Political Science and Peace and Conflict Studies at the University of Manitoba. He is a regular media commentator and author of numerous works, including *Politics in Manitoba: Parties, Leaders, and Voters* (University of Manitoba Press, 2008).

Fletcher Baragar is an associate professor in the Department of Economics, University of Manitoba. His publications include works on the Manitoba economy, the Canadian economy, and heterodox economic theory, and in the field of the history of economic thought.

Malcolm G. Bird is an associate professor in the Department of Political Science at the University of Winnipeg. He is fascinated by the evolution of state-owned enterprises in Canada and abroad.

Curtis Brown is a partner in Probe Research, a public opinion research firm based in Winnipeg. In addition to providing public opinion research to various clients and commentating on politics and policy issues, Curtis is also a former contributor to the *Winnipeg Free Press* and the former editorial page editor of the *Brandon Sun*.

Robert Coutts is currently a visiting scholar at St. Paul's College at the University of Manitoba. He is the author of three books, including *Authorized Heritage: Place, Memory, and Historic Sites in Prairie Canada* (University of Manitoba Press, 2021), and is the editor of *Prairie History: The Journal of the West*. Recently, he was named the general editor of the Champlain Society which publishes works in Canadian documentary history.

Joan Grace is a professor in the Department of Political Science at the University of Winnipeg. She is a co-editor of the *Handbook on Gender, Diversity and Federalism* (Edward Elgar Publishing, 2020).

Lauren Hill is a law student at the University of Saskatchewan College of Law. Previously, she completed her Master of Arts degree at the University of Alberta under the supervision of Dr. Jared Wesley, where she studied contemporary Saskatchewan political culture under prolonged Saskatchewan Party governance.

Royce Koop is a professor in the Department of Political Science at the University of Manitoba. He is the co-author of *Representation in Action: Canadian MPs in the Constituencies* (University of British Columbia Press, 2018) and author of *Grassroots Liberals: Organizing for Local and National Politics* (University of British Columbia Press, 2011).

Karine Levasseur is a professor in the Department of Political Science at the University of Manitoba. She is a co-editor of *COVID-19 in Manitoba: Public Policy Responses to the First Wave* (University of Manitoba Press, 2020) and *Mothering and Welfare: Depriving, Surviving and Thriving* (Demeter Press, 2020).

Aaron A. Moore is a professor in the Department of Political Science at the University of Winnipeg. He is an expert on municipal politics and governance and public policy and has authored two books, as well as numerous articles and book chapters, on these topics.

Jeremy Patzer is Canada Research Chair in Comparative Indigenous Rights and associate professor in the Department of Sociology and Criminology at the University of Manitoba. His Métis and Saulteaux roots come from the West Interlake of Manitoba (family names of Spence, Monkman, Pottinger, and Dumas) and his research interests centre on Indigenous rights and the forms of legal-political resolution, repair, and rights protection that develop within settler state contexts.

Andrea Rounce is a professor in the Department of Political Science at the University of Manitoba. She is a co-editor of *COVID-19 in Manitoba: Public Policy Responses to the First Wave* (University of Manitoba Press, 2020) and writes about public servants and the public service.

Kelly Saunders is a professor in the Department of Political Science and Gender and Women's Studies Program at Brandon University. She is a co-author of *Métis Politics and Governance in Canada* (UBC Press, 2019) as well as numerous articles on political parties and politics in Manitoba.

Mary Agnes Welch is a partner in Probe Research, a public opinion research firm based in Winnipeg, and works with clients in various sectors while providing media commentary on Manitoba politics and public policy issues. She worked for many years as a public policy and political reporter with the *Winnipeg Free Press*, as well as with newspapers in Ontario and Texas.

Jared Wesley is a professor of political science and associate dean in the Faculty of Arts at the University of Alberta. He leads the Common Ground Politics initiative and publishes widely on democracy in western Canada.

www.ingramcontent.com/pod-product-compliance
Lightning Source LLC
Chambersburg PA
CBHW031326230426
43670CB00006B/253